Radio Comedy Diary

# Radio Comedy Diary

*A Researcher's Guide to the*
*Actual Jokes and Quotes of the Top*
*Comedy Programs of 1947–1950*

GARY POOLE

McFarland & Company, Inc., Publishers
*Jefferson, North Carolina, and London*

**Library of Congress Cataloguing-in-Publication Data**

Radio comedy diary: a researcher's guide to the actual jokes and quotes
of the top comedy programs of 1947–1950 / [collected by] Gary Poole.
p.    cm.
Includes index.
ISBN 0-7864-0968-1 (softcover : 50# alkaline paper) ∞
1. American wit and humor.   2. Radio programs — United States.
I. Poole, Gary.
PN6165.R33   2001
791.44'6 — dc21                                         2001041018

British Library Cataloguing data are available

Manufactured in the United States of America

*McFarland & Company, Inc., Publishers*
*Box 611, Jefferson, North Carolina 28640*
*www.mcfarlandpub.com*

# Preface

This book is a collection of jokes, gags, one-liners and quotations from what many have, and rightly, called the Golden Age of radio. Underlying every entry is an acknowledgment of the expertise and dedication of those radio performers, comedy writers, directors, producers, sound effect specialists, musicians, engineers, advertising agencies, broadcasting networks and others who were engaged in bringing laughter to America through the magic of radio over fifty years ago.

The material contained herein is intended to serve mainly as a reference work for historians and students of broadcasting who wish to engage in an analysis of radio comedy writing. I have been careful to give proper credit, where possible, for all material included. Since a lot of radio broadcasts often "borrowed" material from each other, proper ownership is always a question. Milton Berle made a career out of being called "The Thief of Badgags," and a lot of comedy writers followed suit. Taking jokes and switching them was common practice and if, by doing so, one could improve upon it, so much the better.

The material in this work was broadcast over fifty years ago and is derived from notes taken when I was about sixteen through eighteen. This book, with proper credit acknowledged, is presented in part also as a *tribute* to the performers. It is my hope that it will stimulate the interest of its readers to investigate this marvelous era further through existing recordings, CDs and cassettes, which are available from a variety of sources. Though primarily intended to serve scholars of radio, this book is also the proverbial labor of love.

— *Gary Poole*

# Contents

*Preface* v

*Introduction* 1


**1947** 5

**1948** 41

**1949** 99

**1950** 188


*Notes and Comments* 193

*Index* 211

# Introduction

I consider myself a very fortunate person because I was privileged to grow up during the golden age of radio. That was a period of time when the whole family would gather around a huge box in the living room, stare into space and simply listen while the voices emanating from that box swept us away in our imaginations.

Those voices and sound effects took us behind the squeaking door and into the *Inner Sanctum* with spooky tales that would haunt us later in our dreams. *Lights Out* and *Suspense* sent chills up our spine, while the *Whistler* walked by night spinning tales of strange people who lived in the shadows.

In the afternoons *The Lone Ranger* and *Superman* took us along with them in their quest for truth, justice and the American way, complete with moral lessons that helped shape our lives.

*Fibber McGee & Molly, Amos 'n' Andy, Jack Benny, Burns & Allen, Henry Aldrich* and a host of others showed us that life in America could be just one great big situation comedy when viewed from their perspective, and taught us another great moral lesson — how to laugh at ourselves.

*Edward R. Murrow, H. V. Kaltenborn, Gabriel Heatter, Walter Winchell, Louella Parsons* and *Hedda Hopper* kept us informed on what was happening around the world and in that tinsel town called Hollywood. So instantly, we knew what was going on in all four corners of the globe. No matter where — radio was there. When Franklin D. Roosevelt died in Warm Springs, Georgia, we knew about it just minutes after. The live broadcast of the Hindenburg tragedy as it happened is a classic in on-the-spot reporting. Then, of course, there was the greatest broadcasting hoax of all time, *The War of the Worlds*, which wasn't meant to be a hoax at all, but was merely a radio drama featuring the Mercury Players. That broadcast sent people fleeing into the streets in fear and made Orson Welles a star.

As radio grew, so did I. Totally enthralled with it, I wanted nothing more than to be on the radio myself, and so, at age sixteen, began writing radio scripts. I performed one of those scripts for an audition at our local radio station and, fortunately for me, they liked what they heard and gave me my own afternoon fifteen minute time slot three times a week, Monday, Wednesday and Friday, on a sustaining basis to do with as I pleased. It was a golden opportunity in a golden age. I was in heaven.

There I created my own sitcom and began to learn my craft, writing, performing, playing all the characters via voice changes and even doing my own sound effects. To help myself in this endeavor, I began taking notes nightly on all the classic comedy radio shows — Jack Benny, Bob Hope, Red Skelton, Burns & Allen, Fred Allen, Jimmy Durante and so on. These notes helped jump-start me into writing my own scripts. In the beginning I stole jokes outright, having, at age sixteen, absolutely no shame. Gradually, I learned how to "switch" jokes and make them my own. Ultimately, I learned that the best comedy comes from characterization, situations and story lines and that the comedy should evolve naturally from that. Pretty soon, I was able to write my own little plots and draw humor from them.

As the years passed, these notebooks, written in pencil on spiral notebooks, swelled to eleven in number. By then it was 1949, the year of my high school graduation, and time for me to head to New York to study at the American Academy of Dramatic Arts. So the notebooks ended in early 1950, at the point when I went out into the world to prepare myself for a career. By then, of course, television had already become a force to be reckoned with. *Ed Sullivan's Toast of the Town, Kukla, Fran & Ollie, The Goldbergs, Howdy Doody, Captain Video* and others were beginning to implant themselves in the American consciousness. A new era was upon us. Radio as we knew it was on its way out, to be taken over by disk jockeys, music and news.

The comedies and dramas, all performed live, were soon to become a phenomenon of the past, and were replaced by yet another box in the living room. Only this time the box had a screen and we could see the performers and the newscasters right in our own home. All of this prompted that great comedian Fred Allen to say, "The reason they call television a medium is because so little of it is well-done." And Bob Hope's writers put these words into his mouth, "You know what television is, don't you? That's where you see where the smell is coming from."

Obviously, the radio stars were reluctant to give up radio. Who can blame them? Television loomed before them and they would be forced to memorize lines instead of reading them off scripts. Cue cards and teleprompters came into being and they were off and running.

As the years passed, I continued my career, first as a writer of comic books, putting action and words into the mouths of Bugs Bunny, Tweety & Sylvester, Underdog, The Munsters, Little Lulu and a host of others for Gold Key comics. In the fantasy genre, I wrote stories for Rod Serling's *Twilight Zone* and Boris Karloff's *Tales of Mystery*, plus *Flash Gordon* and *The Phantom*. This led to my becoming editor-in-chief of Golden Magazine at Golden Books in New York and, finally, the author of some twenty books, including *The Apple Dumpling Gang Rides Again*, which was also a movie starring Don Knotts and Tim Conway.

The writing continues, and recently, while going through the attic with visions of a yard sale dancing in my head, I came across those spiral notebooks from long ago. There they were, all eleven of them, stacked in the bottom of a cardboard box, still intact. Still readable.

I took them out, sat on the floor and began reading. It was as though I had stepped into a time machine, so complete was my transformation back to those nights when I sat by my radio taking notes. I was sixteen again, and I could still hear those voices spouting those words written on the pages in front of me.

I knew then that this was a treasure that should not be left in a box in the attic. It was something that must be shared. That is how this book came to be. I have transcribed those notes exactly as I wrote them down over fifty years ago. There are jokes, one-liners, snatches of dialogue and occasional plot summaries, which I think will bring back memories for those of you who were lucky enough to have been around during radio's heyday. For others, this will provide basic research material for an understanding of radio as it once was — glorious, silly, informative and above all, entertaining.

Everything you see on television today has its roots in radio. There is nothing new under the sun. Only the technology has improved. Now computers are challenging television and the pendulum is swinging toward the Internet. Soon the events seen in *Star Wars* and *Star Trek* will be a reality, and we will find ourselves living in a world first populated by Flash Gordon and Buck Rogers. We seem to be there already.

Each of us owes a debt of gratitude to radio, because it gave us the opportunity to use our minds and imaginations and helped create the technology we have today. But there's one thing we should remember. Radio got there first.

My notes began in the fall of 1947. I did not keep track of actual broadcast dates until October 12th, however, so the first few entries are undated. They were broadcast during the beginning of that fall season on radio. A lot of the jokes will seem corny now, but some are still very funny, especially if you remember those wonderful characters who first uttered them.

# — 1 9 4 7 —

## Red Skelton

- RED: (*After being introduced*) Thank you, thank you! It's nice to know that every person in the audience is my friend.
  (*SFX: Gunshot*)
  RED: Hah! Missed me!

- COWBOY: Something's funny about this money. Lincoln has his hand over his mouth.
  DEADEYE: Shh! That's hush money!

- CLEM: (*Inviting someone in his house*) Come in quickly! I don't want the fresh air to get in!

## Amos 'n' Andy

- ANDY: That picture shows my bad side.
  KINGFISH: What side is that?
  ANDY: The side my face is on.

- KINGFISH: You're having a party? Why didn't you invite me?
  ANDY: We were afraid you'd accept.

- KINGFISH: My eyesight is perfect. See them ants on the post over there? One has a piece of bread in his mouth. Hmm...whole wheat!

## Jack Benny

- DENNIS DAY: I swear I'll never have anything to do with girls! And when I have kids, I'll bring 'em up the same way!

5

- PHIL HARRIS:   I got the stuff, boy, I got the stuff!
  JACK:   Oh, yeah? Well, I *dream* adventurous stuff!

## Fibber McGee & Molly

- MOLLY:   Every year McGee goes to the car show and makes a Nash of himself.

- FIBBER:   I love cars. I like to tinker with 'em.
  MOLLY:   Yeah, you're the biggest tinker in town.

- MOLLY:   I see where Betty Grable is watching her figure.
  FIBBER:   Yeah? Well, that makes two of us.

  *(Note: Sometimes when a joke doesn't get a laugh, they repeat the last line and the audience laughs.)*
- SALESMAN:   I've been to 500 homes and nobody answers. Think I should knock?
  FIBBER:   *(After joke)* That was too fast for him, he didn't get it! After I heard it I didn't care too much for it myself!
  FIBBER:   *(To Gildersleeve)* Why didn't your mother have a baby?

## Edgar Bergen & Charlie McCarthy

- MORTIMER:   Seems like yesterday.
  BERGEN:   What?
  MORTIMER:   Yesterday.
  BERGEN:   Mortimer, can you say your ABC's?
  MORTIMER:   Okay. A...B...C...
  BERGEN:   And the rest?
  MORTIMER:   There's more?

## Milton Berle

- BERLE:   At my show I've looked at more empty seats than a tailor.
  BERLE:   *(Extolling the virtues of his old girlfriend, Cynthia)* Ah, Cynthia! Golden memories of Cynthia! You were so slim! Remember how we used to pull her through the guns to clean them out! She was a skinny little thing! And Cynthia! Remember how we laughed when we looked in the mirrors at the Fun House! I wish you looked that good in real life!

## Bob Hope

- HOPE:   You're spoofing, Colonna!
  JERRY:   No, I'm Professor Colonna! Spoofing Colonna is my brother.
  HOPE:   You're out of your head.
  JERRY:   Egad! Am I supposed to be in it?

- HOPE:   I got an electric blanket. Now my dreams are shocking.

# Red Skelton

- RED:   Those kids are so young, they're still smoking tobacco.

- GUEST:   Today is the 30th. Tomorrow is the first.
  CLEM:   Hey! Same thing happened last year!

# Durante & Moore

- DURANTE:   (*After Garry Moore punchline*) Dat's my boy who said dat!

- DURANTE:   (*To annoying guest*) Come over to my house and we'll toin on the gas jet!

- MOORE:   Boy, were they wealthy! At dinner they served only money.
  DURANTE:   That's nuthin'! I've rubbed elbows with famous people! (*Aside*) They wouldn't shake my hand.

- DURANTE:   (*To drummer*) Another outburst like that and your drums will go back to Sears and Roebuck!

- DURANTE:   (*After blooper*) It ain't fair! They're using woids wit letters in them!

- DURANTE:   (*After being left out of dialogue*) Attention Farmers! Throw out ya' smudge pots! (I didn't have anything to say, so I thought I might as well throw in a frost warning!)

- STOOGE:   (*Knocks on door*) Turn me around! Turn me around!
  MOORE:   Why?
  STOOGE:   I'm Portia! I wanna face life! (*Door slam!*)

# Fred Allen

- FRED:   I just heard Jack Benny's neighbor threw his radio out the window. Benny's back on the air on Sunday, October 5th!

- FRED (*To announcer*):   Cut it out or I'll have you arrested for impersonating a human being.

- TITUS MOODY (*To Fred Allen*):   Where I come from we bury people who look better than you!

- TITUS MOODY:   Don't turn your back or I'll sneak one by you!

- FRED:   That town in Vermont was so small. When I went to the public library there was a sign on the door that said, "The book is out."

# Alan Young

- ALAN:   I've met her! The girl I'm going to marry! The mother of my children! She doesn't love me, but our children will bring us together!

- ALAN:   You should have seen me play football. Running, passing, kicking! I made nine touchdowns and on the last play I stiff-armed an opposing player! Tore her dress, too!

- ALAN:   I'm tough!
  GIRL:   Say it again!
  ALAN:   I'm tough!
  GIRL:   Say it again!
  ALAN:   I'm tough!
  GIRL:   Say it again!
  ALAN:   Ah, shut up! (*Like a tough guy*)

## Bob Hope

- BOB:   I wanted to take my girl to the football stadium, but she wanted to go when there was a game going on.

- BOB:   What do you like to do on a date, Colonna?
  COLONNA:   I like to park the car, get close and turn out the lights...
  BOB:   And then?
  COLONNA:   See if her wrist watch lights up!
  BOB:   I've heard when you're with a girl, all you want to do is spoon. (*Kiss*)
  COLONNA:   How else can I stir my sugar?

- BOB:   (*In a cowboy routine*) That posse's been ahead of us all day. How come?
  COLONNA:   They have horses!

## Red Skelton

- RED:   Get in the back room! They'll never find us there!
  ANNOUNCER:   Why not?
  RED:   We have no back room! (*Ad-lib*) Now that's brilliant dialogue!

- STOOGE:   You're not a drinking man, are you?
  CLEM:   Naw, I never drank a man in my life!

- GIRL:   Do you like the way I'm wearing my hair on my shoulders?
  CLEM:   Yeah! Why don't you try wearing it on your head? (*Ad-lib*) Boy, I'm sorry we left that baby in there!

- RED:   So you lost your boy friend! Remember, there are plenty of other fish on the beach.
  LULU:   Yeah, but the ones I get are washed up!

- LULU:   The man that gets me gets a prize!
  RED:   What's the prize?

- CLEM:   (*On losing his hair*) I been drinking hair oil and for all the good it does me, I may as well have rubbed it on my head!

## October 12, 1947*

### *Jack Benny*

- ROCHESTER: Cheap, are you kidding? To save food, last week Mr. Benny locked me in a closet.
  DON: Really?
  ROCHESTER: But I fooled him. I ate the doorknob!
  DON: You ate the doorknob?
  ROCHESTER: Yeah, now every little thing turns my stomach!

- JACK: (*Thinking about girlfriend*) Hmm, I wonder how she'd look in a dress. I wonder how she'd look out of a dress. I wonder how she'd look in a bathing suit. Hm, I wonder how she'd look … oh, now I'm being silly!

- JACK: (*To Frank Nelson*) I hate everybody now, and you're all of them!

### *Edgar Bergen & Charlie McCarthy*

- BERGEN: What I lack in muscles…
  CHARLIE: You make up in flab.

- BERGEN: I tore my pants!
  CHARLIE: Well, I knew you'd come through.

- MORTIMER: I have a sure cure for hiccups. Fill your mouth with water.
  BERGEN: Yes…?
  MORTIMER: Then sit on a stove until it boils.
  BERGEN: You're not feeling well, Mortimer? Stick out your tongue.
  MORTIMER: Which end?
  BERGEN: Now, look into my eyes and count ten.
  MORTIMER: You only got two!
  BERGEN: You know, Mortimer, you can cure your hiccups by scaring a person.
  MORTIMER: Okay…boo!
  BERGEN: Not me! I'm supposed to scare you. Mortimer, your stupidity is beyond comprehension!
  MORTIMER: How'd it get way over there?
  CHARLIE: This breakfast cereal! It doesn't snap, pop, or crackle! It just lies there in the bowl! The silence is driving me mad!

### *Fred Allen*

- FRED: (*After bad joke*) Services for that joke will be held tomorrow morning in the chapel.

*At this point in my notes I began keeping track of broadcast dates.*

- ONE LONG PAN: Man who eats macaroni is using his noodle.

- TITUS MOODY: I was up till all hours last night. Why by the time I got to bed it must have been eight o'clock! I was down in the dumps yesterday. Boy, did I get dirty.

- SHIRLEY BOOTH: (*Guest*) Last week I was on the Bell Telephone Hour. I was the only wrong number.

- FRED: The brewer's son. Now there's a lad with a head on his shoulders.

- FRED: (*About women wearing dresses longer*) I know I'm in style. I just let the hem out of my underwear.

- FRED: I understand Campbell's soup even looks good spilled on your vest.

## Alan Young

- ALAN: When I was a baby I had a nurse who used to kiss me and kiss me. By the time I was six months old, the thrill was gone!

- ALAN: (*Private eye sketch*) My name is Joe. I'm a private detective. For weeks I followed a woman in a long dress. Then I found out it was the judge! I was sitting in my office, tired, worried, discouraged, depressed when the phone rang... (*SFX: Phone ring*) Hello? Yeah? I've been laying low. That's right, laying low. The slats in my bed broke. What's that? You want me to find your husband? He has a wart on his face, no ears and no hair? How will I know him? Oh, he'll be wearing a white carnation. (*Hangs up phone*) Finally, I had a job. I poured myself two fingers of whiskey and got my clothes all wet. My fingers slipped.

- ALAN: The door's locked. I'll just shoot it off its hinges. (*SFX: Gunfire*)
  BUTLER: (*Arthur Treacher*) You rang, sir?

- BUTLER: The master is dead and doesn't wish to be disturbed. He was brutally murdered.
  ALAN: Badly?
  BUTLER: His wife is in the study.
  ALAN: Don't worry. I wouldn't touch her with a twenty foot pole.
  BUTLER: Don't you mean a ten foot pole?
  ALAN: Why be half-safe? (*Slogan of a current deodorant commercial*)

- ALAN: The table is set for dinner. There are no knives. Egad, I'll be soup spooned to death!
  BUTLER: The murderer is somewhere nearby.
  ALAN: Don't worry! I've locked all the windows, the attic, the basement.. (*SFX: Creaking sound*) Whatta ya know! I forgot to lock the door!

- ALAN: Got a match?
  BUTLER: Yes.
  ALAN: Ah! Need a cigarette! This match tastes awful!

## Screen Guild Players Starring Bob Hope in "My Favorite Brunette"

- GIRL: I'm in hot water!
  BOB: What else could it be with you in it?
  GIRL: I don't know how to thank you.
  BOB: Oh, we'll think of something.

- BOB: It was one of those big ritzy estates. You know the kind...so big you could shoot quail in the hallway.

- MAN: (*Describing woman*) She's dumb, stupid...
  BOB: And how is she mentally?
  MAN: She's an amnesia victim.
  BOB: Just my luck. I find a dame who's nuts about me, and whatta 'ya know? She's nuts!

- BOB: Just because you're pretty and let me put my arm around you, you think you can make me do anything. (*Sigh*) What do you want, baby?

- BOB: Hi 'ya, Warden. Did the Governor call?
  WARDEN: No!
  BOB: Now I'll know who to call next time! This is the biggest frameup since Whistler's mother!

## Milton Berle

- BERLE: I had the audience in the palm of my hand. That'll give you an idea of how many were there. Ah, Cynthia! Memories of Cynthia with your coal black hair that you wore in a snood. And how I used to help you shovel it in!

## Amos 'n' Andy

- KINGFISH: Of course, I changed the sheets! From one bed to another!

## Bob Hope

- BOB: All characters in this play are characters and must not be confused with people.
  (*SFX: Door opens. Woman screams*)
  BOB: It's our ghost. And she hasn't got her sheet on!

- GIRL: Love me?
  BOB: Forever Amber!
  GIRL: Like me?
  BOB: Forever Amber!
  GIRL: Want me?
  BOB: Forever Amber! Folks, they call this a supporting role!

- GIRL:    (*Sobbing*) What are we going to do? What are we going to do?
  BOB:     Don't over do it. Bette Davis has to eat, too, you know!

- COLONNA:    The baby was born with two heads. Looks like the mother *and* the father!

- GIRL:    (*In a scary situation*) Oh! Something's clinging to my chest!
  BOB:     Don't be a coward, it's me!

- COLONNA: I'll find out! I'll look into my crystal ball. (Gad, I need a shave!)

# October 14, 1947

## Red Skelton

- RED:    Hey, as long as I've got a dollar in my pocket, I can buy twenty-five cents worth of anything!
  RED:    (*Supposed ad-lib*) Will those ten people in the audience who laughed at that joke explain it to me? I don't get it!

- RED:    I saw a sign that said "Formerly $2.00 — Now Just .75." So I got it. I don't know *what* I'm going to do with the sign now that I've got it!

- RED:    (*As Deadeye*) I'm a good shot. See that fly on that dog's tail? (*SFX: Bang!*) Oh, well, he can learn to wag something else!

- RED:    Gotta git me some money outta the bank. (*SFX: Long footsteps. Then gunshot* [Bang!] *More long footsteps*). Sorry, to keep you waitin', but it takes a long time to fill out them slips!

- MAN:    (*Playing poker*) You cheated!
  RED:    What makes ya think so?
  MAN:    You're the only one whose got any cards!
  RED:    Well, if you want to play a sissy game!

- MOM:    Where's the stewed chicken?
  RED:    (*As mean widdle kid*) Maybe he sobered up and went back to the chicken house.

- RED:    (*As Junior*) Are you gonna believe me or Joe?
  MOM:    I'm going to believe the truth!
  RED:    Joe, huh?

- MAN:    What did your parents teach you?
  RED:    (*As Junior*) Never to get married.

- CLEM:    I don't hang around saloons! I lay flat on the floor!

- GIRL:    I'm going to tell father about you!
  CLEM:    Aw, he already knows about me!

- RED: (*Ad-lib*) Can I borrow your hanky? I kind of broke myself up on that last one.

## October 15, 1947

### Sweeney & March
Bob Sweeny and Hal March teamed up briefly, before Hal was host of the $64,000 question.

- (*SFX: Knock on door*)
  BOB:  Open up!
  HAL:  Why?
  BOB:  My arms are full of bundles.
  HAL:  (*Opens door*) I don't see any bundles.
  BOB:  What'd 'ya know? I left them on the bus!

### Durante & Moore
- DURANTE:  (*After announcer laughs*) Dat laugh was so dirty, even Duz couldn't clean it up!

- DURANTE:  Beauty is only skin deep. I just happen to have deep skin.

- DURANTE:  (*Various asides*) Junior, stop sneakin' the pecans outta my Hershey bar! Wait a minute! Let me get these lines straight! Whatta spot for Durante! Involved in the infernal triangle! Oh, Durante, you adorable adolescent!

### Milton Berle
- BERLE:  I'd make you eat those words, but this is meatless Tuesday!

- BERLE:  Ah, Cynthia! Golden memories of Cynthia! How you used to eat an apple every day! On a plate in Lindy's window! Cynthia! How you used to touch up your hair…with paste…to keep it on your head!

- MAN:  I'm an undertaker.
  BERLE:  I'm afraid I don't dig you. (*Ad-lib*) Please, let's not have too much noise in the audience, only laughs.

### Amos 'n' Andy
- KINGFISH:  Your girl is a fat horse!
  ANDY:  I'll punch you in the nose! You're speaking of the fat horse I love!

### Bob Hope
- BOB:  Television. That's where you can see where the smell's coming from.

- BOB:     Look at my face!
  COLONNA:  Pass the Tums.

# October 21, 1947

## Red Skelton

- MAN:   Go inside.
  CLEM:  Where?
  MAN:   Right through that door.
  (*SFX: CRASH!*)
  MAN:   Open it first!

- RED:   Never play cards with a man that cheats. That's why I quit playing solitaire.

- RED:   Here comes a stagecoach without any wheels!
  MAN:   What holds it up?
  RED:   Bandits!

- RED:   (*As Deadeye in a card game*) I'll raise you.
  MAN:   I'll raise you.
  RED:   I'll raise you!
  MAN:   Where are you gettin' all them cards?
  RED:   Out of your pocket!
  MAN:   Are you trying to cheat?
  RED:   No.
  MAN:   Well, I am, so shut up!

# October 22, 1947

## The Bickersons

- BLANCHE:  All this reading hurts my brain.
  JOHN:     Don't worry about a little thing like that!

- JOHN:     Your sister! She's the only girl in the world with chewing tobacco in her compact!
  BLANCHE:  She's perfectly normal!
  JOHN:     Normal? You call a gal with a crew haircut, hip boots and a sheepskin dress, normal?

## Durante & Moore

- DURANTE:  (*At piano*) Iturbi plays best on the white notes! Rachmaninoff plays best on the black notes! But as for me, I play in the cracks! I'm in a class by myself! Now I'd like to play something by Tchaikovsky but a voice keeps saying, "Don't do it! Don't do it!"

MOORE: Who?

DURANTE: Tchaikovsky!

- DURANTE: (*Various ad-libs*) Hang around until wash day. I want to send your head out with the flatwork! I'm so mad I could crush a Rice Krispy! (*After Garry Moore delivers a line with big words in it*) I'm glad I didn't have to say that! We'd be here all night!

- MAN: (*In audience*) I think you're great! You're great!

  DURANTE: Why don't you applaud?

  MAN: I can't with my hands in this strait-jacket!

- DURANTE: Women the lifeboats! Women the lifeboats!

  MOORE: Don't you mean, man the lifeboats?

  DURANTE: You fill your boat, I'll fill mine!

# October 26, 1947

## Fred Allen

- FRED: I hope we both live to be as old as that joke.

- FRED: That was Guy Lombardo and twenty-five reasons why he doesn't have his own show.

- FRED: As the old flour bag said, "I've been through the mill." (*Ad-lib*) I just said that to kill time. We had 5 seconds left and what was I going to do? Just stand here and look at you?

- FRED: (*Doing a doctor sketch*) Scalpel … forceps … needle … thread … blotter! That's it, finished! His head looks like a briefcase, but he'll live!

  FRED: I don't trust that doctor. He's wearing gauze dungarees.

## Alan Young

- ALAN: You'll have to excuse my looks today. Got bad shave. The tweezers broke.

- ALAN: (*In a western sketch*) I'm wearing muh buffalo hat, buffalo shoes and buffalo skin coat. Hmm, that cow over there is making eyes at me!

- ALAN: (*To girl*) Gimme a kiss!

GAL:   No, no!
ALAN:   Just as I thought. Women is purdy but they's yellow!

- ALAN:   Come on! Gimme a kiss.
GAL:   Well … okay. (*SFX: Kiss, kiss, kiss!*)
ALAN:   Just think. All mah life I been wastin' mah lips on eating!

- ALAN:   I'm a good shot! Why I kin shoot that cigarette outta yore fingers! (*SFX: Bang!*) Did I do it? Did I shoot that cigarette outta yore fingers?
STOOGE:   What fingers?

- ALAN:   I'm tied to a stake! A fire is burning! It's burning my feet, my legs, my hips … yeow! it's the end!

# October 28, 1947

## Milton Berle

- BERLE:   You saying that I lay eggs hurts my feelings. (So I'll lay smaller ones.)

- BERLE:   A joke like that never dies. (It has to be beaten to death!)

- BERLE:   Ah, Cynthia! Golden memories of Cynthia! I'll never forget the day I caught you. You bent four of my harpoons! And I'll never forget the day you had your face lifted. Unfortunately, the guy brought it back. Ah, Cynthia, I loved your tinkling little laugh when you slid down the Washington Monument. (*Boing!*)

- BERLE:   I won't say he's vain, but I caught him putting leg makeup on his bald spot. He's an old salt. For years I've been trying to shake him.

- BERLE:   Sorry I'm late. On the way here I was mugged by a pigeon.
ANNOUNCER:   How can a grown man get mugged by a pigeon?
BERLE:   Two of his friends held me down!

## Amos 'n' Andy

(*Discussing having children*)
ANDY:   You know, most homes have little ones running around the house.
KINGFISH:   We had 'em, too, but we set traps for 'em.

## Fibber McGee & Molly

(*One of the Old Timer's stock lines*)
- OLD TIMER:   That's pretty good, sonny, but that ain't the way I heered it!

- FIBBER:   Hello, Autumn boy.
GILDERSLEEVE:   Autumn boy?
FIBBER:   Fall guy.

- FIBBER:    Why didn't your wife go with you?
  PEAVY:    Oh, I carelessly put a beartrap in her shower.

## Bob Hope

- BOB:    (*Doing monologue*) I went to a nightclub last night. It was so crowded, I danced for two hours before I had a partner. I didn't have a date. I investigated Hedy Lamarr...but the ladder broke. Gypsy Rose Lee was there. She spoke. She had nothing to hide. Saw Frank Sinatra there. Poor Frank, he started out with a shoe string. Now he is one. Have you tried that new hand lotion? If you're not satisfied just send them the bottle back with your fingers in them.

## Red Skelton

- CLEM:    I entertained some oil drillers.
  ANNOUNCER:    Crude?
  CLEM:    Well, a couple of 'em ate with their knives.

- CLEM:    (*Singing*) I'm always chasing rainbows... (I'll chase anything with curves). I'm going to the barber shop to get my hair trimmed so I won't trip over it.
  BARBER:    A haircut will cost you a dollar and twenty-five cents.
  CLEM:    What does that include?
  BARBER:    Both heads!
  CLEM:    You know, I used to cut my own hair until my lawnmower broke down.

  (*Sometimes, Red would close his show with a serious message.*)

- RED:    Stop paying teachers peanuts and the children will stop acting like monkeys. Thank you, and God bless.

# October 29, 1947

## The Bickersons

- BLANCHE:    John, do you love me?
  JOHN:    What have you done?
  BLANCHE:    I bought a mink coat.
  JOHN:    Ohhh, no. How much?
  BLANCHE:    You better sit down.

- JOHN:    I went to the doctor. He took X-rays and they were horrible!
  BLANCHE:    Why?
  JOHN:    I looked like a skeleton!

## Durante & Moore

- DURANTE:   Folks, if you don't laugh, we have a brand new audience warming up in the basement.
  MOORE:   You better watch your mouth!
  DURANTE:   Hey, I'd get rid of my mouth, but it's a handy place to keep my teeth!
  MOORE:   I could bite my tongue for saying that.
  DURANTE:   Bite it? You'll have to catch it first!

- DURANTE:   (*Singing*) She's a little bit this and a little bit that,  a little bit short and a little bit fat, her nose turns up, mine turns down! When we kiss...we lock bumpers! (Ha, ha, ha, ha! I gotta million of 'em!)

- DURANTE:   Our house dirty? Are you kidding? This morning while dusting I found another room.

- MOORE:   Women like a man who has lived!
  DURANTE:   I've lived!
  MOORE:   I mean recently.
  DURANTE:   Remind me to reward you with a soggy Tootsie roll!

- MOORE:   That's stupendous!
  DURANTE:   (*Aside*) There's no laugh there, folks, but it helps you follow the story.

  (*Detective sketch*)
- CROOK:   I killed him! I killed him!
  DURANTE:   (*As detective*) Words! Words! I'm looking for clues!

# November 2, 1947

## Bergen & McCarthy

(*Fred Allen was a guest*).
- CHARLIE:   Where's my pitchfork? I'll get you in the end!
  FRED:   I do a one man show. During intermission, I sell popcorn. Jack Benny is too cheap to afford a psychiatrist, so he just lies on the couch and talks to himself.

## Alan Young

(*Guest Tony Martin*)
- TONY:   Ah, tonight I'll be out on the town, champaigning, dancing and kissing!
  ALAN:   That's nothing. I'll be home bathrobing, slippering and hot milking!

TONY:   Don't you ever go out on a date?
ALAN:   Sure! I have a date tomorrow night. And I want you to know, I'll be driving with one hand.
TONY:   Cuddling close, huh?
ALAN:   No, I have to hold the fenders on with the other one.

# November 4, 1947

## Milton Berle

- BERLE:   Our coach has a real head for football. It's full of air and comes to a point. (I made a bet on that last joke. I lose!) Football that's a game you play for four years so you can get a letter to put over the place where your ribs used to be. Ah, college! I spent 14 wonderful years in college. I was there so long ivy kept growing up my legs. Ah, Cynthia! Golden memories of Cynthia! She was our homecoming queen. I'll never forget her tinkling little laugh before the big game when they threw her on the bonfire. She was my old flame. But she made an ash out of herself.

Frank Gallup was Berle's announcer and often got some zingers in at Berle's expense.

- BERLE:   George Washington is dead. I'm alive!
  GALLUP:   Don't bet on it.
  BERLE:   Boy, am I tired, you know, Mr. Gallup?
  GALLUP:   Yes, I know him very well.
  BERLE:   I really am tired. Watch out! Don't trip over my tongue!
  GALLUP:   Berle, we laid an egg, let's not cackle over it.
  BERLE:   That's a good yolk.

- BERLE:   (*Talking about W.C. Fields*) I could run my car all winter on his breath.

- BERLE:   I'm so much taller than my girlfriend, I keep tripping over her.

## Amos 'n' Andy

- KINGFISH:   He's a groom to a horse.
  ANDY:   I knew no girl would have him.

## Fibber McGee & Molly

- FIBBER:   His pants are so baggy it looks like he's smuggling coconuts. Being a literary fellow, the judge threw the book at him. I need some invisible ink. For writing checks on my invisible bank account. Wait! I have a small skeleton key. For opening small skeletons.

## Bob Hope

- BOB:　Oklahoma. That's an oil field that made good on Broadway. I took a plane here. Had a very unexciting trip. The hostess turned out to be a relative. When I arrived out West, I walked up to an Indian and said, "Me brave!" He said, "You must be. I heard your show!"
  COLONNA:　(*On telephone, whispering*) Hello, Mr. Hope?
  BOB:　Colonna, why are you whispering?
  COLONNA:　Someone else is using the phone!

- COLONNA:　While walking in the mountains I met a ferocious bear and he looked me straight in the face!
  BOB:　What did the bear do?
  COLONNA:　He climbed a tree!

- BOB:　(*To a female guest who has refused his request for a date*) There are plenty of other fish in the ocean.
  GIRL:　Good, then I'll go out with you.
  BOB:　You will?
  GIRL:　Yes, I could use a worm for bait.

## Red Skelton

- CLEM:　Hello, I'm Clem!
  ANNOUNCER:　Well, don't blame me.
  CLEM:　Who are you? I ain't got muh glasses on.
  ANNOUNCER:　It's me.
  CLEM:　I'm glad I ain't got muh glasses on!

- CLEM:　I hate gettin' a haircut. It means I have to start wearin' a shirt again!

  (*Red as the mean widdle kid*)
- MOM:　Look at you! You're a mess!
  KID:　Did you see that mud puddle?
  MOM:　No.
  KID:　Neither did I!
  MOM:　You didn't fall in the mud with your clean pants on, did you?
  KID:　I didn't have time to change.

# November 5, 1947

## The Bickersons

- BLANCHE:　What's the matter, John?
  JOHN:　It's the pain!
  BLANCHE:　What pain?
  JOHN:　It's in my head! I've had it off and on for three weeks.

## Sweeney & March

- GIRL:   Get your hands off of me!
  SWEENEY:   I'm sorry. I just washed my hands and can't do a thing with them!

## Durante & Moore

- DURANTE:   Let me hear those violins! (*SFX: trumpet blare*) There's nothing wrong with the violins!

- DURANTE:   When I sing, my voice fills the studio.
  MOORE:   Yes, I just saw a couple leaving to make room for it.
  DURANTE:   Folks, we love this tune and know you'll love it too, it's gonna be another Inka Dinka Doo!

# November 9, 1947

## Jack Benny

- JACK:   Waiter, there's lipstick on this glass.
  WAITER:   Well, there's water in it, too. Wash it off!

- ROCHESTER:   You want hot chocolate? Good luck. Mr. Benny's idea of hot chocolate is a Hershey bar and a match.
  DENNIS:   Gee, Mr. Benny. I see you have a new refrigerator. What quiz program did you win it on?

(Plot summary: Dennis Day phones Jack and disguises his voice to sound like Roland Coleman inviting Jack to a costume party. Jack gets his girlfriend and heads for the Coleman's house. They see Jack coming so they sneak out the back door and go to a movie. Later, while Jack is away, they go into his house to finally get some rest.)

## Bergen & McCarthy

(*Guest Lulu McConnell of* It Pays to Be Ignorant)

- BERGEN:   I'm a real lover of horses.
  LULU:   Is that why you rode with your arms around his neck?
  BERGEN:   I wasn't afraid. Look at me. I'm as calm as a dead fish.
  LULU:   You never looked better. Say, just who is this handsome man?
  BERGEN:   I'm Edgar Bergan.
  LULU:   Not you chowderhead!

- MORTIMER:   Did you hear about muh new job?
  BERGEN:   No, Mortimer. What is it?

MORTIMER: Well...I'm a...uh...uh...Ah, what do you call a man who washes windows?
BERGEN: A window washer.
MORTIMER: That's it!

• CHARLIE: Lulu, if I do a show with you, I'll be glad to forget half my salary.
LULU: Good! And I'll forget the other half.

## Fred Allen

• FRED: The studio's so cold, the audience is clapping to keep warm.

• FRED: (*Sings*) Cheers, cheers for old Notre Dame, It's getting monotonous, they win every game! You'll know me. I'll be standing between Mary, Margaret and McBride.

## Alan Young

• ALAN: I'm so nervous today. This morning I was taking a shower and it missed me!
ANNOUNCER: Well, here's the mail.
ALAN: It's no use. I'm too nervous to open it.
ANNOUNCER: It's a postcard!

• ALAN: (*In cowboy sketch saying goodbye to his horse*) I'm going, old Paint! Goodbye, old Paint! I'm a going fast, old Paint! Let me kiss you, old Paint! (*SFX: Kiss*) Hm, tastes just like old paint!

• (*SFX: Huge crash*)
ALAN: Thanks for layin' out my underwear!

And now a play entitled: "She was a comely wench, but he gave her the brush."
• ALAN: Spray a little cologne on me. (*SFX: Spray*) Spray a little more, my shirt's still dry!
GIRL: Je ne sais pas?
ALAN: You can't fool me with that phony accent. I know you're French! Look Fraulin, or Senorita! Everybody is dead! Murdering thieves are on the loose!
GIRL: Yeah? What else is new?
ALAN: They're dying like flies!
GIRL: Who?
ALAN: Flies.

• ALAN: My car has a motor made by the Singer sewing machine company. Every time I drive, it hem-stitches the white line.

# November 11, 1947

## Milton Berle

- BERLE: Here we are in Washington where it's cooled in the summer by the river and warmed in the winter by a lot of hot air. Right now, folks, we're just in time to watch a congressman pass a bill.
  CONGRESSMAN: Hi, Bill.
  BILL: Hi, Congressman!
  BERLE: I hear the Democrats are looking for a new donkey.
  GALLUP: I'm sure you could prove an asset.
  BERLE: Thank you, Frank, for being behind me and supporting me where I need it most.

## Bob Hope

- BOB: When I arrived in New York City, I stepped out of Grand Central, looked up at the tall buildings and said, "Ahh!" When I looked down, my bags were gone. It was so cold in New York, I saw a squirrel wearing his brother.

- BOB: (*To Vera Vague*) You're just bitter because your parents wanted a girl.
  VERA: When you were born, I'll bet the doctor didn't know which end to slap.

- COLONNA: (*As cab driver*) This is the lover's delight cab!
  BOB: Lover's delight cab?
  COLONNA: No rear view mirror.
  BOB: Take me to the docks. The Queen Mary is at Pier 40.
  COLONNA: Does the King know about this?
  BOB: Say, how come you charge more than the other cabs?
  COLONNA: They're all yellow!
  BOB: I just noticed something. There's an elephant in the back seat!
  COLONNA: He's only going a block. Don't get excited!
  BOB: Yeah? Well, tell him to stop breathing peanuts in my face. And why are you driving on the sidewalk?
  COLONNA: Less traffic!

- BOB: His mother wore long underwear. She started from scratch.

## Red Skelton

- RED: (*As Clem*) I gotta start looking better. Look at me. Just look at me! I'm a mess. Either I've stepped in a shoe, or out of one! I'm afraid to get another haircut. The last time I got a haircut, I found out my nose outnumbered my eyes!

ANNOUNCER:  (*As Clem bathes*) You've got soap in your ear.
CLEM:  That's okay, it'll go out the other one.

## Durante & Moore

- MOORE:  I can't fire the maid. Her slacks fit me perfectly!
  MAID:  (*Very sexy*) I don't know what the fuss is about. I'm just like the girl next door. (*SFX: Huge Crash*)
  DURANTE:  That's the sound of ten thousand men rushing next door!

- DURANTE:  Ah, Esther Williams! That girl brings out the salmon in me. I'd like to go up stream with her. Thanks for laughing, folks. Now you'll all be my guests for dinner!

# November 16, 1947

## Jack Benny

During this period, a new fashion was introduced called the "new look."
- JACK:  I have the new look.
  MARY:  Yes, but with old parts.

- JACK:  (*To Dennis*) One more interruption and I won't take you to see "Forever Amber!"
  MORE LINES:  You shouldn't be walking behind Don Wilson. You need the sunshine, you're looking pale.

- ROCHESTER:  (*Driving the Maxwell car*) We're riding fine, now. Anything else I can do?
  JACK:  Yes, get off the sidewalk!

## Bergen & McCarthy

- BERGEN:  And so, Charlie, you tinkered around?
  CHARLIE:  Yes, little tinker that I am.

(*Discussing Charlie's wild night driving the car.*)
- BERGEN:  Did you go through any red lights?
  CHARLIE:  No, we took 'em with us!
  BERGEN:  Did you have a load?
  CHARLIE:  No, we were cold sober!
  BERGEN:  I'll bet you made the pedestrians nervous.
  CHARLIE:  One went to pieces!
  BERGEN:  And so you were stopped by the police.
  CHARLIE:  Yes, I go to court tomorrow. At least my hotel worries will be over!

- BERGEN: So you don't know what to say to your new girlfriend?
MORTIMER: Nope. I can't talk when I see her. I'm unspeakable!
BERGEN: Mortimer, your girlfriend is a dummy.
MORTIMER: Oh, no! I don't want a girl who's smarter than me!
BERGEN: Even so, your romance is warming up?
MORTIMER: Yup. Her love letters are so hot they steam themselves open.

- CHARLIE: Bergen, I need five dollars.
BERGEN: Five dollars! What do you take me for?
CHARLIE: Five dollars, I hope!

- BERGEN: Our guest tonight is Lana Turner.
CHARLIE: Ah, it's a long road that has no turner.

- LANA: (*Reading Charlie's palm*) I've never seen such lines!
CHARLIE: I could say the same thing. (*Ad-lib*) Stick around, folks, we got lots more good ones!

## Fred Allen

- FRED: From the song, "I was in love with the bearded lady, but she gave me the brush." I read that in the society column of the Hobo News.

- FRED: Her dress was so expensive, it was just a big diamond with sleeves. What an opening! I've never seen so many fur coats. In fact, the furs were so plentiful, two bears got in the audience and nobody noticed it. That is until it got hot and two ushers tried to help the bears off with their coats.

- FRED: If I could get my dues back, I'd resign from the human race.

- FRED: Money. What is money? Money is round. It rolls away. Money is nothing but the devil's confetti.

## Alan Young

- ALAN: Ah, the Fall! The air is just like wine. Just like wine! (Hic) Walking in the park, I saw a bird drop a worm into each opened mouth. I yawned and got fed.

(*Doing a sketch about Alaska.*)
- ALAN: Here we are hunting for gold, in the cold snow in Alaska! Look at my hands. They're blue! Blue!
ANNOUNCER: You forgot to take off your mittens.
ALAN: Last night while fixing dinner, I dropped frozen meat on my foot.
GUEST: Blubber?
ALAN: No, I didn't cry a bit.

- ALAN: (*Speaking to woman*) I haven't seen a girl in months. Last night, I dreamed about a girl wearing perfume, and now that I'm with one, it's driving me mad! Mad, do you hear? Mad!

GIRL:    ...Well?

ALAN:    Gimme a drink of that perfume!

*(In Saloon, challenged to a gunfight by villain.)*

• VILLAIN:    Okay, go for your gun! (*SFX: Sound of footsteps*) Hey, where're you going? I said go for your gun!

ALAN:    I am, it's in San Francisco!

# November 18, 1947

## Milton Berle

• SOME LINES:    Once I was in a Broadway play that was so hot, I had to make up in Unguentine. I don't know what I'd do without you, but I'm willing to give it a try. That's what I get for letting the ushers write my material. Is this an audience or a jury? That violin was confusing. He didn't know which chin to put it under. Thanks for the flowers, folks. Now every where I play, I smell. Okay, let's adjourn to the dummy room and stare at each other.

## Red Skelton

• CLEM:    Well, here I am! Do..do..di..do! I don't feel so good. Just had my distemper shots. But I'm ready to go. Let's see, I fed the dog, fed the cat, fed the pig. Pig! That reminds me, I ain't et, yet!

• RED:    The boss thinks I'm his brother. After each show he says, "Oh brother!" Did you hear about the new pedestrian fountain pen? It writes under cars.

• RED:    Look at this trick mirror! I look stupid.

GUEST:    I got news for you. It ain't a trick mirror.

• SOME LINES:    Her feet are so big, she has to back out of the room to admire the rug. So ugly she has to sleep with her face under the pillow to keep from scaring the covers off.

# November 19, 1947

## Jimmy Durante

• DURANTE:    I always wear elevator shoes when I'm in high society!

SOCIETY LADY:    Sure you can dance. One, two, three...kick!

DURANTE: One, two three.
SOCIETY LADY: Why didn't you kick?
DURANTE: With you in my arms, I can kick? (*Ad-lib*) I love that joke. I was taught to respect the old and weak.

## November 23, 1947

### Jack Benny

Jack Benny was one of the kindest guys in show business. He seldom, if ever, engaged in "put down" humor. His only retort to an obnoxious guest once was: "Ah, go be nice to people."

### Bergan & McCarthy

- BERGEN: There are many versions of this story.
  CHARLIE: Okay, how about the silent one?

- BERGEN: Hello, Mortimer.
  MORTIMER: Awful letdown, ain't it?
  BERGEN: How can you be so stupid?
  MORTIMER: Oh … I specialize.

### Fred Allen

- ANNOUNCER: There's a time and place for everything and this is the time and the place for … Fred Allen!
  FRED: That's the first one, folks. It gets better later. Well, what else is new? Now there's a gem of a line. What else is new?

- PORTLAND: I hear there's a shortage of psychiatrists.
  FRED: I'll bet the patients won't take this lying down.

  (*Parody of Gilbert and Sullivan.*)
- FRED: (*Singing*) When a boy is big and his brain is small, he can always go to college and play football! (*Chorus repeats that*) When he was in school, he was a mess. He had to get a tutor to get through recess. (*Chorus repeats*) It pays to be ignorant, he's no schmo. When he gets out of college, he'll turn pro.

- ONE-LINER: I'm getting champagne ideas in my 7-UP head.

## November 25, 1947

### Bob Hope

(*Broadcasting from England*)
- BOB: Colonna, what makes you act this way?

COLONNA: You won't tell anybody?
BOB: No.
COLONNA: I'm nuts!
BOB: You know, we're playing Beethoven tonight.
COLONNA: Think we'll win?

- ONE-LINER BY BRITISH GUEST: We ask America for a loan, and they only send us one Bob.

## Sweeney & March

- MARch: He's a fisherman. I could give him a gift of a box of worms.

- SWEENEY: Oh, anybody can dig that up. Perhaps I could sell you a stocking to hang over his fireplace?
  MARCH: That's a good idea.
  SWEENEY: Wait. I'll take off my shoe.

## Jimmy Durante

- DURANTE: (*After making a play for a girl*) Excuse me, folks. My scoutmaster let me out in the world too soon!

- DURANTE: (*Discussing the new fashion design ... the "new look."*) The dresses cover the legs, so there's nothing left to show, now instead of whistling, I'm feeling...mighty low!

- DURANTE: I have loads of books at my house. And they're not just for looks, either. (*Aside*) I press a lot of butterflies!

- DURANTE: (*Discussing a raffle*) I had number 8-3-3-3-3! The guy next to me had number 3-3-3-3-8!
  MOORE: So what did you do?
  DURANTE: I traded my 8-3-3-3-3 for his 3-3-3-3-8 for luck!
  MOORE: And he said okay?
  DURANTE: Right!
  MOORE: Who won?
  DURANTE: The judge's brother with number 6! (Ha, ha! I got a million of 'em!)
  DURANTE: (*After bad joke*) I've got a million of 'em! A million of 'em!
  MOORE: If you have a million of 'em, why did you pick on that one?

- WOMAN: (*Speaking gibberish French*) Vous laize vous, pour quor, je suis nes pas?
  MOORE: Oh, I couldn't!
  WOMAN: Vous lay vous, ouvrey la porte, la fentre?
  MOORE: Oh, I couldn't!
  DURANTE: What's she saying? Maybe I could!

## November 30, 1947

### *Jack Benny*

- MARY: Oh, Jack, you're so handsome!
  JACK: Really?
  MARY: One of the handsomest men I've ever seen. May I borrow your hanky?
  JACK: Why?
  MARY: The air is blowing through this hole in my head!

  (*Courtroom scene.*)
- FRED ALLEN: My name is Fred Allen and I'm a comedian.
  JACK: That's a lie, your honor!

### *Blondie*

- MR. DITHERS: (*Referring to Dagwood*) Come into my office. There's some rubbish in there, but I'll ask him to leave.

- MR. DITHERS: My wife is the melancholy type. She has a figure like a melon and a face like a collie.

### *Bergen & McCarthy*

  (*After Charlie has done something bad.*)
- BERGEN: Intuition tells me that you did it.
  CHARLIE: The squealer!

- BERGEN: Mortimer, what are you sneezing from?
  MORTIMER: My nose!
  BERGEN: But, you're hale and hearty!
  MORTIMER: No, I'm me and Morty.
  BERGEN: If you want to get better, you should go to bed with the chickens.
  MORTIMER: Not since I fell off the roost!
  BERGEN: Do you suffer from headaches?
  MORTIMER: Well, I don't enjoy them.

  (*Guest Edward Everett Horton. Psychiatrist sketch.*)
- HORTON: Doctor, I have a desire to go jump off a building. How can I be cured?
  CHARLIE: Follow your desires.
  HORTON: Doctor, how long will it take me to be cured?
  CHARLIE: Three years.
  HORTON: Three years?
  CHARLIE: Yeah, that's how long it'll take me to pay off my house.

## Fred Allen

- FRED:    Last Sunday, due to technical difficulties, there were five seconds of silence on the Jack Benny program. It was the highlight of the show.
  SENATOR CLAGHORN: I say, I'm Senator Claghorn! Clever Claghorn, they call me!
  FRED:    Well, you could have fooled me.

## Alan Young

(*Tracing his ancestors, filling out a form.*)
- ALAN:    Let's see. Age: 25. Sex: American. Nationality: Male. Some of my ancestors were from the South. That's why they wore over-you-alls. My great grandfather was a pirate. He was the terror of the seven seas. He was all wet. Once he saw a pretty blond girl walking the plank and from force of habit, he followed her!

# December 2, 1947

## Milton Berle

- SOME LINES:    Frank Gallup lost a lot of weight. He's so thin he has to hold his pants up with a wrist-watch. What is this? Laughless Tuesday? I'm wearing open-toed socks to go with my open-toed shoes.

- TO ORCHESTRA LEADER:    Ray, I wish there were two of you. Maybe one of you could play music. It's true. You know music backwards and forwards. And that's the way it sounds. I went camping. 24 hours a day, it was man against beast. (My wife was with me).

## Amos 'n' Andy

- ANDY:    I was so broken up over my girlfriend leaving me, I thought I'd commit suicide. So I went to the bridge and took off my hat and coat and, you know something? If it wasn't so high up and there wasn't water down there, I'd have jumped! I was so upset, I couldn't go to sleep.
  KINGFISH:    Why?
  ANDY:    I didn't go to bed.

## Bob Hope

- BOB:    Well, I've done my bit for England. I came home. What a plane trip home! We flew so low, the pilot had fins.
  ANNOUNCER:    Glad to have you back. You look good, Hope. What did you do, change taxidermists?

BOB:   Hey, whose side are you on?
ANNOUNCER:   Who did you see in England?
BOB:   I don't know. The fog never lifted.

- BOB:   (*On phone*) Colonna, where are you calling from?
COLONNA:   I'm in a drug store and I can't get out.
BOB:   Why?
COLONNA:   It's not open yet! I have to hang up.
BOB:   Why?
COLONNA:   Tired of hanging down.
BOB:   Colonna, I'd like to see what's going on in your head.
COLONNA:   Okay, but no smoking!
BOB:   You're just a plain dope!
COLONNA:   Not everybody can wear ruffles like you do.
BOB:   (*Ad-lib*) You brought a writer with you, didn't you?
COLONNA:   So you're back from England. Do you travel much?
BOB:   No, I buy my own towels.
COLONNA:   Have you seen my monocle? My eye is still in it.
BOB:   While I was away you worked in the stable. Did you curry the horses?
COLONNA:   No, but they were delicious french-fried.
BOB:   You better fire that writer.

## Red Skelton

- WILLIE LUMP-LUMP:   My wife's a very stunning girl. Everytime I come home, she stuns me. I tell you, if it wasn't for my wife, I don't know where I'd be, but I wish I was there. (*To guest*) I'm glad you got that face. I might've gotten it myself.

# December 7, 1947

## Jack Benny
(*Rochester is preparing Mr. Benny's bath.*)
- ROCHESTER:   Let's see, now. When Mr. Benny takes a bath, he wants everything just right. Let's see ... hmm, bathmat, bath salts, bath towels ... rubber duck.
JACK:   Rochester, I don't think I'll take a bath today. Just give me the rubber duck and I'll hold it in the shower.
ROCHESTER:   Okay, boss. You want me to sing to you? (*Sings*) Shine little glowworm, glitter, glitter! Shine little glowworm....!
JACK:   Rochester, it's such a small worm, don't kill it!
ROCHESTER:   Why be half-safe?
JACK:   Never mind. Just gimme the soap.
ROCHESTER:   Gimme, gimme, gimme. What are you a human gimme pig?

## Bergen & McCarthy

- BERGEN:   You have a book with blank pages. How can you read it?
  MORTIMER:   It ain't easy!
  BERGEN:   What else have you been doing?
  MORTIMER:   Well, I watched the sun come up. Took all day.
  BERGEN:   Why?
  MORTIMER:   I was facing the wrong way.

## Fred Allen

- FRED:   Now it's time for our presentation: The Author Meets His Match. So before this small talk gets so small we can't see it, and since I appear to have no more lines, let's get on with it.

  (*H. Allen Smith and Franklin P. Adams were the guest authors.*)
- SMITH:   I was in the third grade for 20 years. The teacher loved me.
  FRED:   Did you know then that the teacher loved you?
  SMITH:   Hey, I didn't know nothing. I was only in the third grade!

- ADAMS:   I didn't get a wink of sleep last night.
  FRED:   Really? What happened?
  Adams:   I didn't go to bed.

  (Note: That same joke was on *Amos 'n' Andy* a week before. It doesn't mean that Allen lifted it. Sometimes, writers come up with the same gags independently. However, Fred was famous for coming up with lines like the following.)

- FRED:   Education is like a hole in the sock. You've got it, but nobody knows it but you.

- FRED:   What is your book about?
  SMITH:   About six inches long and four inches wide.
  FRED:   Well phooey, or a reasonable facsimile of, to you.

## Alan Young

- ALAN:   A big beautiful blond came and sat next to me in the movies. She snuggled up close, and laid her head on my shoulders.
  GUEST:   I hope you took advantage of that.
  ALAN:   I did. I ate all her popcorn!
  ANNOUNCER:   Tell me, what are you going to be, if you grow up?

  (*A boxing sketch.*)
- ALAN:   The boxer's trunks were too tight. So it was a split decision. He was a good boxer. He always came to in time for the next fight. But I'm tough, too! Watch! I'll tear this telephone book in half with my bare hands. Ugh! Ugh! (*SFX: RIP*) There! Now for the second page!
  BOXER:   I'm gonna break every bone in your body!

ALAN:   You do, and I'll flab all over you!
TRAINER:   How come you're crouching?
ALAN:   I laced my gloves to my shoes.

# December 9, 1947

## Milton Berle

- BERLE:   (*To Frank Gallup, announcer*) You know, sometimes I think you have as much fun as people who are alive.

Amazingly, two days after Alan Young did a sketch on prize fighting, here comes Berle with ... you guessed it ... a boxing routine.

- FRANK:   Your opponent tonight is named Ape. Now, just remember, "Ape" is just his name. Got that? It's just his name!
  BERLE:   Then why is he sitting in his corner eating bananas with his feet?
  FRANK:   Just remember, you are top dog! Top dog!
  BERLE:   Yeah, well all I can say to you is ... (Bow-wow!)
  FRANK:   Come on! You're a champ!
  BERLE:   Right! I won 25 fights, then I quit. They wanted me to fight a man.
  BERLE:   (*After fight*) Wow! That was a great fight! Who won?
  FRANK:   The doctor is here. Doctor, this is Mr. Berle.
  DOCTOR:   Lay down, I'll operate!
  FRANK:   Don't worry, Berle. He's a good doctor. Almost as good as those with a license.

## Amos 'n' Andy

- KINGFISH:   Now, let's consider the honest way. (*Pause*) Okay, so much for the honest way. Let's think about the way we know best.

- KINGFISH:   This was knitted by a girl with gloves.
  ANDY:   It would probably fit better if she knitted it with a pair of knitting needles.

## Bob Hope

- BOB:   I tell you, the streets were so crowded, I crossed the street three times without touching the pavement.

  (*Football sketch with Frank Leahy, coach at Notre Dame.*)
- FRANK:   You went to college for three years? I'll bet you never opened a book.
  BOB:   You're supposed to have books?

- FRANK:   Okay, here's the play. X takes out Y. Then Y takes out X. Then X takes out Y.
  BOB:   They must be going steady!

- BOB:   Colonna, why don't you take your head to the coach and show him what a real block looks like?

## Red Skelton

- RED:   I got a trigger brain.
  GUEST:   You got Trigger's body, too!
- RED:   I have a good gag.
  GUEST:   Well, tie it around your mouth.

(*SFX: Loud drums*)
- RED:   Hey, the show's a turkey. We don't need no drumsticks to prove it!

(*Willie Lump-lump as elevator operator.*)
- GUEST:   Relax, it's a good job. A lot of men would like to be in your uniform.
  WILLIE:   Tell 'em to come on, there's plenty of room in here for all of 'em!
  GUEST:   You startled me.
  WILLIE:   Well, now we're even!
  GUEST:   I've never been so insulted!
  WILLIE:   Aw, you must have been!

# December 14, 1947

## Bergen & McCarthy

- CHARLIE:   Well, look what the Yuletide washed in.
  BERGEN:   I guess you know why I'm here?
  MORTIMER:   They're cleaning out your cage?
  BERGEN:   Mortimer, what is your favorite flower?
  MORTIMER:   Hm, whole wheat!

## Fred Allen

- FRED:   (*To announcer*) You have a new writer?
  ANNOUNCER:   Yes.
  FRED:   I sensed it.
  ANNOUNCER:   Gosh!
  FRED:   Are you happy with that line? I went to a restaurant and they charged two dollars a plate.
  ANNOUNCER:   That's all?
  FRED:   Well, if you want food it'll be a bit more.

Fred's guest that night was Walter Winchell, who left us with this thought:
- WINCHELL:   A communist is a guy who believes in democracy until he is powerful enough to deprive you of it.

## Alan Young

*(Shopping for Christmas presents.)*

- ALAN:  My uncle has false teeth, a cork leg, false arm. I'll get him all-pur-
pose glue. I don't know what to get my nephew. Last year his parents
gave him a gun. I wonder what the little orphan wants this year? What
to get my girlfriend? A handkerchief? Naw! I don't know what size her
nose is. Ah, here's a sales clerk. Excuse me, could you give me some information on ladies lingerie?
  CLERK:  Well, only what I've heard...

# December 16, 1947

## Bob Hope

- BOB:  Have you ever had mistletoe?
  COLONNA:  Well, no. But I have had a slight case of athlete's foot!
  BOB:  I've been Christmas shopping. I won't say it's crowded but while driving I stuck my hand out and when I brought it back, it was gift-
wrapped!
  BOB:  This Christmas I thought I'd give all my friends a book, but I don't
know when they'd get together to read it.

- VERA VAGUE:  How do you like my dress?
  BOB:  I've seen better filled popcorn bags.
  VERA:  Better be careful. You know what the plastic surgeon said about
shaking your head.

## Red Skelton

- ANNOUNCER:  Hi 'ya doing, Red old pal!
  GUEST:  Hi 'ya doing, Red old pal!
  RED:  Well, you can see Christmas will soon be here!

  *(Red as the mean widdle kid.)*
- MAN:  You're a bad boy! I wish I could be your father for about ten min-
utes.
  KID:  Well, okay, but I don't think Ma will like it!

  CLEM:  The teacher is loaded with class, and I have no principles.

# December 17, 1947

## The Bickersons

- BLANCHE:  My uncle put rubbing alcohol on his back and he broke his neck
trying to lick it off.

JOHN:   Sad way to meet his end.
BLANCHE:   John, close the window. It's cold outside.
JOHN:   If I close the window will it make it warmer outside?
BLANCHE:   Suppose a burglar breaks in and finds me?
JOHN:   It'll serve him right!
BLANCHE:   John, the phone is ringing. Answer it.
JOHN:   Hello?
BLANCHE:   Go to the phone and answer it!

## Jimmy Durante

- DURANTE:   (*Answering tough question*) If I knew the answer to that, would I be sitting here on this bench marked "Wet Paint?"
  MOORE:   You're younger than Al Jolson.
  DURANTE:   Who isn't?
  MOORE:   I've got a great idea! We'll become bridge builders! We'll build 20 bridges in California, 30 bridges in Ohio, and 50 bridges in Texas! Then we'll start digging.
  DURANTE:   Digging what?
  MOORE:   Rivers to go under them!

- DURANTE:   The wall in my hotel room is so thin I can drive a nail through the wall and the guy next door can hang a picture on it.

- DURANTE:   (*As Santa*) I'll bring my five deers. Donner, Blitzen, Cupid, Prancer and Lana Turner!
  MOORE:   Wait a minute! Lana Turner's not a deer!
  DURANTE:   (*To audience*) I gotta have a long talk wit dis boy!

# December 21, 1947

## Jack Benny

(*Jack doing his Christmas shopping. Used situation gags that were plot driven.*)
- DENNIS:   It's very fortunate that Christmas comes during the Christmas holidays!
  JACK:   (*To Phil Harris*) Where's your Christmas spirit?
  PHIL:   I drank them!

## Bergen & McCarthy

- BERGEN:   My heart is overflowing with pride.
  CHARLIE:   Well, put a pan under it!

- MORTIMER: I'll learn this song or my name ain't ... uh ... or my name ain't ... uh ... my name.
BERGEN: You can do it. You can!
MORTIMER: I can?
BERGEN: Can you?
MORTIMER: I asked you first!

## Alan Young

- ALAN: (*To waitress after ordering lunch*) Have you got everything?
SEXY VOICE WAITRESS: Yes...
ALAN: You can say that again!

(*Private detective sketch.*)
- ALAN: I hate to admit this, but I'm afraid of Christmas. You might say I'm a Noel Coward. Last night someone took a potshot at me. Lucky I have a small pot. Was I shot? I stuck my hand to my face. There was a big hole! It was wet! I screamed! (Then I found out it was my mouth!) Then I heard the crook sneeze! Quick as a flash, I let him have it! (Bless you!) I hurried back to my office. Something worried me. Something I should do. (*SFX: CRASH*) Oh, yes. Open the door! I entered my office and sat down at my desk. Then she walked in. She was beautiful. She was wearing an old potato sack. You couldn't tell where the potatoes ended and she began.
SEXY WOMAN: I need your help. Look at me. Look at my dress. How tight it is, how shabby it is, how dirty it is.
ALAN: I'm still looking at how tight it is.
SHE: You've got to help me find the killer.
ALAN: But I could get killed.
SHE: Well, you can't take it with you.
ALAN: If I can't take it with me, I'll be back!
SHE: Think it'll be worth the climb? Where's your manhood, your courage?
ALAN: I left home in a hurry this morning!

## Red Skelton

- CLEM: If a rooster can crow, how come a crow can't rooster? You know, the early bird gets the worm. Hm, I wonder which bird'll get me? Brrr! It's really cold today. There's an icicle on my nose. I'll break it off. (*SFX: CRASH, Tinkle*) Now that was a stupid thing to do! Oh well, I won't have to worry about getting sniffles this winter! I better light a fire. (*SFX: Scratch, scratch!*) Hmm, this match won't light. That's funny. It did yesterday!

# December 28, 1947

## Jack Benny

- JACK:   Rochester, what are we having for dinner tonight?
  ROCHESTER:   Some good hash. Made from last night's leftovers.
  JACK:   What did you have last night?
  ROCHESTER:   Hash!
  DENNIS:   Mr. Benny, what did you get Mary for Christmas?
  JACK:   Oh, I got her some beautiful alligator shoes.
  DENNIS:   (*Shocked*) You mean some alligator is running around barefooted?

## Fred Allen

- FRED:   (*After bad joke*) That was a little sneaky one. (*To Audience*) We have the doors  bolted, you know. You can't get out. (*While visiting Allen's Alley*) Ah, Titus Moody! What did you get for Christmas?
  TITUS:   A short tail cat.
  FRED:   A short tail cat? Why?
  TITUS:   When the winter gets cold, a short tailed cat don't keep the door open so long!

- FRED:   Portland gave me a great Christmas gift. A dozen handkerchiefs with the word "Ah-choo!" printed in the corner.

- FRED:   (*To announcer*) One more word out of you and I'll take that carnation out of your lapel and thrash the living daylights out of you with it.

- FRED:   (*To guest, Buster Crabbe*) Oh, be quiet. Remember, I've seen your pictures.
  BUSTER:   I have the insane desire to take off your toupee and butter the inside of it.
  FRED:   What do you mean barging into my office? I can't see you without an  appointment. So if you don't leave, I'll have to turn my head.

## Alan Young

- ALAN:   Here's a letter from a fan. "Dear Sir or Madam" She has such a short memory. P.S. I would write more but I've already sealed the envelope.

- ALAN:   You're broke? What did you spend your salary on?
  ANNOUNCER:   I weighed myself.

# December 30, 1947

## Amos & Andy

- KINGFISH:   If I was that kid's papa, I'd talk him into leaving home.

## Fibber McGee & Molly

- GILDERSLEEVE: Well, hello, McGee. I haven't seen you for a week.
  MCGEE:    Yes, it's been a wonderful week for me too.

## Bob Hope

- BOB:    Boy, the traffic is so bad in L.A. the drivers had to get out of their cars to hit pedestrians. The driver next to me was so nervous, everytime I stuck my hand out to signal a turn he bit my fingernails. (The least he could've done was get 'em even!) A scalper sold me a ticket to the Rose Bowl. Turned out to be counterfeit. It was the only Rose Bowl ticket with a picture of Lincoln throwing a pass to George Washington.

- BOB:    Colonna, did you see the Rose Bowl parade?
  COLONNA:    Sure did! There was one float in the parade that was three stories high and two blocks long! It was a big bowl of roses and no motor.
  BOB:    No motor? How did the float go?
  COLONNA:    Underneath each rose, a lady bug on stilts!
  BOB:    Colonna, reason has left you.
  COLONNA:    Yes, but I get custody of the children!

- BOB:    (*To sexy woman*) Why are you so beautiful?
  WOMAN:    Lucky, I guess.
  BOB:    Luckies never come in that good a package!

- BOB:    You know I used to play football. In fact, I was the fastest man ever to put on a football uniform.
  WOMAN:    Really? How long did it take you to put it on?

  (*Doing a football sketch.*)
- HOPE:    Okay, let's run this play and go around the end. (*SFX: Footsteps.. crash!*) Okay, let's try the other end! (*SFX: Footsteps…crash!*) Let's try the center! (*SFX: Footsteps…crash!*) Hmm…wonder how they are at ping-pong?

## Red Skelton

- RED:    (*After bad joke*) Well, now for the funny stuff!

(*Talking to Jimmy Durante*)
- RED:    Jimmy, I want to thank you for your Christmas present.
  DURANTE:    Aw, it was nothing.
  RED:    I know but I want to thank you anyway.
  DURANTE:    I have to go now. I'm going to the Z club.
  RED:    The Z club? Where's that?
  DURANTE:    Right behind the "Y." (Ha, ha, ha! I gotta million of 'em!)

- RED:   (*As Clem Kadiddlehopper*) We had so much snow at the farm I had
  to jack up the cows to milk them. It was so cold I had to break off the
  milk. It looked like spaghetti!
  ANNOUNCER:   Come on! Do you want everybody to think you're a moron?
  CLEM:   Hey, I wanna give credit where credits due! Anyway, I gotta go now.
  I gotta go home and get in my twin bathtubs.
  ANNOUNCER:   Why do you have twin bathtubs?
  CLEM:   So I can wash both feet at the same time!

  (*Red as the mean widdle kid.*)
- MOM:   Junior! You've broken six vases! Can you explain that?
  JUNIOR:   Sunday is a day of rest!

- JUNIOR:   Everytime Ma looks at me she gets up and socks Pop in the nose!

# — 1 9 4 8 —

## January 2, 1948

### *It Pays to Be Ignorant*

This was an outrageous comedy takeoff on quiz shows featuring a lot of old time vaudeville comedians and jokes that were so corny they were funny. The host was Tom Howard. The panelists were Lulu McConnell, Harry McNaughton and George Shelton who gave absurd answers to every question, when and if they ever got around to it. Those zany characters endeared themselves to the audience and the show ran nine years.

- LULU:  New Year's Eve I threw a party down in my cellar.
  TOM:  Really?
  LULU:  My husband was the party.
  HARRY:  New Year's Eve all I drank was milk. I drank so much milk I got the trembles.
  LULU:  Oh, you had the milkshakes!
  HARRY:  I spent the evening pulling a plaster cast off my wife's back. Had a ripping time!
  TOM:  My year started badly. Had to let my secretary go.
  HARRY:  Why?
  TOM:  Her husband walked in.
  LULU:  I went to the movies. The usher said, "How far down do you want to sit?" I said, "All the way down, you idiot!"
  GEORGE:  I own that cinema. Lulu, how did you like my cinema?
  LULU:  Bum!
  GEORGE:  Oh, I get it! Cinema-bum!

41

HARRY:    Well, that takes the cake!
GEORGE:   I was in love with a judo expert. But she threw me over!

# January 4, 1948

## Jack Benny

- STORY LINE:    Things that happen to Jack while waiting in line to get tickets for the Rose Bowl. In line for five hours, finally gets tickets, then
  sells them for seven dollars. Money turns out to be counterfeit with picture of Madman Muntz on it. (*Local car dealer at the time*) While waiting, he meets Mr. Kitzel.
  KITZEL:    (*Singing*) A pickle in the middle and the mustard on top, that's
  the way you like it and it's all fixed up!
  JACK:    Mr. Kitzel! How's the hot-dog business?
  KITZEL:    It's fine, but I don't relish it.

## Fred Allen

- FRED:    In order to lower prices the government is buying up all the sus-
  penders. Soon things will start to drop. During last week's wind storm,
  the wind blew down telephone wires. It was awful. Everybody's con-
  versation was lying all over the ground.
  PORTLAND:    Isn't it time to go down Allen's Alley?
  FRED:    Well, I'm glad you asked me, otherwise this would have been a very
  short program.
  TITUS:    I went to the carnival. Saw a midget mermaid.
  FRED:    What is a midget mermaid?
  TITUS:    Half girl, half sardine.

# January 6, 1948

## Milton Berle

- BERLE:    (*To audience*) Folks, don't applaud. If you like it, just nod! (*To
  announcer, Frank Gallup*) What did you get for Christmas ... blood? Ah,
  Cynthia! What memories we have! Remember those youthful days when
  I sat in front of the fireplace and you came in from the snow? I tried to
  take off your snowshoes, and you screamed! I didn't know they were
  your feet! And remember how we used to slide down the snow hills? We
  went much faster when you waxed your stomach! When you went ice
  skating, you did the figure eight, the hard way. Two fours!

## Bob Hope

- BOB:   Last week I went duck hunting. I'll have to admit I'm a bad shot. In fact, I was such a bad shot that the ducks got their pals to come over and throw rocks at me.
VERA VAGUE:   Bob, you're always making movies with Dorothy Lamour. What's Dottie Lamour got that I haven't got? I can walk around in a sarong, too, you know.
BOB:   Yeah, but her sarong doesn't have suspenders.

## Red Skelton

- AS CLEM:   I'm having a glass of horse radish and tea.
ANNOUNCER:   Horse radish and tea? Does it taste funny?
WILLIE:   It helps!
ANNOUNCER:   What have you been up to?
WILLIE:   Got a job at the zoo selling peanuts. Wore a sign that said, "Buy peanuts and feed the monkeys. I was never hungry!

## Abbott & Costello

- ABBOTT:   Every night I go to the movies with a box of chocolates and sit in the box.
COSTELLO:   Doesn't that squash the chocolates?
ABBOTT:   You know, Costello, in order to make movies you have to act with poise.
COSTELLO:   Naw, I wanna act with girls!
ABBOTT:   No, no! Be a gentleman. Wear clothes with grace.
COSTELLO:   How would I look in Grace's clothes?
ABBOTT:   No, you need new clothes…new attire.
COSTELLO:   What?
ABBOTT:   Something to wear! Attire!
COSTELLO:   How'm I gonna look walking around in a tire?
ABBOTT:   You don't understand. Actors need polish. Lots of polish. Now, do you know how to make money in the movies?
COSTELLO:   Sure. Sell polish to the actors!

# January 7, 1948

## Jimmy Durante

*(Durante was out sick. Bob Hope substituted for him.)*
- PRETTY GIRL:   Bob, you're looking good.
BOB:   When I stop looking, I'll quit.
PRETTY GIRL:   I mean … I think you're handsome.
BOB:   If my scoutmaster is listening, I'm not practicing knots tonight!

BOB:    (*Very dramatic*) Water! Water! Water! Every year I make at least one try for the Academy Award.

# January 11, 1948

## *Bergen & McCarthy*

(*Guest Lucille Ball*)

- CHARLIE:    What do you dream about?
  LUCY:    Same thing you dream about.
  CHARLIE:    Why you naughty girl!
  BERGEN:    What are we going to do tonight?
  LUCY:    Let's play games.
  BERGEN:    I'm game.
  CHARLIE:    Yeah, but you're out of season!

- SOME ONE-LINERS BY CHARLIE:    I never knew anyone like you before on purpose. Aw, go make a noise like a cobweb!

## *Fred Allen*

- PORTLAND:    Are you going to Allen's Alley?
  FRED:    As the old oak tree said in the Fall...I'm about to leave. (Someone snuck in here and wrote that joke!)

- FRED:    We were so poor, the mice went hungry.

- George Burns sings so bad, the water in the bathtub curdles.

# January 13, 1948

## *Milton Berle*

- FRANK GALLUP:    Berle, you are the second choice for women of America.
  BERLE:    Who was the first choice?
  GALLUP:    A man.
  BERLE:    Frank took a four year course in ugliness and made it in two years. He wasn't born. His parents got impatient and took the stork.

## *Amos 'n' Andy*

- ANDY:    (*Talking to girlfriend*) Do you smoke, darling?
  GIRL:    No.
  ANDY:    Well, mebbe I can borrow a cigarette from someone else.

- FAT LADY: I'm swelled with pride!
  KINGFISH: Yeah, you is swelled with something, that's for sure. (*Bidding her farewell*) Well, keep your chins up!

## Bob Hope

- BOB: I can't wait for television. That's where you can see what you smell. I went to the racetrack and found a four-leaf clover. Came home wearing it. Let's all live tonight! Tomorrow we can see a psychiatrist.

## Red Skelton

- RED: I bet on a horse. Whatta nag! He kept turning around to see if his plow was on straight. (*As Clem Kadiddlehopper. Enters singing*) My wild Irish Rose…doo, doo, doo! Boy, I can sing Wild Irish Rose so good you can smell it! What's this, perfume? I'll rub a little of it behind my ears. (*Rubs*) Well, whatta 'ya know? It removes hair, too!

- MOM: Junior! There were three cookies in this jar! You ate two. Why?
  JUNIOR: It was so dark, I didn't see the third one!

# January 18, 1948

## Bergen & McCarthy

- BERGEN: Charlie, I want to tell you the story of the boy and the Lion. Once upon a time…
  CHARLIE: Egads, will this story never end?
  BERGEN: To make a long story short…
  CHARLIE: Isn't it a little late for that?
  BERGEN: He took the thorn from the lion's paw. Later, he was thrown into the lion's pit!
  CHARLIE: And the lions threw him back?
  BERGEN: No, no, the lion recognized him.
  CHARLIE: From the Lion's club?

- BERGEN: Well, if it isn't Mortimer Snerd.
  MORTIMER: You don't have to rub it in!
  BERGEN: How are you, Morty?
  MORTIMER: I've been losing weight. Skinniness has set in.
  BERGEN: Why don't you sing something? I'd rather hear you sing than eat.
  MORTIMER: When did you ever hear me eat?

## Fred Allen

FRED: It's been a busy week. I'm busier than a little boy's tongue when his

ice cream starts to melt. I see where America is giving forty-nine billion
dollars to help feed Europe. Where is Europe eating? At the Waldorf?
(*At dinner*) My, that pie looks good. I wish my nose had a knife and
fork.

# January 20, 1948

## Milton Berle

- BERLE:   (*To Frank Gallup*) I'd like to shake your hand, but I never touch
  fish on Tuesday. Boy, it's cold today. I've got goose pimples where even
  the geese haven't gotten them. My Uncle is the only stockbroker on Wall
  street who didn't go broke in '29. He went broke in '28!
  FRANK:   I hear you're having a party at your house.
  BERLE:   Yes, my parties are a lot of fun. When people come to my house,
  what's the first thing they look forward to?
  FRANK:   Going home.

## Bob Hope

- BOB:   They have a new traffic law in L.A. Now every car going over eighty
  miles an hour must have a driver. I just got back from a skiing trip. Boy,
  was it cold. I used ten blankets! Then fifteen blankets, but I was still
  cold. Then I got mad and went inside the hotel and got a room. I was
  a very good skier, until they made me put them on.

- BOB:   When I was born the doctor slapped me. I thought it was applause,
  so took a bow.

- BOB:   (*To guest Tony Martin*) It's nice to be on a show with you. After all,
  we're both talented, handsome, leading men. (*Silence*) Well, we're lead-
  ing men. (*Silence*) Well, we're men. (*Silence*) I wonder if my dress is back
  from the cleaners?
  TONY:   Bob, where are you from?
  BOB:   Originally?
  TONY:   Never heard of the place. I'm from New York.
  BOB:   I'm from Cleveland. Not much difference.
  TONY:   No, but I can go back.

## Red Skelton

- RED:   (*As Willie Lump-lump*) Whew! I just had a narrow escape! Some guy
  just offered me a job! I used to be a fighter. I walked into the center of
  the ring, took off my robe. Men screamed, women fainted. I forgot to
  put on my trunks!

- WILLIE:   Now, I'm thirsty.
ANNOUNCER:   Here's a bottle.
WILLIE:   (*Gulp*) Gosh, water! Don't ever do a thing like that to me again!

# January 21, 1948

## *Abbott & Costello*

- ABBOTT:   We love the outdoors. The other day my wife and I took a tramp through the woods.
COSTELLO:   I'll bet the three of you had fun.
ABBOTT:   I'll have you know my wife's a cover girl.
COSTELLO:   Magazine or manhole?
ABBOTT:   She looks like a pansy.
COSTELLO:   Yeah, a chimpanzee.

- COSTELLO:   Don't make me mad! You know what happens when I get mad?
ABBOTT:   No, what?
COSTELLO:   I see red. And you know what happens when I see red?
ABBOTT:   What?
COSTELLO:   I wanna fight! And you know what happens when I fight?
ABBOTT:   What?
COSTELLO:   I get my brains knocked out!

- COSTELLO:   If I wasn't bigger than you, I'd slug you!
ABBOTT:   Well, I'm bigger than you!
COSTELLO:   That's an even better reason!

- ABBOTT:   Costello, what you need to do is find a girl who likes to do the same things you do.
COSTELLO:   Where can I find a girl who'll stand on street corners and whistle at other girls?

- ABBOTT:   You know in L.A. a man is run over by a car every five minutes.
COSTELLO:   If I was him I'd move to another town!

(*Doctor sketch*)
- COSTELLO:   Doctor, don't you want to listen to my heart?
DOCTOR:   No, if you've heard one you've heard them all! (*SFX: Snoring*)
COSTELLO:   What's that noise?
DOCTOR:   Sleeping pills.

## *You Bet Your Life*

- GROUCHO:   So you're a grocer, eh? I've never seen one in front of a counter. I had no idea you wore pants. When I got married, I sold my little black book to the telephone company. I had more numbers than they did.

- GROUCHO:    You're getting married? How many children do you want?
  WOMAN:    Around two.
  GROUCHO:    Oh, you don't want any square children, eh?
  WOMAN:    We're expecting in April.
  GROUCHO:    Boy or girl? Tell me, what would you do if a baby started crying?
  WOMAN:    I'd hold him tight, and hug him and kiss him.
  GROUCHO:    (*Crying*) Ma — Maaaaaaaa!

- MAN:    I met my wife on the way to church.
  GROUCHO:    I'll bet you've heard many a sermon since then. Where are you from?
  MAN:    Vancouver, Canada. I came here when I was seven months old.
  GROUCHO:    Did you walk down?
  MAN:    No, no. We're farmers. We go to bed with the chickens.
  GROUCHO:    I've often wondered about people who go to bed with the chickens. I'll bet they have an awful lot of eggs in their pajamas. Okay, it's time to play You Bet Your Life. What's on your mind?
  MAN:    Nothing.
  GROUCHO:    I know, but it's still time to play You Bet Your Life!

# January 25, 1948

## Bergen & McCarthy

- BERGEN:    You know, Charlie, I have more talent in my little finger than you do in your whole body.
  CHARLIE:    Then why don't you team up with your little finger?

- BERGEN:    Charlie, I understand Mortimer talks to himself. Tell me, does he talk to himself when he's alone?
  CHARLIE:    I don't know. I'm never with him when he's alone. I'll tell you what he does, though. He puts his socks on the wrong feet.
  BERGEN:    How can he put his socks on the wrong feet?
  CHARLIE:    They're my feet!

## Fred Allen

- FRED:    (*About his announcer*) He suffered an unfortunate incident in his childhood. He was born.

- FRED:    (*As a psychiatrist on the phone*) I'm sorry tell you this, Mr. Smith, but you are not a horse! Do you understand? You are NOT a horse! What's that? Okay, two dollars on the nose, but I don't think you can do it!

# January 27, 1948

## Milton Berle

- BERLE: I come from a tough neighborhood. We could always tell a new-comer. He had ears! But ah, the memories I have of my old girlfriend, Cynthia. She was a burlesque queen. I used to love the cute way she'd throw her leg up in the air. Then catch it coming down!

## Bob Hope

- BOB: It's really hot here in Palm Springs. It's so hot here the olive drinks your martini before you do. And it's really expensive to live here. I came down here with four thousand dollars and got arrested for vagrancy. Just got back from the Grand Canyon. Boy, those donkeys there are sure-footed. At one point the one I rode used only his hind legs. He had to, he was biting his front nails. (*SFX: Crash, bam! Crash!*)

  BOB: Is that you, Colonna?

  COLONNA: No, the sound man!

## Red Skelton

- RED: (*To announcer*) How are you?

  ANNOUNCER: I feel as good as I look.

  RED: Hop in bed, I'll call the doctor.

  (*As Willie Lump-lump, the punch-drunk prize fighter*)

- TRAINER: I want you to fight clean.

  WILLIE: Okay, I'll go take a shower!

  TRAINER: If you get knocked down, go to a neutral corner.

  WILLIE: Yeah, who's gonna drag me there?

  TRAINER: Just get into your best fighting position.

  WILLIE: Okay, I'll lie down on the floor.

  TRAINER: This is the big one! After this fight, you'll go places!

  WILLIE: Yeah, to the morgue, probably.

  TRAINER: (*As fight begins*) Stop those punches!

  WILLIE: You don't see any of 'em getting past me, do you?

  TRAINER: Don't worry. Next fight I'll pick someone in your own class.

  WILLIE: Okay, but do you think Mary Margaret McBride will accept?

- CLEM KADIDDLEHOPPER: I had a date last night and found out you can have fun without laughing. Up until then I swear, I'd never been kissed.

  GUEST: I don't blame you for swearing.

# January 28, 1948

## You Bet Your Life

- GROUCHO: Do you have a back scratcher? I'm just itching for one. Now, tell me. Why are you getting married?

WOMAN:   Oh, just to have something around the house.
GROUCHO:   Why don't you just get some termites? What do you do for a living?
WOMAN:   I work for United Press.
GROUCHO:   Do you do trousers?
WOMAN:   I'm a reporter.
GROUCHO:   You know I worked on a newspaper for three years. I finally quit. Just couldn't solve that crossword puzzle.

## Jimmy Durante

(*Durante had been ill for several weeks. Returned with hospital jokes*).
• DURANTE:   I was sittin' in my hospital bed and the nurse brings me a new born baby! I sez, wait a minute! Dis didn't show up in the x-rays!

(*Victor Moore was a stooge with Durante during this period*)
• VICTOR:   I'm a thief, murderer ... a killer!
DURANTE:   I better watch dis boy, he might turn crooked!
VICTOR:   I have a gun that's unorthodox. My gun shoots for two hours then stops and throws rocks!

# January 30, 1948

## It Pays to Be Ignorant

• GEORGE:   I spent four years at Harvard. Then I spent four years at Columbia and six months at Vassar.
TOM:   What did you learn at Vassar?
GEORGE:   That I'd been wasting my time at Harvard and Columbia!
TOM:   Shelton, only an idiot could understand you.
GEORGE:   I'm glad we understand each other.

• HARRY:   She was my girl! I'd go through fire, water and snoo for her.
TOM:   What's snoo?
HARRY:   Nothing, what's snoo with you?
LULU:   Oh, Harry, come here and gimme a big kiss. I won't charge a thing!
HARRY:   Lulu, why don't you stay in your shell with the rest of the nuts? How old are you, anyway?
LULU:   Oh no, when I was a little girl I was taught to keep my age in the dark.
HARRY:   Those were the Dark Ages.

• LULU:   My father raised pigs.
HARRY:   You're telling me.
TOM:   Okay, let's get back to the show. What was Mark Twain's real name?

GEORGE: Who?

TOM: Mark Twain. He wrote Tom Sawyer.

GEORGE: That's nothing. I wrote Betty Grable. Got a nice letter from Harry James.

# February 1, 1948

## Bergen & McCarthy

- BERGEN: Mortimer, I've been looking for you all day.
  MORTIMER: Any luck?
  BERGEN: Where have you been?
  MORTIMER: I tried to call you but I couldn't work the pay telephone.
  BERGEN: All you have to do is use a little intelligence.
  MORTIMER: Oh ho! I was using nickels!
  BERGEN: You use your index finger to dial. It's right next to your thumb.
  MORTIMER: Going which way?

- RAY NOBLE: (*Restaurant sketch*) I'm a good cook. I'm noted for my frog's legs.
  CHARLIE: Well, wear your pants long and nobody'll notice. Tell me, is your restaurant clean?
  RAY: Why our dishes are never touched by human hands.
  CHARLIE: How do you wash them?
  RAY: With our feet.

## Fred Allen

- FRED: Jack Benny is tighter than six toes in a stocking.
  PORTLAND: Are you ready to go down Allen's Alley?
  FRED: As the man said when the jeweler arrived with his watch, "The time has come." (*Knock on door. Titus Moody answers*).
  FRED: Mr. Moody. When did you learn about the birds and the bees?
  TITUS: My Pa told me. I went steady with a woodpecker 'til I was twenty-one.
  (*Fred did a satire on the opera* Carmen *using the lyrics: "A Fish Can't Smell Without Its Nose." Sung to* Carmen's *theme.*)

## Bob Hope

- BOB: It's better to give than receive. At least that's what they keep telling me.
  VERA: I gave my boyfriend something for his den.
  BOB: What?
  VERA: Me!

- BOB:   (*In car crash*) Colonna, didn't you see that tree?
  COLONNA:   I hit it, didn't I?

# February 4, 1948

## *Abbott & Costello*

- COSTELLO:   My uncle took a banana boat, but it sunk.
  ABBOTT:   Why?
  COSTELLO:   You can't build a boat outta bananas!

- ABBOTT:   Costello, a dog followed you in here. I think he picked up your scent.
  COSTELLO:   How do you know?
  ABBOTT:   He's holding his nose.

## *You Bet Your Life*

- GROUCHO:   How long have you been a dog doctor?
  DOCTOR:   Six months.
  GROUCHO:   I'll bet you could tell many a tale. (*tail*) How do you get customers?
  DOCTOR:   Mouth to mouth.
  GROUCHO:   You mean dogs tell each other about you? I have trouble dancing with fat ladies. Maybe it's because they're so much closer to me than the others.

## *Jimmy Durante*

- DURANTE:   A dog saw my picture in the paper and fell in love 'wit me and his mother hasn't the heart to tell her I'm not a cocker spaniel.

- ARTHUR TREACHER:   It's so hot in Florida. Everyone sleeps under one sheet.
  DURANTE:   Sounds like a swell way to make friends.
  ARTHUR:   What did you do at the dance last night, Jimmy?
  DURANTE:   Well, there I was tossing hunks of gold to the goldfish, when this gal asks me to dance. So I decided to show her my new steps. I stood up and spun around real fast.
  ARTHUR:   What then?
  DURANTE:   I was flat on my back! (Of course, you have to do it with music or it doesn't look so good.)
  DURANTE:   (*After flubbing a line*) Forgive me folks, my old trouble's coming back. I can't read.
  ARTHUR:   You went to the theater last night. How was the show?
  DURANTE:   It was great. They had thirty bubble dancers!

ARTHUR:   What's so good about that?
DURANTE:   Only twenty-nine bubbles!

# February 8, 1948

## Jack Benny

- ROCHESTER:   I better wake Mr. Benny up. Look at him asleep with his thumb in his mouth. How sweet!

- DENNIS DAY:   It was so cold, my uncle sits with his feet in the fireplace.
  JACK:   Really?
  DENNIS:   Wish we could break him of the habit. He's getting shorter every year!

  *(Jack did a takeoff on Allen's Alley. Called it "Nightmare Alley" based on a current movie by that name.)*

- DENNIS:   *(Talking about his date)* Then the beast in me came out. So I put my arm around her and took her hand.
  JACK:   Then what?
  DENNIS:   There's more?

## Bergen & McCarthy

- CHARLIE:   *(Lamenting breakup with girlfriend)* She lit the flame in my heart, then ran away when it got hot! I'm so sad. I'm going down to the river and take lessons in drowning. I'm going to commit suicide even if it kills me.

- BERGEN:   Mortimer, you act as though your dog was human.
  MORTIMER:   Well, he acts as though I'm human!
  BERGEN:   You're putting on weight. What you need are bathroom scales.
  MORTIMER:   Aw, who wants to weigh a bathroom?

- CHARLIE:   *(Introducing guest Andy Divine)* Here he is. His name is Divine, but his voice isn't. Tell me, Mr. Divine, where have you been?
  ANDY:   Well, you've heard of the stockyards show?
  CHARLIE:   Yeh, we just got wind of it.

## Fred Allen

- FRED:   The Jack Benny show. That's the time when people look at their radios and say, "What else is on?" *(To orchestra leader)* That song is all right except for two things. The words and the music. Folks, this is such a good band. If they can't "send" you, they'll go themselves. Our show is unrehearsed, unprepared and uninteresting. Russia is buying everything from the United States. You might say that Russia is giving us the business.

- WALTER WINCHELL: Now, Behind The International Mess. "Ike" Said That Russia Is In No position to fight a global war. Well, they certainly are in a position to fight a global peace!

# February 10, 1948

## Milton Berle

- BERLE: Frank, I got a kick out of that joke and if you'll turn around I'll give it back. You seem so peppy tonight. You must have changed to a lighter embalming fluid. What an audience! There's a man in the third row wearing a straw hat with holes for the ears. And here's a lady in the third row beating her fur coat to death.
  STOOGE: My uncle was a great horseman. He used to ride bareback, but the cops made him put something on.
  BERLE: (*After that joke*) Don't worry, I liked it!

- PLOT: Berle goes to Hollywood to make a movie, but gets replaced by bit player, Clark Gable. In another movie, gets replaced by Margaret O'Brien. Final movie, gets replaced by Lassie. Sketch ends with Berle saying, "Bow-wow!"

## Amos 'n' Andy

- KINGFISH: Don't worry, I got a perfect record in this court room. I aims to win this case and break my losing streak.

## Bob Hope

- BOB: Washington is so crowded. I got a room and a bath in different hotels.
  COLONNA: I'm in a hotel with no walls!
  BOB: No walls? What holds it up?
  COLONNA: That has become a nasty problem.
  BOB: Colonna, how did you get to be the way you are?
  COLONNA: My mother was frightened by something when I was born.
  BOB: What?
  COLONNA: Me!
  BOB: Does your hotel have a bathroom?
  COLONNA: Yes, and I even have a bathtub.
  BOB: Yeah, well, when were you last in it?
  COLONNA: Ohh, you're supposed to get in it?
  BOB: (*To Vera Vague*) Did you have trouble during the flight here? Or is your broom equipped with radar?

## *Red Skelton*

- RED:  (*After joke bombs*) Well, it all looks funny on paper, you know! (*About announcer*) He looks like his distemper shots didn't take. (*As Clem doing a toast*) Up to the lips and over the gums, look out stomach, here it comes! (*About lost girlfriend*) I've been looking for her since 1940. Here it is 1948. Three years is a long time!
  GIRL:  (*She arrives*) Clem, it's me in the flesh!
  CLEM:  Hmm, loose fit! (*In a dairy sketch*) The cows look at me and it makes them content they're cows. Here, sweetheart. For you, a pearl necklace.
  GIRL:  Couldn't you have taken them out of the oysters first?
  CLEM:  (*Aside to audience*) When she was born, she got offers from Inner Sanctum!

# February 11, 1948

## *Abbott & Costello*

- COSTELLO:  I just moved into a new house.
  ABBOTT:  Really. Do you have a large patio?
  COSTELLO:  Let's not get personal!
  ABBOTT:  Is your roof shingle?
  COSTELLO:  Certainly not! Whoever heard of a married roof?
  ABBOTT:  You know when I come to visit, I'd like a room with a bath.
  COSTELLO:  Well, this is a farm. You get a room with a path.
  ABBOTT:  Must be some house.
  COSTELLO:  It's a house with seven Grables. (*Reference to Betty Grable*)
  ABBOTT:  Grables? You mean Gables.
  COSTELLO:  Listen, when I build a house, it's gotta be well built!

## *You Bet Your Life*

- GROUCHO:  (*To contestants*) We make a nice threesome. A bride to be, a groom to be and a used to be. Tell me, how did you meet?
  GROOM:  Through mutual friends.
  GROUCHO:  Oh, they were in insurance? So you're a judge, eh? How much do you charge per case? (*No, no, forget I said that.*) I may have a case for you judge. I have a friend who's having trouble with his wife.
  GROOM:  What's the trouble?
  GROUCHO:  He's married to her. But he found a solution. Four drops in a cup of tea.

# February 14, 1948

## *Jack Benny*

Today, Valentine's day is Jack's birthday. His birthday cake has thirty-nine candles on it arranged in a question mark.

- DENNIS:   Mr. Benny told me to get a girl, hold her close, put my arms around her and put my head close to hers.
  MARY:   Then what did Jack say?
  DENNIS:   Nothing! After he got that far, he fainted!

- PLOT:   Jack broods because his girlfriend broke his engagement, but was very happy when she returned the ring.

## Bergen & McCarthy

*(Mario Lanza was introduced on this show as a new singer.)*
- MARIO:   I'm looking for a job as a comedian.
  CHARLIE:   Oh, too proud to work, eh?
  MARIO:   You must have heard of my reputation.
  CHARLIE:   Well, we all have something to live down.

## Fred Allen

- FRED:   Jack Benny's birth certificate is on the Freedom Train. (*A train filled with historical documents that was currently touring the nation.*) Abe Burrows has a new record album:   I Speak Spanish Like a Castanet.

# February 17, 1948

## Milton Berle

- BERLE:   Frank you're biting off your nose and with that nose you'll have to be a sword swallower. But, ah, those golden memories of Cynthia, my old girlfriend! How could I forget your eyes. One said, "Come hither." And the other one came over to meet it. Oh, Cynthia! Remember when you were angry, how you'd blow off steam through the hole in your head. And on Lincoln's birthday, you got mad because I wouldn't send him a gift. And how you used to call your friends over in Jersey City. I begged you to use the phone!

## Amos 'n' Andy

- KINGFISH:   Open the letter from your uncle. There might be some good news in it. Like maybe he's dying.

- ANDY:   I know why that doctor wears a mask over his face during an operation. In case anything goes wrong, the patient can't identify him.

- KINGFISH:   He's a killer, a thief and a fiend.
  ANDY:   And he's got some pretty bad habits, too.

## Bob Hope

- BOB:  Last night it was so cold, I looked in my closet and my top coat was wearing my overcoat. I returned to Hollywood on the train. What service! If the ride got bumpy they let me change mailbags. But, there's no place like Hollywood. Not even Hollywood.

- BOB:  (*On phone*) Colonna, why are you always calling me "collect?"
  COLONNA:  I can't remember your real name.
  BOB:  Colonna, is there a school for idiots?
  COLONNA:  Yes, didn't you know?
  BOB:  No!
  COLONNA:  We thought you were playing hookey.

- BOB:  That was Les Brown and his "You can have them, I don't want them, they're too flat for me." (*Berle used same joke on his show earlier. It's a takeoff on song "She's Too Fat for Me" sung by Arthur Godfrey.*)

(*Vera Vague was named honorary Mayor of Woodland Hills, California, hence this sketch.*)
- VERA:  Thanks for the introduction, Bob, but next time I want money.
  BOB:  You, a girl? Mayor? I expected a man.
  VERA:  So did I.
  BOB:  I'll bet you were cold last night. Did you have any trouble wearing those fur-lined bloomers?
  VERA:  No. Do you want them back?
  BOB:  You were in vaudeville, weren't you?
  VERA:  Yes, and it was so bad if someone threw a tomato at us we were glad.
  BOB:  It was rough. I once stayed in a hotel that was so bad the mice ate out.

## Red Skelton

(*As Deadeye, the cowboy*)
- DEADEYE:  Step aside men! I'm not afraid of that gunfighter. I'm tough, see? I'm gonna call his bluff. Here, Bluff! Here, Bluff!
  DANCE HALL GIRL:  Look into my eyes. Don't you see love … romance?
  DEADEYE:  Nope! All I see is eyeballs.

RED:  (*To woman*) Just for that, I'm gonna tell everybody you're Mrs. Calabash! (*Reference to Jimmy Durante's mysterious sign-off.*)

# February 18, 1948

## Abbott & Costello

- COSTELLO:  At the dance tonight I'm gonna wear a red coat and red pants.

ABBOTT:    How about red buttons?
COSTELLO:    What? And have everybody staring at me?
ABBOTT:    You're worried about what others think?
COSTELLO:    Sure! At the last party I wore a red sash, and everybody laughed.
ABBOTT:    Well, why didn't you wear red pants to match?
COSTELLO:    Ohh, you're supposed to wear pants?
ABBOTT:    Right, those legs of yours aren't so hot.
COSTELLO:    Hey, I'll match my legs with Betty Grables!
ABBOTT:    Are you kidding? Your legs don't even match each other.

## You Bet Your Life

- GROUCHO:    (*To a long-winded guest*) That's a very sweet story. I enjoyed
  every hour of it. Tell me, at your wedding, did you forget anything?
  MAN:    I forgot where I parked the car.
  GROUCHO:    Oh well, it was too late to back out, anyway.

## Jimmy Durante

- DURANTE:    I don't mind jokes floppin'. It's just that I hate to face those
  comedians later at the Brown Derby. (*Famous Hollywood restaurant*)

  (*At the Brown Derby*)
- WAITER:    Here we seat you according to your importance. Follow me. Not
  here. Next table … next table … come along … next table…. Here we
  are!
  DURANTE:    Well, as long as I'm here I may as well wash my hands!
  WAITER:    The ham sandwich costs twenty-seven dollars.
  DURANTE:    Twenty-seven dollars for a ham sandwich!
  WAITER:    The ham came from New York on an airplane.
  DURANTE:    Well, take this back and bring me one that hitch-hiked!

# February 22, 1948

## Jack Benny

- DENNIS:    I get my ice cream at the hardware store. They put nuts in it.
  JACK:    (*To audience*) That joke doesn't sound like us, does it?

  JACK:    Mary, did you go horse back riding?
  MARY:    All I know about horses is they don't wear high heel shoes.
  DENNIS:    I went horse back riding. I rode side-saddle.
  JACK:    Dennis, you rode side-saddle? Why?
  DENNIS:    I had to. It was a female horse.

  (*Frank Sinatra in guest appearance.*)
- FRANK:    I don't understand it. Every day I get up, put on my shorts, put

on suntan lotion and lie on my stomach for hours, and I still can't get a tan.

JACK:   I don't understand. The sun has been shining all week outside

FRANK:   Ohh, outside!

- JACK:   (*To Mr. Nelson who is building a house*) You built this house and it has no bathroom. What are you going to do?

NELSON:   I'm gonna give you a flashlight and a pair of slippers!

JACK:   Ohh, outside! I think I'll walk out on the balcony. (*SFX: Crash!*) Mr. Nelson! There's no balcony! Why?

NELSON:   My uncle is a doctor. You're the third one this week!

## Bergen & McCarthy

- CHARLIE:   Here I am, Charlie McCarthy. No other program can make that statement. Well, well, Don Ameche. What brings you here besides an ill-wind?

DON:   I need a favor and I'll pay you for it. How does five dollars strike you?

CHARLIE:   It doesn't even muss my hair.

- BERGEN:   Well, Mortimer. How are you today?

MORTIMER:   More or less.

BERGEN:   Feeling poorly? Well, you can't keep a good man down. Who said that?

MORTIMER:   Uh … musta been a cannibal.

BERGEN:   Mortimer, can anyone be as stupid as you are?

MORTIMER:   Well, they got my permission!

(*Sketch about Income Tax office*)

- VOICE:   Aaaak! Don't beat me! Please, don't beat me!

BERGEN:   My goodness, what did that man do?

CHARLIE:   He had a penny left in his pocket.

BERGEN:   You know, Charlie, you can pay taxes as you go.

CHARLIE:   But I'm not going anywhere.

BERGEN:   You will if you don't pay taxes.

## Fred Allen

- FRED:   The way countries are fighting today, you'd think the world was full of relatives and in-laws. That medication the doctor gave me really fouled me up. For two days I didn't know which way the wind was blowing.

PORTLAND:   Is that important?

FRED:   It is if you're chewing tobacco.

# February 24, 1948

## *Bob Hope*

(*Driving with Colonna*)

- BOB:   Beautiful country! Wonder when they'll build a road through here? Colonna, you're driving too fast!
  COLONNA:   I'm only doing sixty.
  BOB:   Yes, but in reverse?
  COLONNA:   I wondered why the Burma Shave signs didn't rhyme!

# February 25, 1948

## *Jimmy Durante*

- DURANTE:   I'll admit I've got a nice profile, but Clark Gable's got a whole face. I went to the races yesterday. Lana Turner was standing at the finish line. It was the first time a jockey came in ahead of the horse.

## *Jack Benny*

- JACK:   I'll never forget the day I met her. I was walking down the street, fell in an open manhole, and there she was.

## *Fred Allen*

- PORTLAND:   How are you today?
  FRED:   If I felt any better, I'd charge admission.
  PORTLAND:   Time for Allen's Alley?
  FRED:   As the butcher said when he stood on his scales, "I'm on my weigh."

# March 2, 1948

## *Milton Berle*

- BERLE:   (*To Frank Gallup*) I've always wanted to write a book about you, but somebody beat me to it ... "The Hound of Baskervilles."

## *Bob Hope*

- BOB:   (*Broadcasting from USC*) I always like to do my show at a college, so I can blame the smell on the chemistry class. This place is co-ed. Coed, that means, see you later I gotta go meet the student body. I love it here, but I never should have asked that girl to let me carry her books. How was I to know she was a librarian? When I was in college I used to write the answers on my sleeve. My shirt graduated two years before I did.

COLONNA: Hope, I've got something for you and I want you to keep it under your hat.

BOB: What?

COLONNA: A new head.

BOB: I see you have a picture of me.

COLONNA: Yes, somebody wrote on it, "Slow, this may happen to you."

## Red Skelton

- CLEM: I went to a rally and heard a politician speak for two hours.
  ANNOUNCER: What did he talk about?
  CLEM: He didn't say.
  ANNOUNCER: I heard you went to a party. Did you enjoy yourself?
  CLEM: I must have, I feel lousy.
  ANNOUNCER: I'll bet you made yourself look stupid.
  CLEM: I did not! I was born this way.
  ANNOUNCER: Oh, stop being funny.
  CLEM: If I do, we starve!

# March 3, 1948

## Abbott & Costello

ABBOTT: Didn't your Dad tell you about the birds and the bees?

COSTELLO: Yeah, he didn't know anything about girls.

ABBOTT: Do you want to be the kind of guy who thinks of nothing but girls!

COSTELLO: Is there any other kind?

ABBOTT: You're just like a kid. I think I'll get you a doll and some games.

COSTELLO: You get the doll. I'll think of the games.

## Bing Crosby

*(Jack Benny was the guest. Scene: A soda fountain.)*

- JACK: I'll have a Coke. You'll have the same?
  BING: No, I take mine in a glass by itself.
  JACK: *(Looking over selections in Jukebox)* Let's see what we have here. Hm, Bing Crosby...nope. The Andrew sisters. Gosh, there's three of them! Hm, the Ink Spots. There's three of them, too. Hmm, Fred Waring's Glee Club! Now, there's a buy if ever I saw one! Gee, if I play this, do all these people sitting around here get to listen to it, too? They do? Well

... okay, everybody! Gather around! This ones on me! (*Finally puts nickel in and plays jukebox.*)

- JACK:  Bing, how would you feel if I didn't play the violin? (*No answer*) Let me put it another way. (*Benny tunes his violin briefly.*)
  BING:  That was great! So long, Jack!
  JACK:  Now cut that out!

## Jimmy Durante

(*Durante sang song, "I'd Make a Wonderful Skywriter If I Only Knew How to Spell."*)

- VICTOR MOORE:  Jimmy, you're the greatest!
  DURANTE:  Ah, you're just trying to raise my ego.
  VICTOR:  No. My salary. Speaking of flying, my Dad jumped out of a plane without a parachute.
  DURANTE:  Nobody can do that.
  VICTOR:  You can...once!
  DURANTE:  Are you going flying?
  VICTOR:  No, I get dizzy looking at airmail stamps.

# March 7, 1948

## Bergen & McCarthy

- BERGEN:  Charlie, this story is a favorite among the Greeks.
  CHARLIE:  Well, go find a Greek and tell it to him!
  BERGEN:  (*After telling the story*) What did you think of my story?
  CHARLIE:  Well, there is a word for it, but they won't let me use it here.

- BERGEN:  Do you think she'd be happy with a man like me?
  CHARLIE:  Well, if he's not too much like you.

# March 9, 1948

## Milton Berle

- BERLE:  (*To Frank Gallup*) Frank, you look like something a dog buried and is trying to forget where. What's the matter? Did they forget to put a clean sheet on your slab this morning? My uncle's afraid to go to sleep. Afraid he'll dream about work.

## Red Skelton

- RED:  Did you hear about the movie star who got married and liked his wife so much he held her over for another week!

- MOM:   Junior, I told you to go upstairs and wash thoroughly!
  JUNIOR:   I did, but thoroughly wasn't up there! I have a split personality. One part is bad and the other part is worse!

## March 10, 1948

### Jimmy Durante

(*Arguing over girlfriend*)
- MOORE:   If I date her, I'll take her for a ride in my car.
  DURANTE:   I'll take her for a ride in my car.
  MOORE:   I'll take her to a show.
  DURANTE:   I'll take her to a show.
  MOORE:   After that, I'll take her to Ciro's. (*Classy nightspot*)
  DURANTE:   I'll take her to Ciro's.
  MOORE:   Yes, but I'll take her inside!
  DURANTE:   Sneak! Here's a friendship that could ripen into nothing!

### The Bickersons

- JOHN:   (*In hotel*) How much do they charge for this broken down room?
  BLANCHE:   Be quiet! This is the elevator.
  JOHN:   Good thing all I brought was my tooth brush and overnight bottle.

## March 14, 1948

### Fred Allen

- PORTLAND:   Are you ready to go down Allen's Alley?
  FRED:   As the pool ball said, "If you want me to go just give me the cue."

- FRED:   The sky is poor tonight. The moon is down to its last quarter.

- FRED:   If you play post office, you may get married and go through life with a dead letter.
  DOCTOR:   Do you mind if I examine your head?
  FRED:   Okay, but hurry and get to the point.

## March 16, 1948

### Milton Berle

- FRANK GALLUP:   It's income tax time! Here's Berle and, as he opens the income tax envelope, we can hear him say: (*SFX: Woody Woodpecker laugh*).

BERLE:    Thank you. Folks, he's always behind me and supports me where I need it most. What's the matter, Frank? Been dreaming you're alive again?

• BERLE:    At breakfast, I just sit and look at my wife....who can eat?

## Fibber McGee & Molly

• FIBBER:    I got a pretty good army record. (*I'll play it for you sometime.*)
GILDERSLEEVE:    I have to leave. I'm going away.
FIBBER:    Really? What's the charge?
GILDERSLEEVE:    I really must go. I'm in a hurry.
FIBBER:    What's the rush? I just came though the post office and your picture is not on the wall.

## Bob Hope

• BOB:    We had a power shortage. The electricity was so weak, when I opened the refrigerator, the little light struck a match! It's raining and it's income tax time. Don't worry about the weather. The government will soak you plenty.

• COLONNA:    Hope, take off your hat and show the geometry class what a real square looks like.
BOB:    Do you believe in being a criminal, a killer, a rat?
COLONNA:    Sure. Keeps me out of mischief!

## Red Skelton

• CLEM:    I don't know what to get my girl for Easter.
ANNOUNCER:    Get her an Easter outfit.
CLEM:    To wear or color eggs?
ANNOUNCER:    You're a mess! Look behind your ears!
CLEM:    If I could do that, I'd pick up a pretty penny in a sideshow!

# March 23, 1948

## Milton Berle

• BERLE:    (*To audience*) There must be people out there, I hear snoring.
(Note:    During this period, Milton Berle had a hit song called, "I Wuv a Wabbit."
Also on *Amos 'n' Andy*, James Baskett, who played Gabby the lawyer, won

a special Academy Award for his voice-over work in the Disney movie, *Song of the South*.)

## Bob Hope

- BOB:   At the Academy Awards, all the actors were there and they were great sports about losing. I had to "boo" alone. Loretta Young won for *The Farmer's Daughter*. *The Farmer's Daughter* … I still don't see how they made a movie out of that story. Anyway, I found out why those stars got Academy Awards. They do it in a sneaky way. They act.

## Red Skelton

- RED:   What a world! Any day now, I expect Stalin to give the world three days to get out!

- RED:   I won't say the Academy Award show was long, but the kid in front of me grew up!

- CLEM:   (*Enters singing*) Doo, doo, doo!
  HOST:   Excuse me. We cannot permit singing!
  CLEM:   Somebody singing?
  HOST:   Come now! You're letting your mind wander.
  CLEM:   Well, that's all right. It's too weak to go far.

- CLEM:   I met a girl. I just opened my wallet and there she was.

- RED:   (*As Junior, the mean widdle kid*) I know what I'll do! I'll fill my tub with bubbles and it will foam, and my mother will think I've gone mad, and I'll never have to take another bath again!

# March 24, 1948

## Abbott & Costello

- COSTELLO:   My uncle milked a cow for ten minutes before he found out he was shaking hands with himself!

- ABBOTT:   What's your girlfriend like?
  COSTELLO:   She's just like Lana Turner. Except that her head is bigger, she's fatter, and she's shorter … aw, the heck with Lana Turner. Ever see Lassie?

- ABBOTT:   (*In jungle sketch*) Come on, Costello! You're acting like a coward!
  COSTELLO:   I'm not acting!
  ABBOTT:   When you're hunting, first the lion gets your scent. Then you get the lion's scent.

COSTELLO:   Well. Now he's got me matching pennies with a lion!

- COSTELLO:   You know if it wasn't for that beard you'd look just like my wife.
  ABBOTT:   I don't have a beard.
  COSTELLO:   No, but my wife does.

## Jimmy Durante

- MOORE:   You know, where I come from the population is so small the mosquitoes go around biting each other.
  DURANTE:   Where I come from, men are men and women are women. (Which is a nice arrangement on those long winter nights!)

- GAME WARDEN:   Hey! It's against the law to fish here!
  DURANTE:   We're not fishing!
  WARDEN:   Oh, yeah? Well, how did those two fish get in that frying pan!
  DURANTE:   Suicide?

# March 28, 1948

## Fred Allen

- FRED:   This is going to be a battle of wits. Too bad you didn't come prepared.
  ANNOUNCER:   Those kids won the Pepsi-Cola scholarship. "Pop" is sending them to college.
  FRED:   A line like that I wouldn't throw to a drowning man!

- TITUS MOODY:   They were drinking to forget.
  FRED:   Forget what?
  MOODY:   What they're drinking.

# March 30, 1948

## Red Skelton

- RED:   I gave an exhibition dive at a swimming pool. I climbed up a hundred foot diving board, walked out to the edge, looked down and....
  ANNOUNCER:   Then what?
  RED:   You know, it's harder to climb down a ladder than go up one?

- JUNIOR:   I learned that word from my mother when she dropped that hot iron on her toe.
  MAN:   Are you his mother?
  JUNIOR:   She'd be awfully silly dressed like that if she was my father!

- RED:  Just do it!
ANNOUNCER:  I don't have to DO anything, except die.
RED:  Yeah, but you keep putting it off!

# March 31, 1948

## Jimmy Durante

- DURANTE:  I used to know a guy named Joe. Boy, what a show-off. Now he's married and has twelve kids. Once a show-off, always a show-off!

## Bergen & McCarthy

- BERGEN:  Boy, that W.C. Fields was so funny, I had to hold my sides.
CHARLIE:  With me, it was my nose.
BERGEN:  *(After reading poem)* Quote the Raven, "Nevermore."
CHARLIE:  Here's your hat and there's the door.

## Fred Allen

- PORTLAND:  Isn't it time for Allen's Alley?
FRED:  As the two men said when they invented the Tootsie Roll, "Let's make it short and sweet."

Fred Allen loved to write lines like that. Here's another one he used later on in the show.

- FRED:  As the eyebrow said to the tweezer, I'll go along with you in a pinch.

# April 6, 1948

## Milton Berle

- BERLE:  At my show people always leave here with aching sides.
GALLUP:  Big laughs, huh?
BERLE:  No, narrow seats!
GALLUP:  Oh, Berle, you kill me.
BERLE:  I'd like to, but I think somebody beat me to it.
BERLE:  Memories of my old girlfriend Cynthia! Remember, dear, when I rode past your house and you'd come running? Barking and snapping at the tires. Later we parked the car in a romantic spot and you kept shaking your head, no! no! I didn't know you had your nose caught in the windshield wiper.
BERLE:  My father was fine until he had a horrible accident.

GALLUP: What was it?
BERLE: Me!
GALLUP: What was he expecting?
BERLE: A baby.

## Amos 'n' Andy

• SAPPHIRE: With this money we could pay some bills that's been laying around here for six months.
KINGFISH: Forget them! Let's pay the old ones first.

## Bob Hope

• BOB: (*After flubbing a line*) Excuse me, folks. I couldn't get my tongue into high. Colonna, what's the orchestra doing?
COLONNA: We're playing Beethoven.
BOB: Anything wrong?
COLONNA: Plenty. We're losing.

## Red Skelton

• CLEM: Well, here I am. America's answer to germ warfare.
ANNOUNCER: Clem, I hope you didn't come here to make a fool of yourself.
CLEM: Nope, I took care of that before I left home. I think I put on the wrong head when I got up this morning!

(*In a western sketch as Deadeye.*)
• BARTENDER: Hey, you're getting to be a regular customer.
DEADEYE: Yeah, them swinging doors fool me!
BARTENDER: So you're a good shot? You must have good eyesight.
DEADEYE: Yeah, once I ate carrots for five months.
BARTENDER: Did your eyesight get better?
DEADEYE: No, but my ears grew three inches.

# April 7, 1948

## Henry Morgan

Along about this time a new comedian was introduced by Fred Allen. His name was Henry Morgan and he brought an offbeat, sophisticated style of humor to radio.

• MORGAN: As a child I wasn't like other six year olds on the block. I was nine.

• MORGAN: (*In sketch*) Darling, we've been married eight years.
WIFE: Yes.
MORGAN: Now you can call me by my first name.

- MAN: Sir, I don't like the way you've been flirting with my wife!
  MORGAN: Well, how do you want me to do it?

- MORGAN: She attempted suicide and threw herself on the railroad tracks. but the trains were so slow, she starved to death.
  MORGAN: (*Doing gag commercial*) Don't forget, "Stuno" spelled backwards means you're showing your ignorance.

## April 11, 1948

### Fred Allen

- FRED: Jack Benny's program ran overtime and he was cut off. Gad, that means you'll never hear the end of Benny! Time for Allen's Alley. As the two inventors said when they invented the garter, "Let's make it snappy!"
  ONE LONG PAN: Man who commit murder with clock, end up doing time.

## April 13, 1948

### Bob Hope

- BOB: Colonna, where did you go during your high school days?
  COLONNA: Grammer school.

- BOB: (*To attractive woman*) I had an awful time catching up with you. I could run faster if I wore a belt. You should go out with me. Let's face it. Some guys have it, some don't.
  WOMAN: Well, maybe you can buy it, Mr. Hope.

- WOMAN: Oh, look. There's dad out digging in the garden.
  BOB: Hasn't he found that bottle, yet?
  WOMAN: I can't resist you. You're so handsome! So ragged!
  BOB: That's rugged!

### Red Skelton

- ANNOUNCER: Now that's what I call a stupid question.
  CLEM: Get ready for a stupid answer.
  ANNOUNCER: I hear you have a new girlfriend.
  CLEM: Yeah, and she's so lazy she sleeps on the stove so she can have breakfast in bed.
  ANNOUNCER: Does she cook?
  CLEM: Well, she simmers a little. I don't know what I'd do without her. But I'm waiting for suggestions.

- RED:    (*Insult line*) Why don't you go play cops and robbers and try to solve yourself?

# April 14, 1948

## Jimmy Durante

- DURANTE:    Me, a circus fan? Oh boy, am I! Why I knew hippo when he didn't even have a potamus! (*Talking to Garry Moore*) That's a great idea you put in my head, and it was a neat trick because I had my hat on! (*About to tell a story*) I'll grab my shirt, for thereby hangs a tale! It all started just the other day.... (*Intro to comedy sketch*)

# April 17, 1948

## Abe Burrows

The broadway playwright, director, songwriter and sometime play "doctor," Abe Burrows had his own radio show for a brief period. He was also the uncle of Woody Allen. He did a lot of song parodies and some great lines like: "I have two electric blankets. One is portable for walking in my sleep."

# April 18, 1948

## Bergen & McCarthy

- MORTIMER:    Well, you know the old saying...
  BERGEN:    What old saying?
  MORTIMER:    Oh ... any old saying will do. I ain't fussy.
  BERGEN:    Mortimer! What about your self-respect?
  MORTIMER:    Oh ... that old thing!

- BERGEN:    Charlie, I'm getting hot under the collar.
  CHARLIE:    Well, you better, you're not so hot above the collar.

## Fred Allen

- FRED:    I hope I live to be as old as that joke. Jack Benny is the only man in Hollywood who has a burglar alarm on his garbage can. When you go to the Stage Delicatessen, try the tongue sandwich. Their tongue sandwiches speak for themselves. Now, it's time for a stroll down Allen's Alley.

PORTLAND:  Shall we go?
FRED:  As the stocking said when the garter broke, there's nothing holding me up.

## Bob Hope

- DIRECTOR:  Colonna, this part calls for a curvaceous girl.
  COLONNA:  I know, but I'm tired of Hope getting all the good parts.

- HOPE:  (*To beautiful girl*) Darling, I'm at your feet. What do you want?
  GIRL:  Scratch my big toe, it's killing me.
  HOPE:  Come on, will you marry me?
  GIRL:  Marry you? Then what?
  HOPE:  We'll settle down and raise cattle.
  GIRL:  I'd rather raise kids. Anyway, I can't marry you. You're a fool, an imbecile, a half-wit, an idiot…
  HOPE:  Not so fast. You went past me.

# April 21, 1948

## Jimmy Durante

On this Wednesday night, April 21, 1948, Jimmy Durante reunited with his old partners Lou Clayton and Eddie Jackson. Before radio, they were a successful comedy song and dance team in nightclubs. Lou was a dancer, and Eddie was a strutting singer. They remained lifelong friends.

- DURANTE:  (*As Lou Clayton dances*) Folks, you'll notice while Lou is dancing his feet never leave his ankles! (*While Eddie Jackson sings*) Bing Crosby, if you're listening … start packin'!

# April 27, 1948

## Bob Hope

- BOB:  Lana Turner got married. Of course, I was at the wedding. I won't say how I got there, but I was all right until somebody counted the bridesmaids. Colonna, are you sure you got the right head back from the cleaners?
  COLONNA:  Why, is yours on too tight?
  BOB:  Are you the floorwalker?
  COLONNA:  You don't see me on the ceiling, do you?
  BOB:  Don't be so smart, they're starting the draft again, you know.

(*Bob's guest on this show was Jimmy Durante.*)
- DURANTE:   Drug stores love me as a customer.
  BOB:   No wonder. Every time you come in it boosts their sale of Tums.
  DURANTE:   I want to buy some perfume.
  BOB:   This perfume costs four hundred dollars an ounce.
  DURANTE:   For that price it oughta smell like money.

- BOB:   (*After Durante sings*) What a voice. It sounds like the mating call of a pair of corduroy pants. So, Jimmy, you're from Brooklyn, right?
  DURANTE:   Yeah, don't let dis Harvard accent fool 'ya!
  BOB:   You're a composer? That's nothing. Mozart was composing music when he was only four.
  DURANTE:   Why not? He was too young to go out wit' girls!

## Red Skelton

- RED:   I went to the baseball game. The stadium was so big and the tickets so complicated, they had St. Bernards for ushers. Then the umpire made a bad call. Anybody could see it was a strike. A jerk could see it. I saw it right away! I got so mad, I jumped to my knees ... (*To announcer*) You wanna read a commercial? I'm really lost here!

  (*Now as Junior, the mean widdle kid*)
- JUNIOR:   I got a secret to tell you.
  MAN:   What is it?
  JUNIOR:   It's so secret, I don't know it myself.
  MAN:   You're too big for your britches.
  JUNIOR:   So that's what's been sneakin' up on me!

  (*As Willie Lump-lump, the punch-drunk fighter*)
- WILLIE:   So he said, "I'll pin your ears back!"
  MAN:   What happened?
  WILLIE:   Hmm?
  MAN:   What happened?
  WILLIE:   Speak up, I don't hear so good with my ears pinned back.

# April 28, 1948

## Jimmy Durante

- DURANTE:   I have a secret. I take bubble baths. Don't tell anybody.
  MOORE:   (*Loudly*) Ladies and gentlemen! Jimmy Durante takes bubble baths!
  DURANTE:   Good thing I didn't tell a blabbermouth!

- DURANTE:   Tyrone Power? I look like him. If you look closely you can see the resemblance. We both have faces.

*(In comedy sketch. Durante plays a house-husband whose wife works in an office.)*
- WIFE:    Honey, I'm home! Where are you? Oh, there you are. That apron and dust cap fooled me.
  DURANTE:    Fooled the ice man, too!

# May 2, 1948

## Jack Benny

- MARY:    Oh, Jack, you know I think you're wonderful. So handsome, talented...
  JACK:    Keep going, we have a half-hour.
  MARY:    Where's Don Wilson?
  JACK:    Any place you look!
  MARY:    *(After someone mentioned the cost of dinner to Jack.)* Why doesn't he fall down? I know he's fainted.

# May 4, 1948

## Amos 'n' Andy

- SAPPHIRE:    I'm trying to look glamorous.
  KINGFISH:    So is the hippopotamus, but he ain't gettin' nowhere.

*(Andy and Kingfish come upon a man drowning in the river.)*
- MAN:    Help! Help! I drowning!
  KINGFISH:    Go ahead, Andy. Save him.
  ANDY:    You save him.
  KINGFISH:    No, you save him.
  ANDY:    You save him!
  KINGFISH:    Let's not argue. If you won't save him, I'll do something!
  *(SFX:    Sound of huge SPLASH)*
  ANDY:    Kingfish! You done pushed me in the water!

## Bob Hope

BOB:    I come from a musical family. In fact, the day I was born they sang, *How Deep Is the Ocean?* Just got back from the racetrack. My horse lost and for a very good reason. When the starting gun went off he had his hearing aid turned off. I learned one thing. Stay away from bookies. You know what a bookie is, don't you? That's a pickpocket who lets you use your own hand.

GIRL: You're a good dancer.
BOB: Thanks.
GIRL: How about trying it with me?
BOB: (*Now seated on couch with beautiful girl*) Sweetheart, will you get mad if I ask you something?
GIRL: No.
BOB: May I look under the cushions for loose change?
(*Her kid brother enters*)
GIRL: This is my kid brother. He's ten.
BOB: Ask him if he wants to be eleven. Say, Junior. Do you go out with girls?
KID: You got any better suggestions?

- BOB: (*On phone*) Hello, Colonna. Where are you?
COLONNA: At the bottom of page six. Join me?

(*At the time of this show, Hope was filming the movie,* Sorrowful Jones.)
- BOB: I'm working in a picture. It's a story about a bookie and a horse.
COLONNA: Which are you?
BOB: Don't let this blanket fool 'ya. I was taking a nap.

## Red Skelton
- CLEM: When I was in school, I was the only kid who could vote.
ANNOUNCER: What school did you attend?
CLEM: It was a correspondence school.
ANNOUNCER: Did you have trouble with correspondence school?
CLEM: Yeah, the first day I got caught in the mailbox.

(*As Junior, the widdle kid*)
- MOM: Why when I was a child…
JUNIOR: Please! No pilgrim stories tonight!
MOM: I was going to ask you. Would you like to sleep with grandpa tonight?
JUNIOR: Do you think there's room in the gutter for both of us?

# May 9, 1948

## Jack Benny
- JACK: (*Cleaning out the attic. Finds picture of old girlfriend*) Rochester, you should have seen her long blond curls. And when she smiled her teeth … her teeth were like pearls.
ROCHESTER: She shoulda give 'em back to Pearl.
JACK: And look. Here's a picture of me sleeping with my teddy bear when I was young. Hmm, it's almost as big as the one I sleep with now.

*(Jack goes to visit his neighbors the Ronald Colemans, who can't stand him.)*
- RONALD:    Benita, who is that at the door?
BENITA:    It's Jack Benny. He's come to say, good-bye.
RONALD:    (*Yells*) Good-bye!
JACK:    Ronald, since you're going away, I brought you this book.
RONALD:    Hmm, nice of you to return it.
JACK:    In London you should buy some tweed, because they're a good buy.
RONALD:    (*Loud*) Good-bye!

## Bergen & McCarthy
- CHARLIE:    (*Flirting with girl*) How about a date?
GIRL:    Please! These are business hours!
CHARLIE:    Well, I mean business.
GIRL:    I can't go out with you.
CHARLIE:    Hey, I've been around. I know my onions.
GIRL:    Well, stand back. I'm beginning to make their acquaintance, too.

## Fred Allen
- PORTLAND:    Time for Allen's Alley. Shall we go?
FRED:    As the water said when it got to the top of the glass, "I think I'll run over."

- FRED:    When the play was over, the audience yelled, "Author!" Then the audience rose, as one man ... which it was....

- BRITISH MAN:    I'll be good to her, old man!
FRED:    Be good to her old lady, too.

# May 11, 1948

Side note:    Red Skelton will not be on tonight because of a political speech by Henry Wallace.

## Bob Hope
- BOB:    What a hotel we're staying in. Only wealthy people come to this hotel. Only poor people leave. This place is so ritzy, they don't change the sheets. They just throw out the beds. The carpets are so deep everyone looks like they're calling for Phillip Morris.

- GUEST:    Bob, when you sing you stand too close to the mike.
BOB:    How far away should I get?
GUEST:    Have you got a car?

- BOB:    Colonna, if you want to attract women you should wear after shave cologne.

    COLONNA:    Does after shave cologne make you attractive?

    BOB:    Yes, put it on after a bath.

    COLONNA:    After a bath! I knew there was a catch to it!

# May 16, 1948

## Jack Benny

(*Jack was absent from the show. Robert Taylor took his place.*)

- DENNIS:    Hello, Don Wilson!

    MARY:    That's the control booth. Don's over here.

- DENNIS:    When I was born my mother drew my middle name out of a hat.

    MARY:    What's your middle name?

    DENNIS:    "Sweatband." I used to play a musical instrument, but one day my mother got mad and threw it at my father and broke it to pieces.

    MARY:    What did you play?

    DENNIS:    The piano.

(*In this scene they approach Frank Nelson who is a photographer. Nelson was always Jack's nemesis, giving him or anyone a hard time. Every week he had a different job: sales clerk, ticket agent, etc. He dealt mainly in sarcasm.*)

- DON:    Is that your camera? That little black box?

    FRANK:    Ooo, no! That's my darkroom! I've got two midgets working inside. I'm Mr. Nelson. They're half-nelsons. Aren't you glad you asked?

    DON:    How about a picture of me?

    FRANK:    Sorry, I don't take landscapes.

    DENNIS:    I had only one picture made when I was three years old.

    MARY:    You haven't had any pictures made since you were three?

    DENNIS:    No, every year my mother would use the same picture and have it enlarged.

    MARY:    Really?

    DENNIS:    In my last picture, I was nine feet tall and wearing a diaper.

At the end of the program Mary said to Jack, who was listening in New York, "Goodnight, doll."

## Bergen & McCarthy

- BERGEN:    Bing Crosby works like sixty.

    CHARLIE:    Well ... isn't he?

    BING:    Watch it, Charlie. I'm easily offended.

    CHARLIE:    Good! Then we won't have to try so hard.

## Fred Allen

- FRED:   That baby is a spendthrift. Every two hours he calls to his parents for a little change. I'm busier than a worm making plans for National Apple week. How could I write a song about nature, after what nature did to me. Want to go into business? Start with a popcorn machine. Maybe somebody will build a theater around it.

# May 18, 1948

## Bob Hope

- BOB:   I'm playing golf to raise money for the cancer fund along with Bing Crosby, Jack Benny, Red Skelton and others. Golf tournaments ... that's when the stars show their form ... and the men come, too. Jane Russell will be there. She's a nice girl well-reared.

- BOB:   Colonna, you'll be the death of me yet.
  COLONNA:   Promises ... always promises!
  BOB:   You're playing in the tournament?
  COLONNA:   Yes, my mother would be proud of me. Maybe, I could get her pardoned.

## Red Skelton

- ANNOUNCER:   Do you fish?
  RED:   Oh, I do a little fly-casting.
  ANNOUNCER:   What do you catch?
  RED:   Flies.
  ANNOUNCER:   What else did you do?
  RED:   Went mountain climbing. The guide charges fifteen dollars to take you to the top of the mountain, then looks down and says, "Ain't that beautiful?" And I says, "If it's so beautiful down there, why did you bring me up here?"

  (As Willie Lump-lump.)
- WILLIE:   It's Mother's Day. That's the day you borrow a buck from mom to buy her a box of your favorite candy. Did you know that my mother and me are the only two people who know the size of my underwear?

# May 23, 1948

## Jack Benny

JACK:   Ladies and gentlemen, for those of you who listened last week, I'm not Robert Taylor.

MARY:   Well, I don't blame you for being mad.

PHIL:   Tell me, Jackson, are you taking bows or is your head so big it keeps bending you over?

*(In this scene they are visiting an old farm house.)*

- JACK:   Here's the kitchen. Hm, there's dust on the stove.

  FRANK:   Blow it off. *(SFX: Loud Crash)*

- FRANK:   Have you tried Sen-Sen?

  JACK:   *(Milking a cow)* Gee ... I can't seem to find ... oh, wrong end! *(Later)* Lots of interesting animals on the farm. Here's a kitty with a white stripe down its back. Gee, if that isn't the cutest thing ... ah ... kitty ... have you tried Sen-Sen?

- JACK:   Are you a neighbor?

  FARMER:   Yup. I live down the road.

  JACK:   What house?

  FARMER:   No house. Just down the road.

## Bergen & McCarthy

*(Guest: Groucho Marx)*

- GROUCHO:   Hello, Mr. ... er ... Mr. ... ah...

  BERGEN:   Bergen.

  GROUCHO:   Mr. ... ah ... Mr. ... eh...

  BERGEN:   Bergen! Bergen!

  GROUCHO:   How can I think of it if you keep talking?

  BERGEN:   Are you hard of hearing?

  GROUCHO:   I went to eight ear specialists

  BERGEN:   What did they say?

  GROUCHO:   I don't know, I didn't hear it.

*(Some lines by Groucho on this show.)*

- GIRL:   *(Applying for job)* Do you have a job for me?

  GROUCHO:   Well, first I need to know your experience, your education, and what you're doing tonight.

  GIRL:   I want to be a girl cop.

  GROUCHO:   Well, at least the badge will be in interesting surroundings.

## Fred Allen

- FRED:   I went to a party that was so swanky, I had to wash and iron my shirts before I sent them to the laundry. This must be Bing Crosby's house. I just saw a horse go in the other door. You can't get married today, madam. We're out of rice.

# May 25, 1948

## Bob Hope

- BOB: I'm a born swimmer, thanks to my father. He didn't tie enough rocks around my neck. At the beach, girls are wearing the latest thing in bathing suits. Some look like they haven't been delivered yet. One girl had on a bathing suit made out of handkerchiefs, but she got arrested. She forgot she had a cold. I'm making a new picture. You know what pictures are? Television without a bar.

## Red Skelton

- RED: Bob Hope called me a ham. Well, I'm not a ham. Hams can be cured.
  ANNOUNCER: Do you have any relatives living?
  RED: Yes, but they're having a hard time proving it.
  ANNOUNCER: They live together? How big is the apartment?
  RED: Including the kitchen?
  ANNOUNCER: Yes.
  RED: One room. They moved in with me, so I bought some hospital beds and cranked them all outta shape. One slept in bed so long he got a job as a model in a pretzel factory.

# May 26, 1948

## Jimmy Durante

- DURANTE: I came on stage and the crowds were yelling, "We want Durante! We want Durante!" And if it hadn't been for the riot squad, they'd of had me! Now I know I ain't never had my name in Who's Who, but I did get a mention once in, "What's this?" I used to be a boxer. I fought and fought and in the fifth round, I had my opponent worried. He thought he was gonna kill me!

# June 1, 1948

## Bob Hope

- BOB: I went out in the woods. It's really wonderful to get out with the birds and the bees and hear their side of that story. While there, I ate so many fish, the only way I can breathe is to lift my arms gently. I saw a girl wearing a dress that was designed for nightclubs ... no cover.

(*In comedy sketch with girl.*)
- GIRL:   I don't have to marry you.
  BOB:   Now she tells me!
  GIRL:   I've had other offers, you know.
  BOB:   So why didn't you take that job in the circus?
  GIRL:   You know, kissing spreads germs.
  BOB:   So what? We'll buy them girdles.

- COLONNA:   When I was born the doctor slapped the stork.
  BOB:   Colonna, how did you get past the usher?
  COLONNA:   I just held these jokes under his nose and then stepped over him.

## Red Skelton

- RED:   Thank you for the applause. It was better than the way we rehearsed it. I feel bad. This is our last show of the season.
  ANNOUNCER:   Well, I'll be back.
  RED:   That's what I feel bad about.

(*People you'll meet, sooner or later.*)
- CLEM:   (*As the roadhog*) I drive on the left side of the road so cars can't sneak up behind me and get me nervous.
  COP:   You have a big mouth.
  CLEM:   You're right! My mouth is so big every time I yawn my ears disappear.
  COP:   And you don't have a driver's license. Wait until the judge hears about this!
  CLEM:   He already knows about it. He took it away from me.
  COP:   And you've been to a party. Did you have fun?
  CLEM:   I must have, they threw me out!

# June 2, 1948

## Jimmy Durante

- DURANTE:   (*Sings a note*) I borrowed that note from Bing Crosby, but how can I return it? I bent it!
  ANNOUNCER:   Jimmy, the bathroom of the future is a long way off.
  DURANTE:   Dat's nothin'! The bathroom of the past was a long way off, too!
  ANNOUNCER:   You like that girl? I don't think she's all there.
  DURANTE:   Maybe not, but what's left is enough to make it worthwhile.
  GIRL:   I have twenty-three kids.
  DURANTE:   Gosh, a thing like that could lead to marriage.

# June 6, 1948

## *Jack Benny*

(*Show about him preparing for trip to Detroit to appear at Fox Theater.*)

- JACK: (*In department store*) I bought thirty-six pairs of underwear. Gee, that underwear salesman was a good one. I only wish he'd sold them to me in the men's department.

# June 8, 1948

## *Bob Hope*

- BOB: Television ... that's when your eyes prove your nose is right. I finished my show and everyone said, "Hail to Hope!" Of course, my friends changed the spelling a little. It was quite a show. Didn't my act kill them?
  COLONNA: Suicides don't count, Hope.
  BOB: Anyway, I think I'll take a quick shower. (*SFX: Loud splash*) That's fine. Now help me take off my clothes.

- BOB: I hear a voice! Who are you?
  VOICE: I'm your conscience. I'm in your head.
  BOB: What's going on in there?
  VOICE: Nothing. Mind if I whittle?

Comedy shows took a summer hiatus. So did I. Resumed taking notes in October, 1948. I turned 17 on October 6th.

# October 10, 1948

## *Jack Benny*

- MARY: While on vacation, Jack took a cruise and got a souvenir, a barnacle off the side of the ship. He must have got that while diving for coins.
  JACK: What a vacation. I met this girl and drank champagne from her slipper. It was very romantic until I choked on Dr. Scholl's footpads. Now, every time I think of her a lump comes into my throat.
  JACK: Dennis! You're wearing glasses.
  DENNIS: Yeah, but I don't need them.
  JACK: Then why are you wearing them?
  DENNIS: My uncle died and left them to me.
  JACK: How could he be dead? Today I saw him walking down the street.
  DENNIS: That was my aunt. He left her his clothes.

JACK:    Look, just because he left them, you don't have to wear them.
DENNIS:    Really? Wanna buy a set of teeth?
JACK:    Now cut that out!
MARY:    Jack, I want one of your dollar bills.
JACK:    Why?
MARY:    I want to see what Washington looked like when he was a boy.

## Bergen & McCarthy

- SEXY GIRL:    I'm your new secretary. I'm here to carry out your every wish and command.
CHARLIE:    You ARE?? I mean …ah … you are. What are you doing tonight?
GIRL:    I think I'll curl up with a good book.
CHARLIE:    How about me making like a bookend?
GIRL:    You have some good lines.
CHARLIE:    Yours aren't bad, either.

During this time a short feature began appearing on the *Bergen & McCarthy* show. It was first called *The Honeymoon Is Over* and later became *The Bickersons*, and starred Don Ameche and Francis Langford. Later they got their own show.

## The Bickersons

- BLANCHE:    All I've ever wanted from you is a little attention.
JOHN:    I give you as little attention as anybody.
BLANCHE:    You aren't considerate. You don't stop the car to pick me up. I have to jump in.
JOHN:    Well, I slow down, don't I?
REDCAP:    (*At train station*) Redcap! May I carry your luggage?
JOHN:    No! She can manage!

## Fred Allen

- FRED:    Tonight our program is unrehearsed, unprepared and uncalled for. Food has gotten so expensive, a lot of people are eating money. They can't afford meat. In Russia, everybody is a nobody. One hundred million people have made a mass of themselves.

# October 17, 1948

## Jack Benny

Jack's plot tonight concerned him going to the movies to see *Sorry, Wrong Number*. All gags plot-driven.

## Fred Allen

- FRED: I'm through with doctors.
  ANNOUNCER: What if you get sick?
  FRED: I'll get down on all fours and see a vet.
  ANNOUNCER: You were in vaudeville, weren't you?
  FRED: Yes, playing all the hick towns. I played one town where the theatre was so far back in the woods, the manager was a bear. On closing night he liked me so much he shook my hand and tore half my sleeve off.
  FRED: (*After a commercial*) Where do you find these sponsors? In the police lineup?

# October 24, 1948

## Jack Benny

- PLOT: Jack has invited his neighbors, the Ronald Colmans, over to his house for dinner, much to their dismay.
  JACK: Rochester, the Ronald Colmans are coming over. I'll bet they're tickled pink.
  (*Musical bridge. Cut to their house*)
  RONALD: Oh, Benita, must we go? Tell him I broke my leg.
  BENITA: You did that last time. It didn't work.
  RONALD: Well, this time I'll break it!
  BENITA: Look at it this way. At Jack's house it wouldn't be so crowded.
  RONALD: No, not until the Greyhound bus stops and they all come in for sandwiches.
  BENITA: That's Benny for you. Candlelight and seven-up!
  RONALD: Come on. Let's go. (*SFX: Loud crash*) Hooray! We don't have to go! I broke my leg! Hooray! Six weeks away from Benny! Six glorious weeks in the hospital! Benita, put me in the maternity ward. He'll never find me there!

## Bergen & McCarthy

(*The Bickersons.*)

- BLANCHE: John, I don't feel good. My liver is run down.
  JOHN: Well, wind it up and go to sleep.
  BLANCHE: Listen to you. You've always been a conceited, stuck up, stingy, brute!
  JOHN: Well, why did you marry me?
  BLANCHE: I didn't know it then.
  JOHN: You did, too! Everybody knew it.
  BLANCHE: There's better fish in the ocean than the one I got.

JOHN:    There's better bait, too.
BLANCHE:    If you were married to Gloria Goosebee, you'd have to pay for her kisses.
JOHN:    I'm not married to her and I get them for nothing!
BLANCHE:    You're cheap, John. Cheap!
JOHN:    I'm not cheap! I sacrifice everything for you. I sew collars on old bloomers and wear them for shirts! My only bathing suit has a hole in the knee!
BLANCHE:    You got new shoes.
JOHN:    New shoes, my eye! I painted my feet black!

# October 26, 1948

## Bob Hope

On this show, Bob introduced a new comedy team. Dean Martin and Jerry Lewis.

- JERRY:    My father was a great man. My grandfather was a great man. Then I came along.
DEAN:    Well, their luck hadda run out sometime.
JERRY:    Where's Bob Hope?
DEAN:    Over there. See that guy with the big nose?
JERRY:    That's a nose? I thought it was his date. No wonder she had two holes in her head.

- BOB:    (*After Dean sings*) When you sing, you sound like Bing Crosby.
DEAN:    Well, I been sick.
BOB:    Who did you ever sing with?
DEAN:    Kate Smith, just to name a few.
BOB:    (*To Jerry Lewis*) Why don't you get married and have a kid? Don't wait until it's too late like your father did.

# October 27, 1948

## Milton Berle

- BERLE:    Frank Gallup, why are you tip-toeing?
FRANK:    I don't want to drown out your laughs.
BERLE:    Hey, I'm getting laughs all over the place.
FRANK:    Really? Your mother must be on roller skates tonight.
BERLE:    You know, it's a good thing I have an open mind.
FRANK:    I know, with that hole in your head. You ought to be ashamed. Your wife slaves over a stove all day while you're out stealing jokes.

BERLE:   You're right. No more fighting with Henny Youngman over Bob Hope's jokes.

## You Bet Your Life

- GROUCHO:   (*To a female contestant*) How old a bachelor are you interested in?
  WOMAN:   Between forty and fifty.
  GROUCHO:   I didn't say how many, I said how old?
  WOMAN:   Well, I'm approaching forty.
  GROUCHO:   From which direction?
  WOMAN:   My first husband worked on the atomic bomb.
  GROUCHO:   Well, I hope he got off it.

## Bergen & McCarthy

- CHARLIE:   Go ahead, Bergen. Tell your story and make it snappy.
  BERGEN:   I do not tell snappy stories. Oh, hello, is that you Mortimer?
  MORTIMER:   Uh ... wait! I'll ask myself. Is that you, Mortimer? Hmm, must be! I'm wearing my clothes.
  BERGEN:   Mortimer, about the election. How do you think it will come out?
  MORTIMER:   I don't know. How did it go in?
  BERGEN:   Have you no brains?
  MORTIMER:   (*Pause*) Well ... (*Pause*) ... not with me!
  BERGEN:   What do you think of Russia?
  MORTIMER:   I think that's a good place for it.
  BERGEN:   What about suffrage? The right to vote?
  MORTIMER:   Everybody votes ... everybody suffers.

## Fred Allen

- TITUS MOODY:   Had some excitement. My wife ran her arm through the washing machine wringer.
  FRED:   That's awful.
  TITUS:   Couldn't holler for help, so she stuck her arm under the door and beckoned to me.
  FRED:   Is her arm in a sling, now?
  TITUS:   No, an envelope.

- FRED:   I went to the Stage Delicatessen. Their tongue sandwiches sell for eight ninety-five. I offered them two dollars.
  ANNOUNCER:   What happened?
  FRED:   The tongue spit at me. I feel awful today. My mouth tastes like the linoleum on a pet shop floor.

# November 3, 1948*

## *Milton Berle*

- BERLE:   We had to rewrite the whole show. Anybody want to buy six pages of Harry Truman jokes? And now, I, Milton (Bing) Berle will sing… (*SFX: Loud Foghorn*) Is that an opinion? What a team! My voice and the band behind me. Eight bars behind me.

# November 4, 1948

## *Burns & Allen*

- GRACIE:   I'm taking up a hobby.
  GEORGE:   Like what?
  GRACIE:   Be a doctor and operate on people.
  GEORGE:   That's a nice hobby.
  GRACIE:   But, it's dull. If you've seen one appendix you've seen them all. Maybe, I'll be a writer.
  GEORGE:   You can be a writer?
  GRACIE:   Sure, I've got a pencil. I've already written a story. Would you like for me to read part of it to you?
  GEORGE:   No.
  GRACIE:   Then I'll read all of it to you. It goes like this. "I heard my husbands footsteps … clump, clump, clump, clump, clump, clump, clump."
  GEORGE:   Wait a minute! How many clumps did you write in?
  GRACIE:   Three pages. I'm getting paid by the word. To continue… "Then he hit me, beat me, threw me down the steps and kicked me in the face. I resented this."
  GEORGE:   You're some writer. You could be another Pearl Buck. She wrote "Dragon Seed."
  GRACIE:   That's silly. Who wants to know how to grow dragons?

Gracie sells the story to a "True Confessions" magazine. It's fiction, of course, but the editors think it's true and that George is a wife-beater. The magazine sends photographers over to take a picture of this awful man. George thinks they are there to interview him about his acting ability. Lots of mistaken identity gags follow.

MAN:   When did you start doing it?
GEORGE:   When I was a kid. I used to try it out on my mother. But now that I'm married, I do it to entertain friends.

---

*\*Harry Truman won the election over favored Thomas Dewey.*

MAN:   What?

GEORGE:   Yeah, I may even do it in the Hollywood bowl. (*SFX: Slap*) Hey, why did you slap me with that magazine?

MAN:   Isn' it true, you beat your wife?

GEORGE:   Of course not.

MAN:   (*To Gracie*) Has he ever raised a hand to you?

GRACIE:   No, if he wants to leave the room, he just goes on out.

MAN:   You sold me a piece of fiction! I'll sue!

GEORGE:   You can't sue her. She's not quite bright.

MAN:   You mean she's sort of...

GEORGE:   Not sort of … she's just plain of….

## November 5, 1948

### Jimmy Durante

- DURANTE:   Ah, Durante! How can one man have so much and conceal it so well!

  WOMAN:   (*In a sketch about the Roman Empire*) I may look like a queen, but underneath these royal clothes hides a woman! What have you to say?

  DURANTE:   Peekaboo?

  WOMAN:   Listen! Caesar gave his life for me! Brutus gave his life for me! Mark Anthony gave his life for me! What have you to offer?

  DURANTE:   I got a hangnail!

### Red Skelton

- RED:   I hear Henry Wallace and his party are holding a mass meeting in a telephone booth. (*After bad joke*) I love these jokes. We just shucked them this morning. (*Starting a car*) OK, I'm gonna start the motor. There! It's started. (*SFX: Motor running*) Now stand back while I put it in the car.

- CLEM:   I tried to take a milk bath, but I couldn't get the cow in the tub. So I just hoisted her up and took a shower.

  ANNOUNCER:   You're reading comic books? Don't you realize what an impression they make on your mind?

  CLEM:   Hey, when I was a kid I used to read books all the time and they didn't make a single impression on me.

## November 7, 1948

### Fred Allen

- FRED:   That cafe's ceiling was so low, they served the frog's legs squatting.

- ANNOUNCER: What's all this tax reduction talk?
FRED: Talk.

# November 9, 1948

## Bob Hope

- ANNOUNCER: What are we going to do about Hope? His leg is broken.
JACK: (*Jack Benny was guest*) Too bad he isn't Trigger. We could shoot him. Let me see your leg, Bob. Gosh, it's all twisted out of shape.
BOB: That's the wrong leg! Jack, what a surprise having you here.
JACK: Some surprise. We rehearsed nine weeks already.
BOB: (*Doing commercial parody*) Attention all ladies weighing over four hundred pounds. Do you have the feeling you're being followed? Well, you are, it's you!

# November 10, 1948

## Milton Berle

- BERLE: (*Begins show by heckling the audience*) Sir, would you mind moving? Your bald head is shining in my eyes. I'd like to put my finger in his ear and use it for a bowling ball. It's great to be here in Philadelphia. The mayor gave me the key. Tomorrow he's going to give me the sardines. This is the city of brotherly love. While driving, I stuck my hand out and a cop kissed it. All this brings back memories of my old girlfriend, Cynthia! Ah, Cynthia! Everyone called you sugar. Your face was square and lumpy. And your lips were like petals. Bicycle pedals!

## You Bet Your Life

- GROUCHO: (*After getting kissed by beautiful girl*) Does anybody here want a pair of shoes with the toes curled up? (*To a contestant*) What do you call a boy who brings an apple to school?
MAN: Teacher's pet.
GROUCHO: I imagine they do, but what do you call him?

# November 15, 1948

## Jack Benny

DON: Now, ladies and gentlemen, let's go back one hour before the broadcast.

JACK: (*Riding in his Maxwell car with Rochester driving*) Rochester, not so fast! Slow down! Watch it! There's a red-light! There's a stop sign! Look out for that bus!

ROCHESTER: Not so loud, boss. People will think we're married.

JACK: Look out! (*SFX: Loud crash*)

ROCHESTER: Guess which fender had the Toni? (*Hair permanent lotion*)

JACK: Rochester, did the motor die again?

ROCHESTER: It died twenty years ago, you just won't bury it. You know those new cars are nice. You step down into them.

JACK: Well, you step down into mine.

ROCHESTER: Yes, but the new ones have floors.

JACK: (*Later, at the broadcast*) Let's see, all the stars have dressing rooms. Here's Burns and Allen ... Abbott and Costello ... Ladies and ... Oh, here's my room!

JACK: (*With Dennis Day*) A drive-in? Gee, I've never been to one of those.

DENNIS: I took my girl to one and I snuggled up close and put my arms around her and kissed her on the back of her neck and then, Wham! It happened.

JACK: What?

DENNIS: She fell off the handle bars.

JACK: Hmm. Tell me, is your girlfriend pretty?

DENNIS: No, she's got buck teeth, stringy hair and a wart on her nose.

JACK: Well, why do you go out with her?

DENNIS: It's her bicycle!

JACK: (*To audience*) I can't even look at him!

## Bergen & McCarthy

- BERGEN: Mortimer, where did you come from?
  MORTIMER: I came from the county (if you'll pardon the expression) seat.
  BERGEN: You know, I'm having legal trouble.
  MORTIMER: Does it hurt?
  BERGEN: No, do you know what legal trouble is?
  MORTIMER: Sure, that's when there's something wrong with your legal.
  BERGEN: I have no legal!
  MORTIMER: Well, there's your trouble right there!
  BERGEN: This is the dumbest conversation I've ever been in.
  MORTIMER: Well, you can only blame me for half of it.

## The Bickersons

- JOHN: (*Sneaking home late at night*) Darn, I can't find the light switch. Oh, here it is. (*SFX: Click*)
  BLANCHE: Hello, darling!
  JOHN: Darling? I must have the wrong apartment. Excuse me, madam.

BLANCHE:  John, don't throw your coat on the floor.
JOHN:  It's okay, you can sweep it up in the morning.
BLANCHE:  When you're out at night, you never call me. Max calls his wife.
JOHN:  Calls her what?
BLANCHE:  You're so cheap. Before we were married you told me you were well off.
JOHN:  I was, but I didn't know it.

## Fred Allen

- FRED:  (*Visiting Titus Moody in Allen's Alley*) Where've you been?
  TITUS:  I was guest of honor at a silo warming. They served owls.
  FRED:  You eat owls?
  TITUS:  I just chew the claws.
  FRED:  Chew the claws?
  TITUS:  Yep. Sometimes the owl has stepped in something sweet. Eating an owl is like biting into a feather duster that hasn't been shook out.

# November 18, 1948

## Hallmark Players

- ANNOUNCER:  Jack Benny in Stephan Leacock's "My Financial Career."
  JACK:  (*As narrator*) My name is Stephan Leacock. I have a son age twelve, a daughter age twenty and a boy six months old. I don't believe in rushing things. When I was thirty-seven years old I ran away from home. I met a girl named Alexis Lujack. She was a chocolate dipper in a candy factory. I loved to hold hands with her and then run home and lick my fingers.

# November 21, 1948

## Jack Benny

- DENNIS:  I've been on a cruise. Here's a picture of my stateroom.
  JACK:  Oh, look at that porthole.
  DENNIS:  Porthole? I thought it was a Bendix and threw all my clothes in it.
  JACK:  (*To audience*) He's such a stupid kid!
  MARY:  He is not!
  DENNIS:  I am, too! Mr. Benny, I've been working for you for nine years and I haven't had a Sunday off.
  JACK:  That's the day we do our broadcast!
  DENNIS:  Excuses! That's all I get, excuses!

## The Bickersons

- BLANCHE:   John, be quiet, you'll wake the baby.
  JOHN:   I don't care.
  BLANCHE:   Then you'll have to rock him to sleep.
  JOHN:   Okay, where's a rock?
  BLANCHE:   How can you say that? Look at him. Isn't he a doll?
  JOHN:   Yeah, turn him over and let me see his face.
  BLANCHE:   That is his face!

# November 23, 1948

## Bob Hope

- BOB:   Nowadays, girls wear so much padding, falsies, the minister says, "I now pronounce you man and stuff."
  JERRY:   (*Martin & Lewis in return engagement*) Where I come from men are men and women are women.
  DEAN:   What about it?
  JERRY:   Well, I'm in there somewhere. (*Dean and Jerry did a routine where Jerry throws lines while Dean sings.*) We're lovely! We're engaged! We use Drene! Tell me, folks. (*Holds Dean close*) Which twin has the head?

# November 25, 1948

(*On a Thanksgiving Special*)

## The Bickersons

- BLANCHE:   John, no other man snores like you do.
  JOHN:   How do you know?
  BLANCHE:   I talk to my friends. Honest John, who carries on like that?
  JOHN:   Honest John!
  BLANCHE:   Did you feed the cat?
  JOHN:   Yes.
  BLANCHE:   What did you feed him?
  JOHN:   The canary.
  BLANCHE:   Did you lock up? Suppose a burglar breaks in and finds me?
  JOHN:   It would serve him right.
  BLANCHE:   John, how much do you love me?
  JOHN:   How much do you want?
  BLANCHE:   John, let me tuck you in.
  JOHN:   Okay.

BLANCHE:   There! Are you comfortable, my sweet?
JOHN:   Yes.
BLANCHE:   Good! Now get up and tuck me in!

# November 26, 1948

## Jack Carson

The comedy actor, Jack Carson, had a radio sitcom for around two years. His co-star was Dave Willock, who played his dopey nephew. Arthur Treacher also appeared as Carson's butler.

- DAVE:   (*At breakfast*) Pass the cream.
  JACK:   Okay.
  DAVE:   Pass the sugar.
  JACK:   What are you having?
  DAVE:   Cream and sugar.
  JACK:   What time is it?
  DAVE:   Wait. I'll look at my Gruen watch.
  JACK:   What does it say?
  DAVE:   Gruen watch.
  JACK:   I'll turn on the radio and they'll have the time. (*SFX: Click!*)
  RADIO:   (*SFX: Bong*) You have just heard the time!
  JACK:   (*In bathroom shaving*) Hmm, what's this? A grey hair? Gee, kinda makes me look distinguished. Sort of intelligent. Too bad it's on my chest.

## Red Skelton

- GIRL:   I won't take another step until you say I'm beautiful.
  CLEM:   Okay. I'm beautiful!
  MAN:   (*To girl*) Are you his date?
  GIRL:   Yes, I'm paying off an election bet.
  MAN:   I ought to punch you in the nose!
  CLEM:   Oh, yeah? Well, go ahead and see what happens! (*SFX: Smack*) See! It bleeds!

# November 28, 1948

## Ozzie & Harriet

- OZZIE:   You know, every time I bring in the newspaper everybody takes part of it and all I'm left with are the want ads.

RICKY:   Okay, go ahead and read it, Pop.
OZZIE:   Thanks.
RICKY:   Uh …you don't want the funnies, do you?
OZZIE:   No … here.
DAVID:   Ah, you don't want the sports pages, do you?
OZZIE:   No … here.
HARRIET:   You don't want the society pages, do you?
OZZIE:   Uh … no. Here you go. (*Long pause*) Wanted: Man to clean floors.
HARRIET:   Our new neighbor is kind of pretty, isn't she?
OZZIE:   I suppose so. She said I had broad shoulders.
HARRIET:   You always do when you wear your new coat.
OZZIE:   It's not the coat! Look, I'll take it off. There! Now do I have broad shoulders?
HARRIET:   Sure you do. Now hang them in the closet.

## Jack Benny

- ROCHESTER:   (*Singing*) Night and day….
JACK:   (*Calling*) Rochester!
ROCHESTER:   (*Singing*) You are the one…
JACK:   (*Calling*) Rochester!
ROCHESTER:   (*Singing*) Only you and you alone under the sun…
JACK:   (*Calling*) Al Jolson!
ROCHESTER:   Yes, boss! Say, are you wearing that tuxedo to dinner tonight? It's so old, it's green.
JACK:   It's not green!
ROCHESTER:   Well, stay away from the salad bowl, you might get stabbed with a fork.
JACK:   (*Doorbell rings*) I'll get it.
ROCHESTER:   (*Sings*) Night and day … how was that?
JACK:   You better sing another chorus. The turkey isn't dead, yet.
PHIL:   (*Enters*) Hand me a bottle opener, my boys are thirsty. Say, Jack you're not wearing that old tuxedo, are you?
JACK:   It's not old!
MARY:   (*Enters*) Well, if it isn't the Green Hornet!
DON:   (*Enters doing the Congo dance*) Da, da, da, da, da … DAH! Da, da, da, da, da … DAH! (*SFX: Loud crash*)
JACK:   Don, if you can't control it, don't swing it!
MARY:   (*At dinner*) I'll have a little more of that white meat.
JACK:   That's my leg!
MARY:   You should have told me sooner. I put gravy on it.

## Bergen & McCarthy

- CHARLIE:   I was a child once.
BERGEN:   You were.

CHARLIE: A boy, I believe I was.
BERGEN: You know, Charlie, if you lie about something, your veins swell up and you choke.
CHARLIE: Oh, don't be silly.
BERGEN: Allright, where were you last night?
CHARLIE: I was home all evening. (*Cough! Cough! Cough!*)

# December 2, 1948

## *Burns & Allen*

- GRACIE: (*Talking about girlfriend*) I've always tried to outdo her. I even told her you were six feet six, since her husband is tall.
  GEORGE: But I'm not tall.
  GRACIE: Well, do a little something for me.
  GEORGE: What?
  GRACIE: Grow for me.

Plot concerns Gracie pretending George is dead so her girlfriend won't know that he's not tall. Tells everyone George is the butler. Confusion reigns as cops arrive believing George has been murdered.

GRACIE: He's a wonderful butler. Is there anything you'd like him to butt?
COP: Lady, homicide is murder.
GRACIE: Yes, it is dull in those small towns.
COP: (*To George*) Why did you kill George Burns?
GEORGE: I am George Burns!
COP: Don't kid us. George Burns is six feet six.
GEORGE: I'm an entertainer. Look, I'll prove it. (*Sings*) "Down in the garden where the roses grow..."
COP: That does it! You're under arrest!
GEORGE: Gracie, help me! They may give me life!
GRACIE: Well, you could use some.

# December 7, 1948

## *Bob Hope*

- SANTA: Ho, ho, ho! Merry Christmas!
  BOB: Same to you, jolly old St. Nick.
  SANTA: Who's jolly? I'm sick and tired with sore feet.
  BOB: Things that bad, eh?
  SANTA: Things are horrible. Put some money in the pot, boy.

BOB:    What's the money for?
SANTA:  For all the Eskimos in Los Angeles.
BOB:    There are no Eskimos in Los Angeles.
SANTA:  Can you prove it?
BOB:    No.
SANTA:  Put some money in the pot, boy.
BOB:    (*In department store*) Get a load of that floorwalker with that silly gardenia.
BING:   Bob, all floorwalkers wear gardenias.
BOB:    In their hair?
BING:   Bob, has your nose always been like that or did you have a ball-point put on it?
BOB:    I was by your house yesterday, but nobody was home.
BING:   Oh, what a shame!
BOB:    I must've rung your doorbell five times.
BING:   Six times.

# December 8, 1948

## Milton Berle

- FRANK:  Ladies and gentlemen...
  BERLE:  They know what they are....
  FRANK:  Here's Milton Berle! (*Applause*)
  BERLE:  What applause! I think I'll quit while I'm ahead. Goodnight!
  FRANK:  I see there's an article about you in *Life* magazine. I want to ask you, why didn't I get my picture in there?
  BERLE:  Frank, the name of the magazine is *Life*, not *Death*.
  BERLE:  (*In prison*) Here I am on Death Row. I'm going to die. Now I'm walking toward that little green door at the end of the hall. That little green door! Here it is. I'll open it. (*SFX: Woman screams*) Excuse me, madam! How did I happen to be in prison? It all started years ago. I was at home, the phone rang and my wife tenderly asked...
  WIFE:   (*Tough*) Put down the paper, 'ya big slob and answer the phone!
  BERLE:  Oh, no! It's big Louie! Big Louie! (*But let me start from the beginning!*) It was ten years ago. I was in a bar when a man came in and told me that No-Nose was after me! Oh, no! No-Nose! Not No-Nose! (*But let me start from the beginning.*) It was five years ago. I was out with No-Nose's girlfriend. I was drinking champagne from her shoe. For four hours I drank from her shoe. Then I found out she was wearing open-toed shoes. I wonder if No-Nose knows! And if No-Nose knows, what exactly does No-Nose know? Then, Fingers Fink entered.
  FINK:   Ready Eddie is after you!
  BERLE:  Ready Eddie! No, not Ready Eddie! (*But let me start from the begin-*

*ning.*) I ran to my room and they were there! There were five of us in it together, Big Louie, Ready Eddie, No-Nose, Fingers Fink and me.
FINK:    You ran out on us! For that you die!
BERLE:   What did I do?
FINK:    You broke up our basketball team!

# December 19, 1948

## Ozzie & Harriet

* OZZIE:   (*Knock on door*) Oh, hello, Thorny. What are you wearing?
  THORNY:   That's mistletoe. Now anybody can take advantage of me and kiss me.
  OZZIE:   Well, don't look at me. I wanted to put up mistletoe, but Harriet didn't think too much of it. I could tell by the way she talked.
  THORNY:   What did she say?
  OZZIE:   She said she didn't think too much of it.

* ANNOUNCER:   When he was young, Ozzie was strong, rough and tough. He played football. In one game it was the last down with thirty-seven yards to go. With only one minute to play, rough, tough Ozzie turned to his players and said...
  OZZIE:   This is hopeless, fellas. Let's quit!

## Jack Benny

* DON:   Let's go down to the local department store where Jack is Christmas shopping.
  JACK:   Pardon me, are you the clerk?
  FRANK:   No, I was just standing here and they built the store around me.
  JACK:   Is this price right? This cowhide wallet cost forty dollars?
  FRANK:   Stop squeezing it. It won't give milk.
  JACK:   I guess I'll take it. Forty dollars, huh. Does that include the engraving? It's a gift for Don Wilson.
  FRANK:   Yes, what do you want on it?
  JACK:   The price.
  MARY:   If you're wondering what to get Phil, remember he goes hunting.
  FRANK:   Does he hunt bear?
  JACK:   Oh, ask me that again.
  FRANK:   Does he hunt bear?
  JACK:   No, he wears his union suit just like everybody else! Ha, ha, ha! Why don't you laugh? Hmp, he thinks he's smart, doesn't he, Mary?
  MARY:   Don't talk to me. I'm pretending I'm not with you.
  FRANK:   How do you want this wallet engraved?

JACK: I'll just put in a card. "This gift is from Jack, oh golly, oh shucks. I hope that you like it, it cost forty bucks."
FRANK: Fine. Now, would you like something else?
JACK: Could you show me something in silk lingerie?
FRANK: Sure, what's your size?
JACK: (*Shouting*) It's not for me!

## The Bickersons

- JOHN: At least you fix my lunch to take to work.
  BLANCHE: John, I haven't fixed your lunch in over two years.
  JOHN: You do, too. Every morning I find it in a brown paper bag on the side of the sink.
  BLANCHE: That's the garbage!

# December 21, 1948

## Bob Hope

- BOB: What an ugly woman. I said to myself, either that's an ugly woman or a handsome man.
  PECK: (*Gregory Peck was guest*) Where's Bob Hope? I've been waiting for months to see the man who says he has so much more than I have.
  BOB: Well, here I am. What'd 'ya think?
  PECK: Have you been sick long? The last time I saw a stomach like that a farmer was sitting beside it with a pail.
  BOB: I come from a poor family. We were so bad off the mice used to come in, take one look around and leave some cheese in the traps for us.

# December 26, 1948

## Jack Benny

This was Jack's last show on NBC. He'd been with them for seventeen years. Now voted nation's number one comedian by *Fame* Magazine. He moved to CBS.

- JACK: Mary, did you like that perfume I gave you for Christmas?
  MARY: Good perfume! I put some on my dress and three moths dropped dead.
  DENNIS: Hello, Mr. Benny.
  JACK: Hello, Dennis. Now as I was saying…
  DENNIS: Merry Christmas!
  JACK: Merry Christmas, Dennis. Now as I was saying…

DENNIS: Happy New Year!
JACK: Happy New Year, Dennis. Now as I was saying...
DENNIS: Can I go home, now?
JACK: Sure. Now as I was saying ... Dennis! Why are you going home, now?
DENNIS: I kissed Mary under the mistletoe. I'm done.
JACK: Mary! Why did you let him kiss you? Mary ... Mary...?
DENNIS: It's no use. She won't be awake for an hour, yet.

## Bergen & McCarthy

- BERGEN: So you drove my car and had an accident?
  CHARLIE: Yes.
  BERGEN: Charlie, yesterday I could have sold it as a new car.
  CHARLIE: Well, today you can sell it as an accordion.

- GIRL: Charlie, I love you because you never change. You're always the same.
  CHARLIE: Well, thanks.
  GIRL: A little rat.
  CHARLIE: Thanks again, I think.
  GIRL: I've a good mind to slice you into venetian blinds.
  CHARLIE: Why the very thought of it makes me shutter!
  BERGEN: A friend in need is a friend indeed, Charlie. Who said that?
  CHARLIE: I ain't sure, but I think you just did.

## Fred Allen

- ANNOUNCER: Jack Benny's no longer on NBC. Gee, it's going to seem funny without Benny around.
  FRED: It always seems funnier without Benny around.

# December 29, 1948

## Milton Berle

- BERLE: I just flew in from Florida. What a flight. You press a button, food comes out. You press the stewardess, your teeth come out.

- ROBBER: Stick 'em up!
  BERLE: How high?
  ROBBER: Don't mix me up, I'm new at this job!

# — 1 9 4 9 —

## January 2, 1949

### Jack Benny

Jack begins his relationship with CBS which will last for the rest of his career and lead to a very successful, long running series on television.

- ROCHESTER: (*Driving Benny in the Maxwell car to the CBS studios*) Don't be nervous, boss!

  JACK: I'm not nervous.

  ROCHESTER: Then stop pacing up and down the running board! (*The car stalls*) Relax, boss. I'll get the car started, but you'll have to close your eyes.

  JACK: Why?

  ROCHESTER: I'm gonna use the whip!

  (*SFX: Horse hoof beats*)

  JACK: Who was that?

  ROCHESTER: Gene Autry.

  JACK: Side saddle? (*At CBS studios*) Hello, Dennis. You look very nice.

  DENNIS: I'm wearing the suit my Dad got married in.

  JACK: There's catsup on the lapel.

  DENNIS: That's not catsup. My father wouldn't say, "I do," so my mother punched him in the nose.

  JACK: Well, why are you wearing hip boots?

  DENNIS: I couldn't find the pants.

  JACK: Why didn't you wear your own pants?

  DENNIS: I did, but I lost them. When I passed NBC, I went on, but my pants went in.

## Fred Allen

- FRED:   I have a headache. My head feels like there's a porcupine inside backing into my eyeballs. My mouth tastes like somebody's using it for an incinerator.

  TITUS:   (*In Allen's Alley*) My horse wasn't so smart. He was a moron. All day long he'd sit in the pasture strumming his lip with his hoof. So we gave him a brain operation.

  FRED:   You gave your horse a brain operation?

  TITUS:   Yep. We put a cat's brain in and the horse thought he was a cat. He used to curl up at the foot of my bed and purr.

# January 5, 1949

## Milton Berle

- TEACHER:   (*Berle is taking singing lessons*) Yes, you have talent! You have a voice!   You have money?

  BERLE:   Yes, I want to be a great singer.

  TEACHER:   Okay, open your mouth. Hmm, you have a small mouth and no teeth.

  BERLE:   That's my ear.

  TEACHER:   I thought your lips were big!

  BERLE:   What do I have to do to be a great singer?

  TEACHER:   A great singer must suffer!

  BERLE:   (*Sings*) Ah, sweet mystery of life at last I've found you!

  TEACHER:   You don't understand. You're supposed to suffer, not me!

- FRANK:   Berle, since you've been on the air we've been flooded with requests for your picture.

  BERLE:   Really? People want my picture?

  FRANK:   Yes, they've been beating up the wrong guy.

# January 6, 1949

## Burns & Allen

- GRACIE:   I wish George would act more romantic like Gregory Peck. Maybe he'll kiss me if I give him the chance. I'll say, "Darling, have you missed me?" Then he'll kiss me and say, "Yes, darling, so very much!" Here goes. "Darling, have you missed me?"

  GEORGE:   I didn't know you were gone.

  GRACIE:   Won't you give me something to warm me up?

  GEORGE:   Here's a match. Go light the furnace.

GRACIE:    George, there's a chair behind me.
GEORGE:    Well, go ahead. Squat.
GRACIE:    Oh, George! Why can't you be thoughtful like Gregory Peck?

(*Later, George meets with Gregory Peck.*)

GEORGE:    I've got a terrific problem, Gregory. My wife wants me to be more like you.
GREGORY:    Relax, George. Remember, good things come in small packages.
GEORGE:    Yeah.
GREGORY:    It's just that you are so loosely packed. I'll tell you what. I'll hire an actress to play the part of my wife and when Gracie comes over, I'll be the meanest, dirtiest rat that ever lived.
GEORGE:    Yeah, then Gracie won't want me to be like you. I'll bring her over.
GREGORY:    I'll be the world's worst husband … unshaven … rude…

(*Later, George enters with Gracie.*)

GEORGE:    Gregory, this is my wife, Gracie.
GREGORY:    So this is Mrs. Burns. Well, bring the old battle-ax in!
GRACIE:    He wants you to come in, too, George.
GEORGE:    Gregory, where did you get those slacks?
GREGORY:    These are jeans.
GRACIE:    Isn't that sweet? He's breaking those pants in for a girl named Jean. And gee, Mr. Peck. It's nice of you to be in your stocking feet so you can be as short as George is. So thoughtful!
GEORGE:    Oh, great.
GRACIE:    He's so masterful! He eats with his fingers to save on silverware. And you, George, sit there with a knife and fork!
GEORGE:    Yeah, I'm a real slob.
GREGORY:    (*Whispers*) I'll go in the next room and pretend to beat my wife. (*Exits and we hear*) Those potatoes were lumpy and you're gonna get yours! (*SFX: Crash*)
GRACIE:    (*Rushing in*) There you are! You woman beater!
GREGORY:    You don't understand. She was just taking a part.
GEORGE:    Now, Mr. Peck's gonna get taken apart. Stand up!
GREGORY:    Okay.
GEORGE:    You didn't have to stand that tall!

(*Enter the real Mrs. Gregory Peck.*)

MRS. PECK:    I'm Mrs. Gregory Peck.
GRACIE:    Well, one Mrs. Peck just left. What are you, the night shift?
MRS. PECK:    I could use a little clarification.
GRACIE:    I know you're upset, but don't start drinking.

(*Later, back home.*)

GRACIE:   George, I like you just the way you are.
GEORGE:   Okay, go to sleep.
GRACIE:   You've got something that Peck hasn't got.
GEORGE:   Good. Now go to sleep.
GRACIE:   I can't. I'll be up all night trying to figure out what it is!

# January 9, 1949

## Jack Benny

- DON:   One of the most popular restaurants is the Brown Derby. Let's go back to yesterday when the waiters are fixing the tables.
1ST WAITER:   Here comes Jack Benny. You wait on him!
2ND WAITER:   Oh, no! You wait on him!
1ST WAITER:   Not me. You wait on him.
2ND WAITER:   Just tell him there are no tables available right now.
1ST WAITER:   Sorry, Mr. Benny. There are no tables available right now.
JACK:   That's okay. I see Jimmy Stewart over there. Jimmy! Do you mind if we join you?
MARY:   How could he say no, you're already eating his roll.
JACK:   There's enough for both of us.
1ST WAITER:   You can move over to this table, now.
JACK:   I thought you didn't have any tables.
1ST WAITER:   We have now!
JACK:   We'll just stay where we are. Oh, waiter! Waiter!
MARY:   Jack, just call him. Don't wave your toupee at him.
STEWART:   (*After dinner*) I'd feel better if I paid the check.
JACK:   Well, if your health is involved … okay! (*Jack ad-libs after Jimmy Stewart flubs a line*) He got an Academy Award and he can't even read!

## Fred Allen

- CLAGHORN:   I had a cousin who was crazy. He thought he was a house! His button was the doorbell, his pockets were windows and he even wore his union suit backwards so he'd have a front door.
FRED:   That's nothing, I had an uncle who thought he was a dog. He kept punching himself in the nose. He thought he was a Boxer. (*Ad-lib*) We might as well say anything. It's better than what we've got written down here.

# January 12, 1949

## Milton Berle

- BERLE:   What a cold winter we're having. You know how the M-G-M lion starts their movies with a growl. Now, he goes, "Brrr!" (*Ad-lib*) I thought that was a clever joke. Wonder whose it is? Oh, hello, Frank Gallup. I didn't see you standing over there in the shadow. In the shadow of your nose.

(*Sketch about a gangster taking care of a baby.*)

- BERLE: (*As crook*) Okay kid, drop that diaper! Oh ... you wanna take a powder, eh? Things been kinda rough lately, huh? There you are kid. I gotcha covered! Allright ... now ... uh-oh! Kid, drop that diaper!

- BERLE: (*Sings*) ...a beautiful sight, we're happy tonight, walking in our winter underwear. Ah, my old girlfriend, Cynthia! Remember what fun we'd have in the winter! How we'd slide down the hills in the snow. We'd go much faster when you waxed your stomach. (*Now, that's a belly laugh!*) Oh, Cynthia, you had that extra tang ... orangatang! And you had an hour-glass figure. Too bad all the sand settled in the bottom.

- BERLE: (*Interviewing high jumper*) What was the longest jump you ever made?
  MAN: Three hundred and fifty feet.
  BERLE: Three hundred and fifty feet? What made you jump so far?
  MAN: I was bending over when someone opened an umbrella.

- ANNOUNCER: Alaska! From the land of cold, where men die for gold came Yukon Berle!
  BERLE: (*To girlfriend*) While I was out on the frozen wastes I was hungry for your lips! Hungry for your cheeks! Hungry for your hair!
  GIRL: Well, here I am!
  BERLE: Sorry, I just ate.
  BERLE: (*In card game*) This is a cold deck.
  GAMBLER: How do you know it's a cold deck?
  BERLE: The Queen of Spades is wearing long underwear.

# January 13, 1949

## *Burns & Allen*

- GEORGE: You know, Gracie it takes thirty minks to make one coat.
  GRACIE: Really? How long does it take them?
  GEORGE: So you've got fur coat fever?
  GRACIE: My sister had a fur coat. It really did something for her figure.
  GEORGE: What?
  GRACIE: It hid it!

- GRACIE: (*Talking to neighbor*) So I took off all my clothes and told George that if he didn't buy me a mink coat, I'd go downtown with no clothes on.

BEA:    What did he do?
GRACIE:    He gave me a letter to mail. (*Pause*) He knew I wouldn't do it.
BEA:    Sure, why should you mail his letters?

# January 16, 1949

## Ozzie and Harriet

- OZZIE:    (*In drug store*) Why doesn't that guy get off the phone? I've got an important call to make and that half-wit is using the phone. Who is he, anyway?
  CLERK:    My brother.
  OZZIE:    No offense, he's probably a good guy.
  CLERK:    No, he isn't. He just hangs around all day staring at me.
  OZZIE:    Why don't you get rid of him?
  CLERK:    I can't, he owns the store.
  OZZIE:    Hey, you! Get out of the phone booth.
  MAN:    I can't. My finger's caught in the coin slot.
  CLERK:    What's he doing with his finger in the coin slot?
  OZZIE:    Maybe he's trying to tickle the operator under the chin.

- HARRIET:    (*Eating steak dinner*) Ozzie, is the steak tough?
  OZZIE:    Oh, no. See? When I press down on this end the other end stands up.
  HARRIET:    Is it good?
  OZZIE:    I'll taste it. (*Cough, gag, cough*)
  HARRIET:    Oh, it's terrible!
  OZZIE:    No, it isn't. It's full of that locked-in flavor. It couldn't get out if it wanted to. (*Pause*) Could you get me another knife? I bent this one.

## Jack Benny

- JACK:    My eyelashes aren't grey. It's just that my eyes are so blue they keep picking up lint.
  ROCHESTER:    Boss, we're out of flour.
  JACK:    I'll go next door and borrow some from Ronald Colman. (*SFX: Door opens, closes, footsteps as Jack walks next door.*) Gee, as long as I'm going, I should've brought a larger cup. (*Jack hums his theme song:* Love in Bloom *as he walks. SFX: Coin clinking into cup—CLINK!*) Thank you. (*Continues walking. SFX: Doorbell. Door opens*) Hi, Ronnie, I'd like to borrow a cup of flour. Shall I come in?
  COLMAN:    No, I'll just sift it to you through the screen door.
  JACK:    I'm making a little paste with flour and water. I'm saving the write-up about my show in the paper.
  COLMAN:    (*Amazed*) You save those?

- MARY: (*Talking about her sister and her boyfriend*) They were going to elope. The ladder was up, the window was up and she was so embarrassed. He wasn't home!
  JACK: What did she do?
  MARY: While she was up there, she painted the house.
  JACK: Well, when a guy gives you the brush...

- DENNIS: Jack, I've got two tickets to the Rose Bowl.
  JACK: Dennis, that game was played three weeks ago.
  DENNIS: I know. That's why they're so hard to get.
  JACK: Do me a favor ... this is silly talk. Go out and come in again.
  DENNIS: Okay. (*SFX: Door slam. Doorbell rings. Door opens. Does impression of Titus Moody*) Howdy, Bub!
  JACK: Titus Moody!
  DENNIS: Yup. I got two tickets to the Rose Bowl!
  JACK: Now cut that out!
  DENNIS: Okay. I'm reading a book about Graphy.
  JACK: Graphy?
  DENNIS: Sure. George Graphy. Right here on the cover.
  JACK: That's geography! Just sing, Dennis. Sing!

## Fred Allen

- TITUS MOODY: It's been tough sledding all week.
  FRED: Tough sledding?
  TITUS: No snow!
  NUSSBAUM: I'm cooking a cake at home.
  FRED: How can you cook a cake at home and be here?
  NUSSBAUM: The cook book says to leave the house.
  FRED: Leave the house?
  NUSSBAUM: It says to mix the batter and beat it for ten minutes ... so I'm beating it!

# January 19, 1949

## Milton Berle

- BERLE: Listen to that applause!
  GALLUP: You mean somebody else's mother is applauding, too?
  BERLE: Frank, you have a wonderful knack for taking a joke and building it into a straight line.

- BERLE: My brother Frank is looking for work. He's very handy. Sort of a jerk of all trades. He's going to school to learn some sort of trade so he'll know what kind of work he's out of.

GALLUP: Berle, you are really corny. You're the king of corn!

BERLE: I know. When I was born it took three storks to bring me. One to carry me, and two to beat off the crows. My parents were worried. They didn't know whether I'd grow or pop. Instead of undressing me, they used to husk me to bed.

- GALLUP: And now, George Washington gives his famous farewell speech!

  BERLE: So long, fellows!

- GALLUP: (*In sea adventure sketch*) Captain, our ship is moving slowly. Could it be because of the barnacles on our bottom?

  BERLE: Could be.

  GALLUP: Or could it be because we're still tied to the dock?

  BERLE: Yes, could be. Who's the dope that did that?

  GALLUP: You, sir.

  BERLE: Smart move!

  GALLUP: Shall I unfurl the mizzenmast?

  BERLE: What?

  GALLUP: Shall I unfurl the mizzenmast?

  BERLE: I didn't know one was mizzen.

  GALLUP: There's an enemy ship off the port side.

  BERLE: Okay, men! Strip for action! (*SFX: Burlesque bump and grind music*) I don't mean that kind of stripping! Mr. Christian! Come here! (I sound just like Charles Laughton, don't I?)

## You Bet Your Life

- GROUCHO: I met my wife in a travel agency. She was vacationing and I was the last resort.

# January 23, 1949

## Jack Benny

- JACK: Dennis, I'm having a party and you're invited.

  DENNIS: White tie or black tie?

  JACK: White jacket. You're parking cars.

- DENTIST: Open wide.

  JACK: Ahh!

  DENTIST: Open wider. Wider ... wider...

  JACK: But, doc..

  DENTIST: Don't talk, you're biting my ankles.

  JACK: How are my teeth?

  DENTIST: Fine, but you'd better have something done about that appendix.

# January 30, 1949

## Ozzie and Harriet

- OZZIE: (*Taking a driver's test*) These questions are easy. Ask me another.
  COP: Okay, if a streetcar is going north at an intersection, and there is a fire station on one corner and a police station on the other, and a man on a motorcycle is coming and a truck full of turnips is making a right turn, and a blimp is coming down for a landing … which has the right of way?
  OZZIE: Was that … turnips?

## Jack Benny

- JACK: Don, just do the commercial.
  DON: Okay, Jack. You know when I look into those blue eyes of yours I'm putty in your hands.
  JACK: Don, that's ridiculous. What would I do with two hundred and seventy pounds of putty?

- ROCHESTER: I gave the parrot a four-way cold tablet.
  JACK: What happened?
  ROCHESTER: He laid a square egg!
  MARY: Jack, that's some toupee you're wearing. The part goes from ear to ear.
  JACK: It does not. Someone yelled and I turned my head too fast!

# February 3, 1949

## Milton Berle

(*Berle out sick with "virus-x." Rudy Vallee subs.*)

- RUDY: (*As private detective*) My name is Sam Shovel, private eye. I can smell a crook. I can smell a clue. They should call me a private nose. On my desk is a picture of a thief. A top drawer thief. I caught him in a room full of top drawers. Yesterday, I was sitting in my office when she came in. She was beautiful. She entered and dropped her eyes. Quickly, I picked them up. She had a turned up nose. Real turned up. Every time she sneezed, she blew her hat off. I told her I would get on her case right away. My mother always taught me that the early bird gets the worm. I tried that. It didn't make me much of a success, but I have about eight million worms. I began to believe this woman was dangerous, because when I kissed her, she gave me a cold. Every man she kissed got a cold. I finally arrested her for winning friends and influenzing people.

## Burns & Allen

*(A couple from the Safety Council are checking the Burns home for possible accident causes. They are pointing out various danger signs.)*

- WOMAN: You shouldn't be chopping celery with such a sharp knife.
- GRACIE: Well, my brother did it all the time.
- WOMAN:: Really? What's his name?
- GRACIE: Three fingers McGoo.
- WOMAN: Joe, get a picture of that antique with the weak leg in the corner.
- GRACIE: George, get in the corner.
- GEORGE: She doesn't mean me!
- WOMAN: And get a picture of that old radio connection running across the rug.
- GRACIE: Run across the rug, dear.
- JOE: How about a picture of that shaky old moose head over the door?
- GRACIE: Hang over the door, George.

# February 6, 1949

## Fred Allen

- FRED: *(Visiting Titus Moody)* Mr. Moody, you're white as a sheet.
- TITUS: I'm whiter than most sheets. I have an upset stomach. I was eating soup when I saw something in the soup. *(And I think it saw me!)*
- FRED: What kind of soup was it?
- TITUS: Squirrel soup. After I ate it, it felt like the squirrel had come to life and was burying things in my stomach.
- FRED: I see you have stained glass windows in here.
- TITUS: Not real stained glass. The fellow who lived here before me chewed tobacco.

# February 8, 1949

## Bob Hope

- BOB: When I was a boy scout, I could fasten a tent flap in ten seconds. Of course, I'd had ten years basic training with long underwear. I'll never forget my first girlfriend. She was nine and I was ten. One night we kissed and our braces locked. (We went around together a lot after that.) What a welcome I got when I returned from my tour. For big stars they have a full orchestra. For medium stars they have a choir. When I arrived, a street cleaner banged two trash can covers together, threw come confetti in the air and sang, "Say it isn't so."

COLONNA: I had a poor childhood, too. We couldn't afford cheese for the rat traps, so we baited the traps with a picture of a piece of cheese.
BOB: What did you get?
COLONNA: A picture of a mouse.

- MAN: How do women dress in Russia?
  BOB: I don't know. They keep the shades down. I showed the Russian ambassador around New York. When we passed a bank, he went (*SFX: Spitting sound.*) When we passed Wall street, he went (*SFX: Spitting.*) When we passed a rich man in a limo, he went (*SFX: Spitting.*) Then we stopped while the driver put the windshield wipers on the inside.

# February 13, 1949

## *Jack Benny*

- DON: Jack thinks he's quite the lover boy.
  MARY: Some lover. He goes to a diner, has a hamburger, squeezes the waitress's hand, then goes home and dreams he's Errol Flynn.
  JACK: Oh yeah? Well, I'll show you. Kiss me, Mary! (*SFX: Loud kiss*) Now, how was that?
  MARY: Thank you, Errol Flynn.
  JACK: You said it. Now, put me down!
  (*To Dennis Day*) Dennis, you seem angry. Why?
  DENNIS: Oh, I'm mad, all right. I'm going to punch my doctor in the nose.
  JACK: Why?
  DENNIS: I just found out that when I was born, he slapped me. My back was turned, too.

## *Fred Allen*

- FRED: (*To Titus Moody*) Your arm is in a sling.
  TITUS: Yep. Got my arm caught in the milking machine. My fingers are now eighteen inches long.
  FRED: Does that bother you?
  TITUS: Only when I scratch. I keep scratching past the itchy spot.
  FRED: (*Talking to Ajax Cassidy*) What are you celebrating?
  AJAX: The birthday of Thomas Edison.
  FRED: Why?
  AJAX: He invented the electric light bulb.
  FRED: So how did you celebrate?
  AJAX: I got lit!

# February 17, 1949

## *Burns & Allen*

- GEORGE:  Gracie, James Mason is coming over for a visit.
  GRACIE:  Oh, I feel like I know Mr. Mason. I've been using his jars for years.

- MASON:  Your cat, is she expecting a litter?
  GRACIE:  Oh no, her boyfriends can't write.
  MASON:  Mrs. Burns, a litter is a bunch of cats. Tell me, what is your method of raising cats?
  GRACIE:  We just put our hands under their tummies and lift.
  MASON:  Do they have pedigrees?
  GRACIE:  No, we keep them very clean.
  MASON:  What do you feed them?
  GRACIE:  We feed them cheese. It helps them catch mice.
  MASON:  How does that work?
  GRACIE:  Well, the mice smell the cheese on their breath and come to the cats. That's my husband over there with one of our cats.
  MASON:  Hm, a bit moth-eaten, don't you think?
  GRACIE:  Yeah, but the cats like him, anyway.
  MASON:  I meant the cat. He's shedding fur.
  GRACIE:  Well, he's part Maltese and part strip-tease.
  (*Gracie has put a sardine inside George's coat pocket to make him popular with cats.*)
  GEORGE:  What's this in my pocket?
  GRACIE:  Ohhh, a cigar!
  GEORGE:  I've looked at a lot of cigars in my life, but this is the first one that ever looked back!
  GRACIE:  Isn't that cute? It has a mouth, too. It can blow its own smoke rings!
  GEORGE:  Gracie, this is a sardine.
  GRACIE:  Oh, is it? Here, I'll light it for you.

- GRACIE:  George, I think that woman has a crush on you.
  GEORGE:  Really?
  GRACIE:  She gave you a double wink.
  GEORGE:  A double wink?
  GRACIE:  Yes, she looked at you and closed both eyes.
  (*Mistaken identity jokes. Gracie goes to the Mason house to get George. However, James Mason thinks she's come to get their cat named George.*)
- GRACIE:  I've come to get George.
  MASON:  Must you? We're so fond of him. My wife lets him sleep at the foot of the bed.
  GRACIE:  Why would you do that?

MASON:    He has such a shiny coat.
GRACIE:   Shiny coat? You should see his pants!
MASON:    And such cute little fuzzy legs.
GRACIE:   (*Surprised*) You saw them?
MASON:    Yes, when I gave him his bath. Could we buy him from you? We'll give you fifty dollars. What's wrong?
GRACIE:   The price is right, but I love him. However, he is a little old.
MASON:    Oh, I don't know. He's a bit frisky around me.
GRACIE:   Oh, he was, too, when I first met him.
MASON:    What diet should we put him on?
GRACIE:   Just tie a napkin around his neck. He'll eat anything!
MASON:    You act like he was a man.
GRACIE:   Yes, and believe that, no matter what people tell you.

# February 18, 1949

## *Jimmy Durante*

- DURANTE:   What a voice! (*Sings*) Lah, lah, lahhhhhhh!
  ANNOUNCER:   Where did you get a voice like that?
  DURANTE:   In the shower. When I backed into the hot water pipe. (*After singing "Deep in the Heart of Texas."*) Ah, Texas! Every morning I'd get up, put on my riding hat, my riding boots and my riding spurs. Then go out and almost freeze to death. I shoulda worn my riding pants!
  ALAN:   So you work in a bank? What's wrong with your vest?
  DURANTE:   I spilled money on it.
  PRETTY GIRL:   Well, little old Alan! Come to visit little old me! In my little old house! How about giving little old me, a little old kiss?
  ALAN:   Better hurry. I'm gettin' a little old.
  GIRL:   Do you like my new dress?
  ALAN:   Yes, I do.
  GIRL:   Sho' nuf?
  ALAN:   Yep, it shows enough.
  GIRL:   Would you be so kind and tie my shoe?
  ALAN:   Okay. Here, I'll kneel down and tie your shoe.
  DURANTE:   (*Opens door*) Hey Alan, no use shoeing that old mare! She looks like she's ready for the glue factory!

## *Red Skelton*

- RED:   She was so bowlegged, the first time I saw her I thought she was delivering ice! She looked like a donut with one bite taken out of it!

# February 20, 1949

## Ozzie & Harriet

- OZZIE:   I can't remember his name. Jones, Smith, Collins...
  HARRIET:   Try to associate his name with something. Where did you meet him?
  OZZIE:   At the bowling alley.
  HARRIET:   Okay. Now think of his face. Now think of the bowling alley.
  OZZIE:   His face. The bowling alley. I've got it!
  HARRIET:   What's his name?
  OZZIE:   Ed Bowlingface.
  HARRIET:   That's not it.
  OZZIE:   Burns? Kennedy? Rogers?.
  HARRIET:   He lives in this block.
  OZZIE:   Bloch? Bloop? Bleep?
  HARRIET:   Use your head.
  OZZIE:   Head? Red? Sled? Hat?
  HARRIET:   His name is Oliver!
  OZZIE:   Oliver? Well, that's a twist.

## Jack Benny

- DENNIS:   Hello, Mr. Benny. I just sold my bicycle for ten thousand dollars. Here's the check.
  JACK:   Let me see. Dennis, it isn't even signed.
  DENNIS:   When a man offers you ten thousand dollars for a bicycle, you don't argue.
  JACK:   What was his name?
  DENNIS:   Napoleon.
  JACK:   Dennis, he's been dead for years.
  DENNIS:   Really? Well, then what does he want with a bicycle?

# February 23, 1949

## Milton Berle

- BERLE:   I put my pants on backwards and looked in the mirror. I thought I was just coming in, so I went back to bed. My uncle was so crooked when he died we didn't bury him. We just screwed him into the ground.

- BERLE:   (*Sketch about the FBI*) I'm Berle of the F.B.I. This is the case of X2Z15, which I call X2Z15. I was sitting in my office when the phone rang. (*SFX: Phone rings*) Being careful not to leave any fingerprints, I lifted the receiver with my teeth. A voice said, "Berle, come to Dirty

Dave's hideout." I quickly decoded the message. He wanted me to come to his hideout. So I went to Dirty Dave's. Was I too late? Yes, I was too late. There it was on the floor. A dead elephant. An ordinary man wouldn't have seen it. I saw it in less than an hour. Then I knew what I must do. I went to India (*SFX: Swoosh*) and met a man who said, "You'll find him in the city of ... ahhhh! (*SFX: Thud! Drops dead.*) I looked through my maps, but I couldn't find a city by the name of Ahhhh! So, disguised as a leechie nut, I went to China. (*SFX: Four gunshots*) Sounded like they were killing the Andrew Sisters! Then I found a note. I analyzed it. It was written on paper! Then I found Dirty Dan who said, "The Chief wants a sandwich." I said, "With or without mustard?" Another case solved by Berle of the F.B.I.

## You Bet Your Life

- GROUCHO:  I don't think they trust me when I get on an airplane. The first thing the hostess does is strap me in the seat. Now, as a traveling salesman, tell me, do you fly?
  GUEST:  Yes, I fly all the time.
  GROUCHO:  Could you fly around the studio for us? (*To a blacksmith*) What do you do for a living?
  GUEST:  I shoe horses.
  GROUCHO:  Do you shoo flies, too?
  MAN:  No, I let the horse do that.
  GROUCHO:  That's a likely tale. (*tail*) (*To a manicurist*) Do you ever get tired of holding a man's hand and looking into his face?
  WOMAN:  No, I don't.
  GROUCHO:  (*To the blacksmith*) Do you ever get tired of holding a horse's hind legs and looking into his ... oh, never mind.

# February 27, 1949

## Jack Benny

- JACK:  Hello, Dennis.
  DENNIS:  I came to say good-bye. I'm running away from home.
  JACK:  What's in the suitcase?
  DENNIS:  I don't know. My mother packed it.
  JACK:  Your mother packed it?
  DENNIS:  Here's a picture of her.
  JACK:  That's Monty Wooley!
  DENNIS:  No, it isn't. I drew a beard on her.
  (*SFX: Doorbell rings*)
  JACK:  Maybe that's Mary. No ... she's in Palm Springs.

DENNIS:   Well, they have doorbells there, too.
RAINS:   Hello, Jack. I'm Claude Rains.
JACK:   You're here early.
RAINS:   I didn't come for my laundry. You're on the Ford Theater with me.
JACK:   That's right. We're doing "The Horn Blows at Midnight" together.
RAINS:   Yes, I sat through that picture twice.
JACK:   You liked it that much?
RAINS:   I could believe what I saw the first time.
JACK:   Then you know the story. I'm an angel and you're my boss and at your request I come back to earth.
RAINS:   At my request, you wouldn't stop there.

## Fred Allen

- FRED:   (*Some one liners*) I know a man who took those reducing pills. He lost twelve pounds. His arm fell off. Had to have a little man come along to tip his hat for him. My uncle had long fingers. He could put his finger in one ear and beckon to you through the other one. My bird is depressed. He's been reading the newspaper on the bottom of his cage.

(*Fred's guest was Henry Morgan, whom Fred liked so much they did a bit about a program that advertised nothing but Henry Morgan. He also did a satire on the quiz program "Stop the Music," which ultimately knocked Fred off the air due to lower ratings.*)

# March 2, 1949

## Milton Berle

- BERLE:   (*To announcer Frank Gallup*) Mr. Gallup, in your own way you have more fun than people who are alive. When Frank cuts himself, his veins send out an I.O.U.
  GALLUP:   Here's a review about your show. It says you are great, wonderful and have a dual personality. Huh, look at the way they spelled dual … D-U-L-L.

# March 3, 1949

## Burns & Allen

(*Gracie had a fender bender, so their car is being repaired. She is trying to keep that fact a secret from George.*)
- GEORGE:   Where's the car?

GRACIE:   What car?
GEORGE:   Our car.
GRACIE:   The one with the windshield wiper?
GEORGE:   Yes, where is it?
GRACIE:   On the windshield.
GEORGE:   Where's the car?
GRACIE:   Have you heard the moron joke about…
GEORGE:   Gracie, I went into the garage and it wasn't there!
GRACIE:   The garage has been stolen?
GEORGE:   Where's the car?
GRACIE:   It's being fixed.
GEORGE:   Dents?
GRACIE:   Oh, I'd love to! Turn on the music.
GEORGE:   I don't feel like dent…cing. What happened?
GRACIE:   A car ran into me.
GEORGE:   Who was driving?
GRACIE:   Nobody, it was parked.

• GEORGE:   (*To guest, Richard Widmark*) Remember me?
WIDMARK:   No, I'm afraid I don't.
GEORGE:   We played bridge together, remember?
WIDMARK:   No, I don't.
GEORGE:   You won four dollars from me.
WIDMARK:   I still don't remember.
GEORGE:   I didn't pay you.
WIDMARK:   George Burns!

## Jack Carson

• CARSON:   (*Private eye monologue*) I was sitting in my office when she walked
in. She was wearing a black, low-cut evening gown and tennis shoes.
She was ready for anything … romance or basketball. She said her uncle's
body was outside in the hall and asked me if I wanted to look at the
body. I looked at the body. Then I went outside and looked at her uncle
(*Returning from a trip, Jack picks up the wrong suitcase by mistake. It turns
out to be a woman's suitcase. To find out her identity, he searches through
it.*) Gee, I wonder what kind of girl she is. I'll look through here. Hmm,
here's a slip, lots of lacy things. What are these? Must be knee guards.
Could be a scrub lady. Oh, look, here's her diary! Should I read it? Of
course not! Reading a woman's diary is just about the lowest, dirtiest
thing a man can do. It would be awful if I read her diary. Only a dirty
rat would do a thing like that. I wouldn't dare do that. Only a lowdown
snake would … (*Pause*) … Dear Diary….
WOMAN:   (*Alone with Carson*) Come closer, my dear. Come on, closer …
closer … closer… Oops, you went past me! Tell me, you want to dance
with baby?

CARSON:    You have a baby?

- CARSON:    (*Talking to himself*) I really like this girl, but her mother might not like me. She's so snooty. I'll bet she's a real blue blood. Yep, she probably won't like me. When she meets me, she won't like me. (*Loudly*) But I don't care! I don't care! Do you hear?
  TUGWELL:    (*Alarmed*) Jack, what's the matter?
  CARSON:    Her mother hates my guts!

- WOMAN:    (*Alone with Carson*) Would you like to kiss baby?
  CARSON:    I'd love to!
  WOMAN:    Fine, I'll call my little brother.

# March 6, 1949

## *Jack Benny*

- JACK:    (*In the Maxwell car*) Gee, it's a pretty day, Rochester. Put the top down.
  ROCHESTER:    The top is down.
  JACK:    Then why is it so dark?
  ROCHESTER:    We ain't outta the garage, yet.
  (*SFX: Car riding along*)
  JACK:    Say, there's a house that looks like mine!
  ROCHESTER:    It is yours. We're still in the driveway.
  JACK:    Ah, this is the life! Riding to the race track with the top down. (*Car stalls, hiccups ... Car sound effects played by Mel Blanc.*) Rochester, the motor is flooded. It's got too much gas!
  ROCHESTER:    What do you want me to do? Throw it over my shoulder and burp it?
  (*They pick up Mary Livingston. Then have a flat tire.*)
  MARY:    Hey, there's Phil Harris!
  JACK:    Yeah, put down that jack, Mary and wave to him. (*Later, at the race-track*) I'd like to get something to eat. What would you suggest?
  NELSON:    (*As waiter*) A bib. You look like the sloppy type.
  JACK:    Are the eggs fresh?
  NELSON:    Ooooooo! Are they!!
  LEONARD:    (*Sheldon Leonard as racetrack tout*) Psst! Hey, bud! Come here a minute.
  JACK:    Who me?
  LEONARD:    Yeah. You gonna eat in here?
  JACK:    Why, yes. I was going to sit at table one over there.
  LEONARD:    Uh-uh. Take table nine. Table one is a card table.
  JACK:    Hey, waiter! Put everything on table nine!

(*Ronald Colman and his wife, Benita, see Jack at the racetrack. Naturally, they want to avoid him.*)

- BENITA:   Ronnie! Look, there's Jack Benny.
  RONALD:   Oh, no! Jack Benny!
  BENITA:   What if he sees us?
  RONALD:   I don't know about you, but I'm going down to the starting gate and run around the track!

## Fred Allen

- FRED:   Remember this. You should live each day as though it were your last day on earth ... and one day you'll be right.
  TITUS:   I've got twelve hens. One day they laid thirteen eggs.
  FRED:   You have twelve hens and one day they laid thirteen eggs?
  TITUS:   One of my hens stutters.

# March 8, 1949

## Alan Young

- LADY:   (*Alan in movie theater unwrapping bag of popcorn*) What are you unwrapping back there, a new Nash?
  ALAN:   I love westerns. Look at all the horses. There's a brown one, a white one, a tan one, a polka-dot one. A polka-dot one? Oh, excuse me, madam!

- DOCTOR:   According to surveys, it's best for women to have children young.
  ALAN:   Naturally. Who wants to have old children?

- ALAN:   (*At racetrack urging horse on*) Come on, horse! Come on, Lady Luck! Come on, Lady Luck! That's it! Now ... the other foot!

## Bob Hope

- BOB:   Colonna! As I live and breathe!
  COLONNA:   Not in my direction. You just singed my eyebrows.

  (*Doing balcony scene from "Romeo and Juliet."*)
- JULIET:   Romeo, Romeo, wherefore art thou, Romeo. Come up the rose trellis and be with me. Hi thee hence!
  BOB:   That's a pretty tall rose trellis. I don't know whether I can hi my hence up that far!
  JULIET:   Hello.
  BOB:   Hello. (*Gee, this is the furthest I've ever gotten with a girl!*)
  JULIET:   (*Dramatically*) Oh, father! Father!
  BOB:   Oh, brother!

JULIET:    (*Overly dramatic*) Now, I die! I die! Ohhhhh, I die!
BOB:    Don't die so loud, I'm the star, you know.

- BOB:    (*Discussing his date*) We licked stamps all evening. Then we kissed. That was a mistake. We got stuck together and had to steam ourselves apart over a tea kettle. She also wore braces. Her face looked like the front end of a Buick. Once I kissed the car goodnight and backed her into the garage.

## March 9, 1949

### Milton Berle

- BERLE:    Ah, that Frank Gallup. He looks like an ad for a famine. He's so thin when he takes a shower he has to move around or he won't get wet.
GALLUP:    Berle, producers are crazy for you.
BERLE:    What producers?
GALLUP:    Crazy producers!
BERLE:    Very clever. This boy has the makings of a clever ex-announcer.
GALLUP:    And now ... Great Moments from Motion Pictures! Who could forget the most romantic scene ever filmed? The Casbah scene in Algiers. The two lovers meet. Tenderly, he says...
BERLE:    (*Low bass voice*) Duh. Duh ... Hedy....
HEDY:    Oh, Pepe! Pepe! Pepe!
BERLE:    Hey, this is as peppy as I can get.
HEDY:    I luf you!
BERLE:    Bon!
HEDY:    But I will have to leave you!
BERLE:    Bon!
HEDY:    I will have to work in a shirt factory!
BERLE:    Bon!
HEDY:    Where I will make buttons for shirts!
BERLE:    Buttons and bon! (*Popular song of the day*)
(*Interruption by Edward G. Robinson impersonation.*)
EDWARD:    Listen here, see? I'm taking over this picture, see? Ya got that, see? 'cause I'm the boss, see?
BERLE:    This picture ain't half over and I'm getting seasick!

- BERLE:    I'm a member of the French Foreign Legion and my name is ... ha, ha, ha, ha! What does it matter, my name? We're made up of the scum of the earth, and doctors who won't smoke Camels. I'll never forget one night. We were in a cafe. The curtains parted and there she was doing the dance of the seven veils. Slowly, she removed the veils until she removed the last of the seven veils and we saw! We saw! (She had seven more!)

## You Bet Your Life

(*Groucho interviewing a motorcycle cop and a woman driver.*)
- COP:   I've been riding a motorcycle for twenty years.
  GROUCHO:   You must be very callous about it. Are you a mounted police-
    man?
  COP:   Well, you could say that.
  GROUCHO:   Okay, you're a mounted policeman.
  COP:   We cops have to use psychology.
  GROUCHO:   Oh, you're a psychologist, now, eh? Do you carry a couch on
    the back of your motorcycle?
  COP:   Not really.
  GROUCHO:   Did you ask this woman out for a date?
  COP:   No.
  GROUCHO:   Why not? You're tall, good looking. Why wouldn't she date
    you?
  COP:   She was short.
  GROUCHO:   Financially?
  COP:   She gave me the eye, though.
  GROUCHO:   She gave you the eye? Now she has only one?
  COP:   And I danced with her for awhile.
  GROUCHO:   And then you gave her the eye back?
  COP:   I was nervous about being on this show.
  GROUCHO:   Why?
  COP:   Well ... you're Harpo Marx and...
  GROUCHO:   I am not Harpo Marx!

# March 13, 1949

## Ozzie & Harriet

- OZZIE:   (*Working on his income tax*) Let's see, now. Name: Ozzie Nelson.
  O ... Z ... Z ... I ... E. Gee, this his harder than I thought. I better
  read this book. "How to Save Money on Your Income Tax" by number
  284957836.

## Jack Benny

(*Jack is upset because he spent four dollars and twenty-five cents.*)
- MARY:   Jack, don't blow your artificial top. It's only four twenty-five!
  JACK:   You're right, Mary. What's four twenty-five? Only the deposit on
    two hundred and thirty-seven Coca-Cola bottles. You know how I feel
    about money. Easy come, easy go! (*Silly giggle*) Let's just forget about
    the four twenty-five.

MARY:   Okay. What time is it?
JACK:   Four twenty-five.
MARY:   Oh, look over there. A fox tail!
JACK:   That's not a fox tail and put it back on my head!
DENNIS:   Hello, Mr. Benny.
JACK:   Dennis, I haven't seen you lately. Where have you been?
DENNIS:   Working in a gas station. I've never seen such silly people.
JACK:   Silly people?
DENNIS:   Yep. One guy drove up in his car and told me to fill 'er up and I put in five hundred gallons.
JACK:   Five hundred gallons?
DENNIS:   Yes, and I could've put in more, but one window was open a little bit.

• JACK:   (*Later, at home*) Gee, I'm so tired. I just want to go to bed. Ah, it's nice to be home and take off this high collar. And this shirt. Hmm, just look at those muscles. Hard as a rock. I gotta stop wearing them in the shower, the buckles are getting rusty. Ahh, here we go. Gee, it's nice to get in bed. Gosh, I'm tired. What a day. There's nothing like a good night's sleep … (*Snores, talks in sleep*) Four twenty-five … four twenty-five … four … twenty-five…
(*Jack dreams he's at the racetrack*)
JACK:   Is the next race ready?
NELSON:   No.
JACK:   Then why is the crowd cheering?
NELSON:   They saw you give me a tip!
VOICE:   Just a minute, bud!
JACK:   Is that you, Mary?
VOICE:   (*Low*) No, I'm her sister, Babe!
JACK:   Wait a minute! You're a horse!
VOICE:   That's right.
JACK:   If you're a horse, how come you can talk?
VOICE:   I can't. The horse next to me is a ventriloquist.
JACK:   That's an old joke!
VOICE:   I can't help it. He's Fred Allen!
ROCHESTER:   Boss! Boss! Wake up!
JACK:   What? Oh … I was asleep.
ROCHESTER:   You must have been dreaming about horses.
JACK:   How do you know that?
ROCHESTER:   You're riding the bed post.
JACK:   What?
ROCHESTER:   Side saddle.

## Fred Allen
- FRED:   Jack Benny. If I had his taste in clothes, I'd spit it out. His pants are so baggy they look like his knees are wearing derbies.

## Here's Morgan
Henry Morgan returned to the air sponsored by Fred Allen. Actually, he was sustaining with no sponsor.
- MORGAN:   Hello, anybody. Here's Morgan. Ladies and gentlemen, where have you been? (*Doing take-off on Hollywood gossip columnists*) This just in! Tyrone Power, Errol Flynn and Clark Gable are three different people! You heard it here first!

ANNOUNCER:   That joke just won't die.

MORGAN:   Give me a stick. I'll beat it to death.

His humor was very sophisticated, and unfortunately, didn't attract a large audience.

# March 16, 1949

## Milton Berle
- GALLUP:   Now it's time for Milton Berle who does his bit every now and then and that's why he's known as a two-bit comic.

BERLE:   Oh, Mr. Gallup.

GALLUP:   Yes, Berle.

BERLE:   (*Imitating his voice, very low*) Yes, Berle! Yes, Berle! What a voice! Tell me, why must you always sound like you're calling a hog?

GALLUP:   You should know. You always answer.

BERLE:   I see you have another review of our show.

GALLUP:   Yes, it says Milton Berle is great, but so and so and so. Then it goes on to say … so and so … and so and so…

BERLE:   Well, now you know what I am.

GALLUP:   Yes. An old so and so.

# March 20, 1949

## Ozzie & Harriet
- OZZIE:   (*Looking through their bookshelf*) Gee, we have books here I haven't even read. Here's one: *The Romance of Dirt*. Where did we get this?

HARRIET:   It came with the vacuum cleaner.

OZZIE:   There must be some good books here. You can learn a lot. Go ahead, pick out any book and I'll read it, and we'll learn something.

HARRIET:   Okay. Here.

OZZIE:   (*Reads*) Always empty the dust bag before using. Oh, well, some days you just can't win. Let's go borrow some books from the library.

OZZIE:   (*At the Public Library*) Shh ... here's a huge book. Gosh, it's heavy! Must be really intellectual.

HARRIET:   Read from it.

OZZIE:   (*Reads extremely complicated sentence.*) Well, how about that?

HARRIET:   What does it mean?

OZZIE:   I haven't the faintest idea.

HARRIET:   No wonder. The last time this book was borrowed was December 1910.

## Jack Benny

- DON:   Jack's show holds rehearsals on Saturday, so let's go back to then.

JACK:   You know, Don, Van Johnson's going to be our guest on the show.

DON:   What a coincidence. I've often been compared to Van Johnson.

JACK:   Don, the van you're compared with has furniture sticking out of it.

DON:   Here he is now! Van Johnson! (*Applause*)

JACK:   Van, I want to ask you. Why do girls like you so much?

VAN:   Girls like me? Why, Jack, most of the glamour girls won't even spit at me.

JACK:   That's funny. They do at me! I mean, they think I'm hot stuff. Look, Van, those freckles of yours are all right for Huck Finn. And your eyes are no good. But mine ... they sparkle! Now, take my hair...

VAN:   Okay.

JACK:   Put that back! And not so far on the side, either.

(*Jack and Van Johnson go to meet their dates at a local restaurant.*)

JACK:   Van, you shouldn't have paid for the parking.

VAN:   I thought somebody should. We've been sitting in the parking lot for four hours. There are our dates. That one's yours.

JACK:   That short one? Hm, not bad! Cute figure!

VAN:   Jack, that's the fireplug.

JACK:   Gee, these girls are all right. In case anyone picks a fight, that tall one can lick her weight in wildcats!

(*Their dates are not the brightest girls in the world.*)

JACK:   (*To his date*) Would you like to dance?

GIRL:   Sure! Wait till I put on my shoes.

JACK:   We should order first. What would you like?

GIRL:   Nothing. I don't feel like eating.

JACK:   Good ... Good!

GIRL:   Maybe, I'll have the Tehboney steak.

JACK:   What?

GIRL:   The Tehboney steak. It's on the menu.

JACK:   That's T-bone!

GIRL:    Okay.

JACK:    Oh, waiter. We'll have the T-bone steak.

WAITER:    We don't have any T-bone.

JACK:    Yes, you do. It's on the menu. See?

WAITER:    That's Tehboney!

## Fred Allen

- ANNOUNCER:    Oh.

FRED:    Now that was a worthwhile retort. You accomplished your purpose and cleared your throat at the same time.

FRED:    (*Visiting Ajax Cassidy in Allen's Alley*) What's the matter?

AJAX:    I've got to get something for snake bite. My wife's been bit.

FRED:    Was it a garter snake?

AJAX:    He didn't go for any particular spot. Just bit what was handy.

(*Fred's guest that evening was the actor, Victor Moore, who was noted for his timid, whiny kind of voice.*)

VICTOR:    The doctor tried to give me a blood test.

FRED:    What happened?

VICTOR:    No blood! He opened one of my veins and it just hissed at him.

FRED:    What did he tell you to do?

VICTOR:    He told me to drink goat's milk to get better teeth.

FRED:    For more calcium? Are your teeth better now?

VICTOR:    Yes, only one thing wrong. They're goat's teeth.

# March 23, 1949

## Milton Berle

- BERLE:    (*Singing*) Ah, sweet mystery of life at last I've found you! Ah! Ah! Ah!

GALLUP:    (*To himself*) Oh, Berle, you are … lousy.

BERLE:    (*To audience that isn't laughing*) How can you sleep with the lights on? Oh, Mr. Gallup?

GALLUP:    (*Very low voice*) Yes … Berle?

BERLE:    He sounds like an answer for Chiloe. Time for our version of *Gone With the Wind*.

GALLUP:    We join Ashley Calhoun Berle as he knocks on Scarlett O'Hara's door.

BERLE:    (*SFX: Knocking*) Open the doe! Open the doe! I've come three hundred miles! Open the doe! I've come to say, good-bye!

SCARLETT:    (*SFX: Door opens*) Good-bye! (*SFX: Door slams*)

BERLE:    Open the doe! Open the doe! If you keep talking they'll go to war without me! (*SFX: Door opens*)

SCARLETT: What'll I do?
BERLE: Keep talking! (*Narrating his story*) Yes, I was in the Civil War. I was a spy. I hid in my union suit. But they found me.
SCARLETT: Why?
BERLE: I couldn't keep my trap shut.

- BERLE: Ah, it's springtime! So lovely in the park! (*Sings*) While strolling through the park one day...
GALLUP: The question is: Did Milton's mother know it was spring when she saw the sap running?

## March 24, 1949

### Burns & Allen

- GRACIE: George, you should be in a western. You have legs like a cowboy.
GEORGE: Thank you.
GRACIE: I can just see you now, during the big stampede. You standing there smiling with the cattle running between your legs.
GEORGE: I'm not that bowlegged.

- GRACIE: If you were in a western, you'd win an Oscar.
GEORGE: I'm afraid my competition would be very stiff.
GRACIE: Oh well, in that case, take a few drinks yourself.

- GRACIE: I have an uncle who's a doctor in an insane asylum.
GEORGE: He must be very smart.
GRACIE: No, he's not a real doctor. He thinks he's Dr. Fu Manchu.

- WOMAN: At the awards I plan to wear a strapless evening gown with a train.
GRACIE: Oh, no! Well, I hope it doesn't happen to you.
WOMAN: What? What happened?
GRACIE: A woman I know wore a gown with a train and someone stepped on the train, and...
WOMAN: Oh! You mean the gown...
GRACIE: All the way!
WOMAN: Oh, my goodness!
GRACIE: Don't worry. If it happens to you ... keep cool!

- JANE WYMAN: (*Guest*) So your husband, George, likes to sing.
GRACIE: Oh, yes. His voice is just like medicine. Every time he sings they say, "Boy, what a pill!"
JANE: Really?
GRACIE: Let him sing you to sleep. Take your choice ... medicine or his voice! Now surely you don't want anything horrible, nasty and icky, do you?

JANE:     No. I'll take the medicine.

- MAN:     I'm the dress maker. I'm here to try on Miss Wyman's gown.
  GRACIE:     Go ahead, but I don't think you'll look good in it.
  MAN:     You've got it all wrong. I just want to get a perfect fit.
  GRACIE:     Well, she'll have one if you try on her gown.
  MAN:     This is imperative!
  GRACIE:     Sorry. Good-bye, Mr. Imperative!

## Al Jolson

- AL:     Folks, I couldn't get Betty Grable as a guest, so I've got the next pret-
  tiest pair of legs … Georgie Jessel!
  JESSEL:     Ah, spring! When a young man's fancy turns to thoughts of love.
  I've been wondering. What does a young man's fancy turn to the rest of
  the year?

# March 27, 1949

## Ozzie & Harriet

- HARRIET:     Ozzie, what are you doing?
  OZZIE:     I'm sitting here saving my energy for this afternoon.
  HARRIET:     What are you going to do this afternoon?
  OZZIE:     I'm going to walk around back and lie in the hammock.

- THORNY:     My wife is unreasonable.
  OZZIE:     So's my wife. When she's house cleaning she gets awfully unreasonable. She wants me to help her.

## Jack Benny

- JACK:     Oh, Rochester! What happened to those pretty lace curtains?
  ROCHESTER:     Oh, those were cobwebs. I swept them down.
  JACK:     (Doorbell rings) I'll get it, Rochester. (Opens door) Well, Dennis Day!
  DENNIS:     Hello, Mr. Benny. I just got a letter from my mother.
  JACK:     Well … how are things with your dear old mom?
  DENNIS:     She says their cow's been sick for two weeks and Pop wishes she
  would get well so he can have his part of the bed back.
  JACK:     The cow sleeps in the bed?
  DENNIS:     She says, "I've always wanted an old fashioned bed and now with
  the cow there I just tied a sheet to her four legs and used it for a canopy.
  JACK:     Dennis, you're making this up.
  DENNIS:     This makes the cow hard to milk. You're pulling against gravity.

## March 30, 1949

### *Milton Berle*

- BERLE:  Wow! What applause! Thank you, ladies and gentlemen, and just for that I'm going to send each of you a photograph of myself … just as soon as I get the negatives back from the F.B.I.

  GALLUP:  (*Low voice*) …Berle!

  BERLE:  What's that noise? Funny time to be delivering coal. Oh, it's you, Frank. I hardly recognized you. What did you do, change embalming fluid? Folks, the reason he looks so formal. He's still wearing the suit he was buried in. Frank, really, you're so thin. You should eat and get fat. Look at me.

  GALLUP:  If I look at you, who can eat?

- GALLUP:  Tonight our theme is travel, and Mr. Berle needs no advice on travel. For years people have been telling him where to go.

  BERLE:  Where shall we go on our magic carpet? Merry England?

  GALLUP:  You know in England the famous London policemen are called Bobbies.

  BERLE:  And the men who beat them up are called Bobby-soxers.

  (*They decide on an ocean voyage. Then change their tickets to third class, and to save even more money, they get eighth class tickets. Now, as they board the ship…*)

  BERLE:  Well, we're traveling eighth class. Here's the boat.

  1ST MATE:  Tickets, please! What's this? Eighth class! Gad, I almost touched them! Get below!

  (*They go down, down, down into the depths of the boat.*)

  SAILOR:  Get in your stateroom!

  BERLE:  What kind of stateroom is this? (*SFX: Cow moo*) Oh, no! Let me out!

  GALLUP:  Someone's scratching on the wall.

  BERLE:  Who's there?

  MAN:  (*Whispering*) It's me in the next cabin. Got a cigarette?

  BERLE:  (*Loudly*) Where are we?

  MAN:  (*Whispering*) Keep quiet! It's ten lashes if you get too loud.

  BERLE:  Okay. Is breakfast ready?

  MAN:  Wait a minute. Here it comes. (*SFX: Cow moo.*)

## April 3, 1949

On this day, Dean Martin and Jerry Lewis made their debut on CBS. They were a huge success in nightclubs and it was hoped that they might become a hit on radio. However, most of their humor was visual, relying on Jerry's elastic face to garner laughs. This did not translate very well to radio. Movies, however, brought them both world-wide fame and acclaim.

## Martin & Lewis

- MARTIN: Well, Jerry. Here we are on radio.
  JERRY: What if we lay an egg?
  MARTIN: Come on! How big an egg could we lay?
  JERRY: Well, if we got a hen and made her hold back for a few years....
  MARTIN: Just relax, Jerry.
  JERRY: I can't. I've got butterflies in my stomach.
  MARTIN: Well, take an aspirin.
  JERRY: I did. Now they're playing Ping-Pong with it.

## Jack Benny

*(Jack is packing for a trip to New York City.)*
- JACK: Let's see ... one ... two ... three ... four ... five ... six ... seven! There, that ought to do it.
  ROCHESTER: Boss, why don't you pack a whole box? Kleenex doesn't cost much.
  JACK: That'll do fine. Gee, I'm hungry. I haven't eaten much today.
  ROCHESTER: What about that egg?
  JACK: Oh that was a mothball.
  ROCHESTER: I wish you'd told me sooner, you had it for breakfast.

## Fred Allen

*(Doc Rockwell and Henry Morgan were guests.)*
- DOC: I was in town buying some mustache wax.
  FRED: But, Doc, you don't have a mustache.
  DOC: I know, but my wife does.

*(Doing takeoff on Mr. Anthony, advice to lovelorn.)*
- WOMAN: I have a problem, doctor. My husband drinks, then comes home, hits me and kicks me down the stairs.
  MORGAN: And what is your problem?

- MORGAN: And finally, these words of wisdom. Please remember, in this great democracy of ours, every parent who has children is a mother and a father. Thank you and goodnight.

## NBC Theater

On this program Bob Hope did a "special" radio adaptation of his movie "The Ghostbreakers." It was an hour long and here are some excerpts from notes taken during that broadcast.

- BOB:   Oh, so won't move, eh? Take that! And that! And that!
  GIRL:   What's wrong?
  BOB:   I can't get this window open.
  GIRL:   I need your help.
  BOB:   Ah yes, don't you all? Poor girl…
  GIRL:   I've inherited a ghost house on Black Island. I have a note here.
  BOB:   Let me see. It says, "Death waits for you at Black Island!" Well, here's your note back, good-bye!

  (*Gangsters are after Hope, so he agrees to go to Black Island to escape from them. Now, on board an ocean liner…*)

  BOB:   What a stateroom on this ship. It's so low I can use the propeller to mix up my shaving cream.
  GIRL:   That note was signed, "Morty."
  BOB:   I know his brother … Rigor Morty. Listen, Mary, I know you're beautiful,…
  GIRL:   And we're going to the haunted house.
  BOB:   Yeah, we won two glorious weeks there on Ladies Be Seated.
  GIRL:   I hear there are Zombies there. They look horrible with green, evil eyes and vacant looks in their eyes.
  BOB:   You mean Republicans?

- BOB:   Well, here we are on the island.
  GIRL:   Look! The zombie walks!
  BOB:   Taxi strike, huh?
  ZOMBIE:   Go away! You'll die! You'll die! What do you want here?
  BOB:   Could I interest you in some magazines?
  ZOMBIE:   You'll die! I'm a zombie!
  BOB:   Well, give my regards to Boris Karloff!

  (*They approach the haunted castle on Black Island.*)
- GIRL:   There it is! I wonder who lived here?
  BOB:   Must have been Jolson. The front porch is down on its knees.
  GIRL:   At least we're alone.
  ZOMBIE:   Ahoooooooo!
  BOB:   That's the first time I've heard a breeze with adenoids. It's a zombie. The walking dead.
  GIRL:   I've never seen any.
  BOB:   You've never played Philadelphia.
  ZOMBIE:   Ahooooooo!
  GIRL:   What did he say?
  BOB:   With men who know castles best, it's zombies two to one.
  (*Takeoff on Lucky Strike commercial of that period. "With men who know tobacco best, it's Luckies two to one."*)
  (*SFX: An organ begins playing*)
  BOB:   The organ's playing and there's nobody here!
  GIRL:   It's playing by itself! I don't like it.

BOB: Petrillo won't like it, either. (*Head of musicians union*) Somebody must have put a nickel in it.

GHOST: Marching men! Marching men!

BOB: Maybe, they're drafting again.

GIRL: The ghost! It's going to that coffin! It disappeared!

BOB: That ghost put on a good show.

GHOST VOICE: Wait 'till you see me in *Hamlet.*

BOB: (*Playing the organ*) Look, when I play the organ the coffin rises up.

GIRL: There's a secret dungeon down there. Let's go down.

BOB: Okay, but remember, I'm lead-off man on the way back. (*SFX: Thud*) Oops, I fell!

GIRL: What did you fall on?

BOB: This is a comedy, what do you think?

GHOST: (*Moaning*) It's mine! It's mine! It's mine!

BOB: Thank you, Gertrude Stein. I'll match you to see who faints first. (*He faints*) Move over! Stop hogging the floor.

(*They search the castle and find a hidden treasure. All is well that ends well.*)

GIRL: This treasure! What will we do with it?

BOB: We can always open a hotel in Texas.

GHOST: Ha, ha, ha, ha, ha!

BOB: Why didn't we have him sit in the audience?

(*After the show.*)

GIRL: Well, Bob I guess you'll go play golf with Bing, now.

BOB: Play with Bing? Would you play golf with a bum?

GIRL: No.

BOB: Well, neither will he.

# April 5, 1949

## Alan Young

- ALAN: She has the skin you love to retouch.
  GIRL: Alan, I have the feeling that he tells you I'm ugly and that I wear makeup to hide it.
  ALAN: Nonsense! I wouldn't care if you didn't use anything to hide it.

- BANKER: We wouldn't lend you a skunk skin even if you could prove you were its father! And you know something? I believe you could!

- GIRL: (*Opening front door*) Oh, it's you, Alan. I wish you'd come to the back door. We have an agreement with the neighbors not to leave rubbish on the front porch.

- ALAN: I'll show you I'm not afraid! You! Behind that trash can! Come out with your hands up! Now! (*SFX: Meow*) Come on out!

GIRL: Alan, it's only a cat.
ALAN: Well ... he pulled a knife on me.
MUGGER: Hold it! I've got a gun in your back.
ALAN: You have? Well, move it a little higher ... more to the left ... higher ... little more to the right ... higher ... there! Ahhhhh!

## Bob Hope

- BOB: We have a new garbage can at our house. It grinds the garbage up and drops it under the house. It works fine, but now our house is three feet off the ground. I bought some lamb chops the other day. They were so skinny they had to hold each other's panties up. Ah, Professor Colonna! You look chipper.
  COLONNA: I just bought a car. It's a runabout.
  BOB: A runabout?
  COLONNA: No floor!
  BOB: How's your singing coming along?
  COLONNA: My teacher told me to sing in the shower. I don't have a shower so I got in the washing machine. You'd be surprised how many high notes you can hit when those paddles come around.

# April 7, 1949

## Abbott & Costello

- COSTELLO: (*To girl*) We could park and you could tell me your problems.
  GIRL: But I don't have any problems.
  COSTELLO: You've never dated me before.

- COSTELLO: He told me not to let the cat out of the bag and to keep it under my hat, but I can't!
  ABBOTT: Why not?
  COSTELLO: It gets awfully uncomfortable with a cat in a bag stuck under my hat.

- ABBOTT: What a frog! He hasn't croaked in three days.
  COSTELLO: Maybe, he has a man in his throat.

- COSTELLO: I was with a girl and I lost all account of time.
  ABBOTT: It was that romantic, eh?
  COSTELLO: No, she stole my watch.
  ABBOTT: She's quite a girl. I hear she comes from good stock.
  COSTELLO: Too bad. She shoulda come from people.

- ABBOTT: She has the map! It may be on the table
  COSTELLO: I'll hold her. You look for it.

ABBOTT:    Not here! It may be in the drawer.
COSTELLO:    I'll hold her. You look for it.
ABBOTT:    Not here! It may be in her stocking.
COSTELLO:    You hold her. I'll look for it!

## Burns & Allen

- GRACIE:    You're a man about town, George. You look like you've lived!
  GEORGE:    Really?
  GRACIE:    And lived, and lived, and lived…
  GEORGE:    All right! All right!

  (*Gracie has an antique teapot and is having it appraised.*)
- APPRAISER:    May I see the pot?
  GRACIE:    Oh, George has gone to the cigar store.
  APPRAISER:    I meant the teapot.
  GRACIE:    Would it be worth, say, a million dollars?
  APPRAISER:    Now, that's a nice round figure.
  GRACIE:    Well, thanks, but keep your mind on business!

## Al Jolson

(*Jolson's guests that evening were Groucho Marx and Oscar Levant.*)
- AL:    At our house we dress for Easter.
  OSCAR:    At our house we dress every day.
  GROUCHO:    (*Entering*) Say, have you got the key to the washroom? I want to rinse out this cigar. Say, who are you?
  OSCAR:    I'm Oscar.
  GROUCHO:    Oscar? That's a strange name. Why weren't you named something normal like Harpo or Zeppo, or even Zazu Pitts?

- GROUCHO:    How would you like to buy an elephant?
  OSCAR:    Why would I want to buy an elephant?
  GROUCHO:    You could make your own piano keys.
  OSCAR:    Tell you what. I'll sell you some piano keys and you can make your own elephant.

  (*Groucho is trying to sell Jolson a girl's baseball team.*)
- AL:    Girl's don't play baseball.
  GROUCHO:    Well, they probably know some other games, too.
  AL:    What teams have they played?
  GROUCHO:    They played the Donut team.
  AL:    The Donut team? Are they any good?
  GROUCHO:    No, I've never seen a donut play a good game, yet.
  AL:    Why are you selling your girl's baseball team?
  GROUCHO:    I can't get to first base with them.
  AL:    Do they have many fans?

GROUCHO:    Last game there were five thousand in the grandstand.

AL:    Any bleachers?

GROUCHO:    Well, a few of 'em are blondes.

AL:    How many bats do you have?

GROUCHO:    Only three. The rest look pretty good.

AL:    Do you have a good pitcher?

GROUCHO:    Sure, you'd like her after a fashion. You'd like her even better after an Old-Fashioned.

AL:    Would they play a double-header?

GROUCHO:    Not if I can get a single headed one.

AL:    That short stop has no glove. How can she stop the ball?

GROUCHO:    With her face. It'll stop anything.

AL:    Who pinch hits?

GROUCHO:    I pinch. She hits.

AL:    Have you had any experience?

GROUCHO:    Remember. I used to play with the Dodgers.

AL:    Brooklyn?

GROUCHO:    No. Draft.

AL:    Anywhere else?

GROUCHO:    I was with the White Sox.

AL:    What did you do with the White Sox?

GROUCHO:    Washed socks. Came up from underwear ... started at the bottom then.

AL:    Did you ever play baseball?

GROUCHO:    Yes. It was a crucial game, but I threw my arm away.

AL:    What happened?

GROUCHO:    It went into the grandstand. Some guy threw it back. It didn't have any mustard on it.

# April 10, 1949

## *Martin & Lewis*

- SEXY GIRL:    Hello, big boy. Could you give me a minute of your time?

JERRY:    Are you kidding? You could use my head to crack walnuts.

DEAN:    Hello, there.

SEXY GIRL:    Well ... two handsome men.

JERRY:    Two handsome men? She must be looking at me twice.

DEAN:    I'd like to sing a song.

JERRY:    Me too! I have a brand new song entitled, "I'm Head Over Heels in Love with You, and I Look Better That Way."

DEAN:    That's dumb.

JERRY:    Hey, I'm only twenty-three years old. What do I know?

## Fred Allen

- FRED: (*To Mrs. Nussbaum*) So you're a singer?

  NUSSBAUM: I been singing with the exterminating company.

  FRED: With the exterminating company?

  NUSSBAUM: I just stand in the house and sing, and all the rats coming running out with their little paws over their ears.

  FRED: Don't they use traps?

  NUSSBAUM: Not when I open mine!

## Henry Morgan

- HENRY: Ah, the circus! The barker! (*Hey, hey!*) The lion (*Roar*) The seal! (*Arf, arf*) The giraffe? The giraffe? Okay, you do a giraffe!

  TREACHER: Henry, where were you born?

  HENRY: Under Taurus, the bull.

  TREACHER: It figures.

  HENRY: We're doing a western sketch tonight.

  TREACHER: Jolly good. I've always had a yen to be a cowlad.

  HENRY: Cowlad?

  TREACHER: We'll call it "Trotalong Treacher."

# April 20, 1949

(*Side bar note: Television is coming to Charlotte, North Carolina, in 60 days.*)

## Milton Berle

- BERLE: Ah, baseball! I love it. When I was a kid the big boys used to let me play on their team. They had to let me play. My stomach was first base.

- GALLUP: Mr. Berle!

  BERLE: Mr. Gallup. The last time I saw a nose like that it was fencing with Errol Flynn.

  GALLUP: Poor Berle. He's carried that egg around since Easter just to lay it here tonight.

- BERLE: (*At baseball game*) There's a cute blond in the stands.

  GALLUP: Joe got a hit! He's trying to get to first base!

  BERLE: So's the guy with the blond.

  GALLUP: What a crowd! The stands are packed.

  BERLE: So's the blond!

  GALLUP: That was a ball! Not a strike! What's the matter with that umpire?

  BERLE: He's the only man who can look through a keyhole with both eyes.

GALLUP:   Did you ever play baseball, Milton?
BERLE:   I was rookie of the year. They took one look at my wife and said, "You've been rooked!"

## You Bet Your Life

• GROUCHO:   So you're a telephone operator? Tell me, why are there no men telephone operators?
LADY:   Oh, women just have more patience.
GROUCHO:   I thought it was because if a man answered everybody would hang up.
LADY:   No, we can put up with a lot more. Try me.
GROUCHO:   Okay, I'll pretend to make a phone call. Hello, information? I want the number of Sam Migozisowitski.
LADY:   How do you spell that?
GROUCHO:   S — A — M!
LADY:   No, I meant the last name ... Migozisowitski.
GROUCHO:   Look, if I could spell it, I'd write him a letter. Enough of this. Now it's time to play *You Bet Your Life.* But, first ... are you married?
LADY:   No, but I've had three chances.
GROUCHO:   Three chances? You struck out, eh?

# April 24, 1949

## Martin & Lewis

• JERRY:   I'm tough. Feel that muscle.
DEAN:   Hmm, you've been eating your spinach.
JERRY:   What does it feel like?
DEAN:   Spinach.
JERRY:   You should have seen me before I worked out. I was so thin I used LifeSavers for a belt. Once I got caught in the rain and my pants fell down six different flavors.
DEAN:   Did your mother drop you on your head when you were a baby?
JERRY:   No, my mother worked. My father hadda do it.

*(Dean and Jerry in a western sketch.)*
• JERRY:   Here we are in the Buzzard's Breast Saloon and I'm tired. I been riding the trail for three days and I'm mighty tired ... mighty tired ... Yep! I'm mighty tired .... mmmmightyyyy tireddddd! Do you think I'm overacting?
DEAN:   I just got back from robbing a stagecoach.
BARTENDER:   Thar ain't been no stagecoach through these parts for four years! How'd you do it?
DEAN:   It was behind schedule.

JERRY:    Get a load of that dance hall gal. She's stacked like a deck of cards. Too bad we don't have time, we could play some pinochle.

DEAN:    Look at this fella. He thinks he's tough!

JERRY:    Yeah, look at him and his tough face and his big gun. BIG GUN? Bye!

DEAN:    Hey, where're you going?

JERRY:    I like my nose the way it is (*SFX: Smack*) ... was!

HOMBRE:    I'm so tough, I lie on the railroad track and let the train run across my legs.

DEAN:    That's tough!

HOMBRE:    Of course, I keep gettin' shorter all the time.

JERRY:    Let's shoot it out!

HOMBRE:    Okay. I'm loading.

(*SFX: Gunshots. Bang, bang, bang, bang, bang, bang, bang, bang!*)

JERRY:    Okay, now let's reload!

(*The sketch ends with them all singing "Ragtime Cowboy."*)

## Amos 'n' Andy

On this show, Andy inherits two thousand dollars. Naturally, Kingfish wants to gyp him out of it. The will states that the money must be used to send Andy to college. So Kingfish starts his own college and tries to convince Andy to enroll for (*you guessed it*) only two thousand dollars. He even hires a girl to pretend she's a co-ed.

• ANDY:    What do you teach at this here college?

KINGFISH:    Oh, math, English, solid geometry ... flabby geometry.

ANDY:    I don't think so. I gotta be going ... well ... hello, baby!

KINGFISH:    She's just a sample of one of them co-eds we got at the college.

• DOCTOR:    (*After giving Andy a physical*) I looked in his ears and what do you think I saw?

KINGFISH:    What?

DOCTOR:    The wall paper on the other side of the room.

KINGFISH:    You mean to say that there is a passage from one ear to the other?

ANDY:    Yeah. On a windy day my head whistles like a piccolo.

## Fred Allen

• FRED ALLEN:    (*Referring to Billy Rose, a Broadway producer who was very short.*) Billy Rose? Yes, I saw him in Lindy's. I happened to look under a table and he was standing there. With his hat on. I saw a sign in front of a liquor store. It said: No Parking. This place for loading only.

• TITUS:    I come from a dumb family. My papa not only didn't know nothing, he didn't even suspect nothing! He didn't even know he was supposed to wash himself. Finally, got the idea from the cat. Every night he'd curl up on the floor and start licking himself.

# April 27, 1949

## Ted Mack's Original Amateur Hour

On this day Frank Fontaine appeared on the Original Amateur Hour and did his soon to be famous John L. C. Sivoney character. This launched his career and he appeared at various times on the Jack Benny radio show. Later, Frank would bring that character to the Jackie Gleason show on television in the 1950s in those Joe, the bartender sketches. Here is a sample of that routine heard on the Original Amateur Hour.

- FRANK: (*As John L. C. Sivoney*) How did I win the sweepstakes? (*Silly laugh*) Well, I was sitting around the house ... I wasn't doing nuthin' ... just hanging around the house. So I says to myself, "John, what are you doing?" and I says, "Nuttin'!" And I was right! I wasn't doing nuttin'! Just sittin' around the house. So I'm sittin' there, listening to the radio and it starts talking to me. Now, I've had that radio for three years and it ain't ever said nothin' to me. I don't speak to any of my furniture. It says the lucky number is 6887534285902478643984720430l (*takes breath*) 3207586034192798! (*breath*) 7839472831998379378! And I says that's me! (*Stupid laugh and then gasps for breath*).

This is an example of how pure characterization can get laughs. Those readers who have been fortunate enough to have seen or heard Frank do this bit will know what I mean. I doubt seriously if anyone else could have gotten laughs with this material the way Frank did.

## Milton Berle

- BERLE: My new sponsor is Texaco. They have a funny way of paying me. They just pump the money into my pocket. In fact, I got a telegram from them. It says: "We have heard your show and decided to give you a raise." Look how they spelled raise — R-A-Z-Z.
  GALLUP: (*His very low voice*) Mr. Berle!
  BERLE: Frank, you look like a million dollars. All green and wrinkled.
  GALLUP: Berle, I could stand here and listen to you for hours and it feels like I already have.

- BERLE: Oh, that Little Orphan Annie! For forty years she's been wearing that same lousy dress. No wonder nobody'll go out with her but that crummy dog. And what a dog! For forty years he's been in the comic strip and all he says is, "Arf!" I've got a little puppy that out talks him and he's only two months old and he knows three words. "Woof, woof, woof!" And that Dick Tracy's new character, Pear Shape! I don't have to read the paper to find pear shape, I can just look at my girlfriend.

# April 28, 1949

## *Abbott & Costello*

- COSTELLO:  I'm a wow with women. It's my personal magnetism. Yesterday I picked up two blondes, a redhead and a rusty nail.
  ABBOTT:  So you're hot stuff with the women?
  COSTELLO:  You bet! I'm the kind of guy women leave home for.
  ABBOTT:  Yeah, when you were born your mother took one look and she hasn't been back since.

- COSTELLO:  My uncle has a new trucking business. He has a new truck, too. It's one inch wide and three blocks long.
  ABBOTT:  What does he haul in it?
  COSTELLO:  Spaghetti.

- COSTELLO:  My uncle drinks a lot. At night the mosquitoes bite him and keep me awake.
  ABBOTT:  If the mosquitoes bite him, how does that keep you awake?
  COSTELLO:  They bite him, then fly over to my bed and hiccup.

- COSTELLO:  My girlfriend has a new electric blanket. She loves to have breakfast in bed. She takes eggs and bread to bed with her so when she wakes up ... it's done! Last night she turned it up too far and today she's the toast of the town!

- ABBOTT:  Costello, you know, money isn't everything. You can't take it with you.
  COSTELLO:  Yeh, but it's nice to have it around to say good-bye to.

*(They do a private detective sketch.)*
- COSTELLO:  I'm Sam Shovel, private eye. I'm sitting in my office playing cards the hard way ... without any cards. Thanks to me, the cops caught three crooks ... Babyface Jones, Babyface Nelson, and Babyface Brown but that wasn't so tough considering they were all babies.
  ABBOTT:  What kind of office is this? An old cracker barrel for a desk, and a soap box for a chair.
  COSTELLO:  Yeah! Would you believe, a year ago I started out with nothing.
  ABBOTT:  We'd better go after those crooks.
  COSTELLO:  Okay, I'll get my gun, my knife, blackjack and newspaper.
  ABBOTT:  What's the newspaper for?
  COSTELLO:  If the others fail, I'll show him the headlines and he'll worry himself to death.

- VICTIM:  Help! I've been shot, stabbed and my legs are broken.
  COSTELLO:  Does it hurt?
  VICTIM:  Only when I laugh.

(*A beautiful woman turns out to be the crook.*)
- WOMAN:   Promise you won't turn me over to the cops. I'll do anything. Just don't turn me over!
  COSTELLO:   Who wants to turn you over? You look great on this side.
  WOMAN:   Just call me, Sally, you big hunk of man.
  COSTELLO:   Okay, Sally, you big hunk of man.

## Burns & Allen

- GEORGE:   Gracie, why are you cooking?
  GRACIE:   Because the last time I baked a cake, you accused me of buying it from a bakery.
  GEORGE:   And you didn't?
  GRACIE:   No. I bought it from a grocery store.
  GEORGE:   What are you making now?
  GRACIE:   I'm making a jelly roll. And watch where you walk on the floor.
  GEORGE:   Why?
  GRACIE:   Well, for your information, jelly won't roll.
  GEORGE:   You know, I can cook ladyfingers. But don't tell a soul. If you do everybody will kid the pants off me.
  GRACIE:   Well, it won't matter. You'll have an apron on.
  GEORGE:   Says here in the cookbook to fold an egg. How do you fold an egg?
  GRACIE:   Uh … fry it first. If you don't you can't get the corners straight.

- BEA:   Does George stick his nose in the cooking?
  GRACIE:   No, he uses a spoon.
  BEA:   Well, I've got to go pick up my husband.
  GRACIE:   Oh. He still can't hold his liquor, eh?

- FARMER:   I feed my pigs three times a day. I fill my pen with garbage.
  GRACIE:   Oh, do you? George fills his pen with ink.
  FARMER:   I meant for the pigs.
  GRACIE:   Oh, don't kid me! Pigs can't read.
  FARMER:   You should come to my farm and see the big fat boar.
  GRACIE:   We'd love to, but that's no way to talk about your wife.

(*George wants to keep the fact that he cooks ladyfingers a secret.*)
- GEORGE:   About my ladyfingers. You didn't spill the beans, did you?
  GRACIE:   No, I only served the ladyfingers. George, admit it! You are the King of Ladyfingers!
  GEORGE:   Oh … I … wish … I … were … dead.
  GRACIE:   George, you look sad. So sad. Like a cow that's been milked with chapped hands.

- BILL:   George, I thought you'd be in the kitchen greasing your pan.
  GRACIE:   Oh, he's too worried to even shave it.

BILL:  I was just kidding. I just thought I'd give him a rib.
GRACIE:  Well, he won't cook that, either.

## Al Jolson

- Oscar Levant: I've lost so many women in the movies, even my wife is beginning to wonder what she saw in me.

- WIFE:  Oh, you don't love me! I'm leaving! I'm going home to mother!
AL:  Well, you don't have far to go, she lives with us.
WIFE:  My mother hates you.
AL:  Don't say that.
WIFE:  Too late. I already said it.
AL:  Then I'm going to join the French Foreign Legion!

(*Segue into French Foreign Legion sketch.*)
- WOMAN:  You've been walking in the desert for ten days. I'll bet your feet are blistered. Why don't you sit down?
AL:  My feet aren't the only place that's blistered.
WOMAN:  This will make you feel better. (*SFX: Kiss*) Ohhhh! The way you kiss!
AL:  It's the hot sand in my mustache.
WOMAN:  How did you get across the hot desert without a camel?
AL:  Oh, easy. Put me down, Oscar. (*Oscar Levant*)

- OSCAR:  I've always worked for my money. Why when I was only five years old I had a paper route. I worked and slaved and worked and saved my money until that unforgettable day when I had five whole dollars. And do you know what I did? I went up to my mother and said, "Here, this is for you."
AL:  Gee, I'll bet she was proud of you.
OSCAR:  You bet. And I was only twenty-nine years old at the time.

## May 1, 1949

## Martin & Lewis

- DEAN:  Baseball catchers wear masks to keep from getting hit and getting their faces all beat up.
JERRY:  I know all about it. I used to be a catcher.
DEAN:  Gee, why didn't you wear a mask?

- DEAN:  See that pretty girl over there? Why don't you ask her for a date?
JERRY:  Aw, she wouldn't wipe her feet on me.
DEAN:  Well, wait'll she gets to know you better. Then she will.
JERRY:  Dean, only a moron would think otherwise.

DEAN:    Folks, meet Jerry Lewis, boy otherwise. Her name is Madeline. Tell her you're charmed to meet her.

JERRY:    (*Fast flat monotone*) Madeline, I'm charmed to meet you!

MADELINE:    Oo! Let me kiss you! (*SFX: Loud kiss and pop*) Well, say something!

JERRY:    (*Exactly as before*) Madeline, I'm charmed to meet you!

DEAN:    What's the matter with you?

JERRY:    The last girl I kissed said, "Murder!"

DEAN:    I'll bet that's what they preferred.

JERRY:    (*To girl*) Oh, my dear ... come! Let us go to the woodland and take off our shoes and tip-toe through the flowers.

DEAN:    Jerry, nobody does that.

JERRY:    I do ... but what do I know?

DEAN:    Take her dancing.

JERRY:    Good idea. I can rumba.

DEAN:    Where did you learn to rumba?

JERRY:    I got a bicycle with a loose seat.

## Jack Benny

- JACK:    Hello, Mary. What's that in your hand?

  MARY:    A letter from my mother. My sister Babe has a new French bathing suit.

  JACK:    Can she swim?

  MARY:    Like a mermaid.

  JACK:    I've noticed the resemblance, but it's just that the wrong half looks like a fish.

  DENNIS:    Speaking of fish. I went fishing the other day.

  JACK:    Did you catch anything?

  DENNIS:    Yep! Caught a sandal.

  JACK:    Oh, for heavens sakes.

  DENNIS:    You should have seen the hip boot that got away!

  (*Comedy sketch was a takeoff on the movie* Treasure of the Sierra Madre.)

- JACK:    (*In Bogart role*) It's a hot, humid, sultry day and here I am roaming the streets of Mexico. Just walking, walking with nothing to eat or drink. I'll go in this saloon. Bartender, gimme three fingers.

  BARTENDER:    Of what?

  JACK:    Just three fingers. I'm hungry. I began talking to a man standing at the bar. He was down on his luck.

  MAN:    I used to work in department store here in Mexico. I worked in the Jose department.

  JACK:    That's hosiery department!

  MAN:    Would you be interested in making a lot of money?

  JACK:    Money? I can take it or love it ... I mean, leave it.

(*Later, high up the Sierra mountains.*)

- JACK: I'm tired! We've been digging in these mountains for months!
  MEL: Si.
  JACK: Are you a Mexican?
  MEL: Si.
  JACK: And you're going to kill us, right?
  MEL: Si.
  JACK: What's your name?
  MEL: Cy.
  JACK: Cy?
  MEL: Si.
  JACK: Now, look Si ... I mean, Cy. I'm getting seasick.

## Fred Allen

- FRED: I've been very busy — busier than a man with a wooden leg in a forest fire.
  FRED: (*Visiting Allen's Alley*) Ah, Titus Moody, what's new with you?
  TITUS: My grandpa. He's a hundred years old. They gave him a party.
  FRED: A party? What did he do?
  TITUS: At a hundred, what can he do?
  FRED: You're right, when a man gets to be a hundred, he's been where he's going.
  TITUS: They gave him a television set.
  FRED: That's nice. I'm sure he enjoyed that.
  TITUS: Not much. They hung his washing on the TV antenna.
  FRED: What happened?
  TITUS: Have you ever seen Toscanini conducting the Philharmonic Orchestra through the back of a union suit?

- FRED: I've been dreaming about a watermelon.
  AL: (*Orchestra conductor*) Watermelon? That's the name of a horse! This is mental telepathy! We gotta get to the track. We'll make thousands!
  FRED: Folks, never belittle a conductor. He may be on the right track.
  TOUT: (*At the racetrack*) He'll win. This is straight from the horse's mouth, and I got the oats on my shirt to prove it.
  FRED: How come you're so sure he'll win?
  TOUT: Look under my coat.
  FRED: Oh, a hypodermic needle two feet long!
  (*The race ends. The horse loses.*)
  FRED: Watermelon came in last! But ... what about my dream?
  AL: Did you ever see a dream walking? (*Song title of the period*)

## Henry Morgan

- HENRY: I went to a French restaurant and ordered the Soup de jour. Guess what? There was not one jour in it!

ANNOUNCER:   Soup de jour means soup of the day.

HENRY:   Well, it tasted like the soup left over from the jour before yester-jour.

ANNOUNCER:   What else did you order?

HENRY:   Meatballs. They gave me one lousy meatball. It was so small I could have sucked it through a straw. A fly walked across my plate and it stuck to his foot.

- HENRY:   (*Doing takeoff on Hollywood gossip columnist, Jimmy Fiddler.*) Hello, this is Jimmy Morgan with news of Hollywooooooduh! Do you remember the acting of Jack Holt fifteen years ago? I don't! In their last movie, Clark Gable and Jean Harlow kissed eighty thousand times! Now, their lips have grown back and they're making a new picture.

# May 4, 1949

## Milton Berle

- BERLE:   I feel wonderful tonight. It's May! Oh, it was so beautiful in the park. The birds were flying, the trees were sighing, the sailors were trying.

GALLUP:   (*Low*) Mr. Berle!

BERLE:   Frank Gallup. He's happy. He can sleep late tomorrow, the morgue doesn't open until noon.

- BERLE:   (*Dreaming that he's alone on an island in the South Pacific with native girl.*) Darling ... don't run around like that you're liable to catch cold. Now go put another flower in your hair. (*He wakes up*) Time to get up. I'm beginning to dream about women with clothes on!

(*They do sea adventure sketch: "Captain Moby Berle, Killer of the Seven Seas."*)

- BERLE:   (*Sings*) Sailing, sailing over the briny deep ... say, what's that up there in the crow's nest? Ah, just as I figured ... a crow!

SAILOR:   Captain, Captain! There's a sail, a sail!

BERLE:   Where?

SAILOR:   In the department store.

BERLE:   That's silly. Where is it?

SAILOR:   It's a thirty degrees latitude and forty degrees longitude.

BERLE:   Quiet! Where is it?

SAILOR:   On our left.

BERLE:   Just leave my union suit hanging, maybe they'll fall into the trap.

SAILOR:   Look at the stars. There's the big diaper. The big diaper!

BERLE:   Egad, the weather's in for a change!

## You Bet Your Life

- GROUCHO:   (*Contestants are a coffee taster and a pest exterminator.*)
  (*To coffee taster*) Ever have a job called off because of wet grounds?
  TASTER:   Coffee doesn't keep you awake. We have proof.
  GROUCHO:   You have proof? What do you do, prowl around bedrooms at
  night? What if people wake up? Do you say, "Don't bother, I'm just see-
  ing if coffee keeps you awake?" Tell me, which hand do you use to stir
  your coffee?
  TASTER:   I use a spoon.
  GROUCHO:   Wait a minute! No jokes! How would you like it if I came to
  your job and gulped coffee?
  (*To exterminator*) So, you're an exterminator, eh?
  MAN:   Yes, did you know a single cockroach can have thirty thousand
  offspring?
  GROUCHO:   A single cockroach can do that? If he ever got married it'd be
  disastrous! Speaking of offspring … do you have any children?
  MAN:   We just had triplets.
  GROUCHO:   Triplets? Tell me, which triplet is your favorite?
  MAN:   I'm not going to have any favorites.
  GROUCHO:   Oh, you're going to dislike them all, eh?

# May 5, 1949

## Abbott & Costello

- ABBOTT:   So do you even know how to get engaged?
  COSTELLO:   Easy. I just heard on the radio … "use Woodbury soap and get
  engaged." So I bought twelve cases.
  ABBOTT:   Did you get engaged?
  COSTELLO:   Heck no! I was too busy washing to get engaged!
  ABBOTT:   I got a girl for you. Her name is Tracy.
  COSTELLO:   Tracy? Is she any kin to Dick?
  ABBOTT:   Don't be silly. Dick Tracy is a character in a comic strip.
  COSTELLO:   Well, your wife is no oil painting.

- ABBOTT:   (*To pretty girl*) Darling, my little bird, let me put my wing around
  you. Now the other wing. Now, I coo in your ear. Costello, what do I
  do, now?
  COSTELLO:   Don't just stand there, drop a worm into her mouth!

- COSTELLO:   I have a new car, now. The motor is in back and so's the steer-
  ing wheel.
  ABBOTT:   Gee, how can I get one like that?
  COSTELLO:   Easy, just run into a Sunset bus.

- COSTELLO:   My uncle thinks he's a chicken.
ABBOTT:   Why don't you send him to a hospital?
COSTELLO:   We would, but we need the eggs.
(*Note: This joke was used by Woody Allen in "Annie Hall."*)

- MYSTERY SKETCH: The case of the murdered florist, or he was caught with his plants down.
COSTELLO:   Just listen to this rain. (*SFX: Bucket crashing*) It's coming down in buckets! (*SFX: Snore … meow … snore … meow*) He's taking a cat-nap.
ABBOTT:   Are you a good detective?
COSTELLO:   Yes! I nailed a crook in New York. Then I nailed him again in New Jersey. I don't carry a gun. Just a hammer and nails.
ABBOTT:   You'll know him when you see him. He has a foul mouth.
COSTELLO:   That's believable. He has a nose like a chicken.
ABBOTT:   Your brother is a crook. I want you to arrest your own brother.
COSTELLO:   Oh, no! A little sad music maestro! (*Band plays* Hearts and Flowers) I said, "Sad!" Not pitiful.
ABBOTT:   There's your brother! The man with the ladder sticking out of his head.
COSTELLO:   He's really my step-brother.

## Burns & Allen

(*Guest is William Boyd who played Hopalong Cassidy.*)
- BOYD:   I'm a Boyd.
GRACIE:   A what?
BOYD:   I'm a Boyd. A Boyd!
GRACIE:   Well, flap your wings and fly back to Brooklyn.

   Situation: A mix-up in names. William Boyd is talking about a girl named Trixie, and since he's a cowboy star, Gracie thinks he's talking about a horse named Trixie.
- GRACIE:   What color is she?
BOYD:   White.
GRACIE:   Solid white?
BOYD:   Well … yes…
GRACIE:   Are there any markings on her behind?
BOYD:   I wouldn't know that. She used to come over to me and…
GRACIE:   …and you'd climb on her back!
BOYD:   No, no…
GRACIE:   Well, bring her over and I'll introduce her to the best horses in town.
BOYD:   (*SFX: Phone rings*) Hello? Okay, fine. I'll see you later. (*Hangs up*) That was Trixie on the phone.
GRACIE:   Wow! You mean she can talk?

BOYD:    Of course! She also sings and plays the violin.

- BOYD:    We're remaking an old movie, and I want you to be in it, George.
  GEORGE:    I'll need an old suit.
  GRACIE:    Yeah, well, just keep the one you have on.
  GEORGE:    Gracie's little joke never works.
  BOYD:    I know, George. Why don't you get a job?

- GRACIE:    George, other men tried to tug at my heartstrings, but when you came along, it was more than a tug … what a jerk!

## Al Jolson

- AL:    How are you and your girlfriend getting along?
  DENNIS:    (*Guest, Dennis Day*) We came to an understanding. She married somebody else.
  AL:    What happened?
  DENNIS:    I was going to elope with her, but she lost her nerve. I waited three hours and she never showed up.
  AL:    What are you doing now?
  DENNIS:    I want to earn some pocket money.
  AL:    Why?
  DENNIS:    I just found a swell place to buy pockets.
  AL:    How do you plan to make some pocket money?
  DENNIS:    I thought I'd be a babysitter.
  AL:    What qualifies you to be a babysitter?
  DENNIS:    Well, this morning I was on a bus and sat on a baby.
  AL:    What did her mother say?
  DENNIS:    Nothing. Before she found out, I was burped twice and diapered three times.
  AL:    How could she confuse you with her baby? Babies are supposed to be soft, warm and tender.
  DENNIS:    Well, I have my moments.

# May 8, 1949

## Martin & Lewis

- DEAN:    You're so skinny. How much do you weigh stripped?
  JERRY:    I don't know, I'm bashful.
  AGENT:    Well, well, where did you boys come from?
  JERRY:    The stork brought us.
  DEAN:    Jerry, he didn't mean that.
  AGENT:    Oh, yes I did! I know you boys backwards and forwards.
  JERRY:    Well, come around front sometime, we got talent around there, too.

- JERRY:   (*Doing takeoffs on commercials*) So, drink Drene! It comes in six delicious flavors ... strawberry, raspberry, orange, lemon and bathtub.
  DEAN:   This program is brought to you by Sloop! The breakfast cereal that makes you wish it was lunch time.
  JERRY:   And also by Slop, the shampoo for baldheaded men. It contains a new secret ingredient ... hair!
  DEAN:   Simply put some wheels on the bottle and, presto! You've got a new Studebaker!

## Jack Benny

- JACK:   (*Ad-lib after Mary flubs a line*) I haven't heard you flub lines like that since you ordered a chiss sweeze sandwich.
  JACK:   (*In a drug store at the soda fountain*) Excuse me, are you the clerk?
  FRANK:   Yessssss!
  MARY:   Oh, Jack, why do you always run into this crazy guy?
  FRANK:   Are you going to order or wait for the floor show?
  JACK:   A floor show? In a drug store?
  FRANK:   Oh, yes! Dr. Shol comes out and does a fan dance with two footpads.
  JACK:   What?
  FRANK:   He's corny, but good!
  JACK:   Okay, I'll take a chiss sweeze sandwich.
  FRANK:   Good! Do you want me to crimm the trust?
  JACK:   And look! There's lipstick on this glass.
  FRANK:   Well, there's water in it, too. Wash it off!

## Fred Allen

- FRED:   Portland and I ate in a restaurant that was so far back in the woods, that if you wanted cream in your coffee, a cow backed up to the table. After the first cup, I took mine black. I just threw that in. We had it left over from last week's show.

# May 11, 1949

## Milton Berle

- BERLE:   Folks, tonight's show is about cars. I know. You came here to see me make a Nash of myself. You know, there's nothing like getting a new car when you're down in the dumps. And that's exactly where I got mine. Oh, Mr. Gallup! Frank Gallup!
  GALLUP:   Yes, Berle.
  BERLE:   Did you hear those belly laughs I just got?

GALLUP:  Yes, they were laughing at your belly.

BERLE:  That's because I'm wearing a Howard suit and Howard's still in it.

GALLUP:  Why tell jokes, Berle? Nowadays people want to hear the news.

BERLE:  But I'm a comedian.

GALLUP:  Now, that's news!

- BERLE:  (*Riding in a buggy with beautiful girl*) Ah, this is lovely. Here I am, stroking your black hair in the buggy.

GIRL:  But my hair is blond.

BERLE:  Doggone that horse's tail!

GIRL:  For twenty minutes we've been looking at the same part of the horse.

BERLE:  That reminds me ... how's your father?

- BERLE:  My brother, Frank, picked me and my girl up and dropped me off at my house. The louse!

GALLUP:  Wasn't that nice? To drop you off at home?

BERLE:  While doing sixty miles an hour?

GALLUP:  I hear when he drives, people are safe on the streets.

BERLE:  Yeah, he drives on the sidewalk.

- BERLE:  Those new cars are built so close to the ground they don't have doors. They have manhole covers. But they seat seven people.

GALLUP:  So what? Lots of cars seat seven people.

BERLE:  In the glove compartment?

- BERLE:  (*As auto corporate executive*) I'm surrounded by yes men! All day all I hear is yes, yes, yes! Why doesn't somebody say, "No?"

MAN:  No.

BERLE:  You're fired!

SECRETARY:  You buzzed me?

BERLE:  Yes, take a letter to all department heads. Dear heads!

# May 12, 1949

## *Abbott & Costello*

- COSTELLO:  Well, here we are in Dr. Ug's store.

ABBOTT:  You idiot! That's drug store.

CLERK:  Excuse me, may I help you. I'm the assistant manager.

COSTELLO:  You are? Boy, what a louse the manager must be. I'd like to buy a dozen golf balls.

CLERK:  Good. Shall I wrap them up?

COSTELLO:  No, just tee 'em up and I'll drive them home.

CLERK:  Hey, Abbott, look at these new toothbrushes. They're made out of the hair of a dog's tail. They're great for a lazy man. You just stick the brush in your mouth and it wags up and down.

ABBOTT:   I don't think so. Look at this. A new pill. Cures all ills.
COSTELLO:   What is it?
ABBOTT:   Poison.
MAN:   (*Strange man interrupts dramatically*) I've been awake for three days and three nights! No sleep! Ahahaha! What'll I do? What'll I do?
COSTELLO:   Go to bed.
MAN:   (*Relieved*) Gee, thanks!
COSTELLO:   (*At soda fountain*) Gimme a banana split with lemon, chocolate, and strawberries.
SODA JERK:   Shall I put a cherry on it?
COSTELLO:   What are you trying to do? Make me sick? (*Notices pretty girl at counter*) How about a soda, baby?
GIRL:   No, I have to watch my figure.
COSTELLO:   Well, you have the soda, and I'll watch your figure. How about a date? We could park and make pictures.
GIRL:   But it's dark. Nothing will develop.
COSTELLO:   You've never been out with me, have you?

- MAN:   I was off on a trip. I sent my wife a telegram telling her when I'd be home. Then, when I got home, I found her in the arms of another man. What do you think?
  COSTELLO:   I don't think she got your telegram.

- COSTELLO:   Yesterday I talked to the Boy Scouts.
  ABBOTT:   What about?
  COSTELLO:   Girl Scouts.

- NURSE:   (*In operating room*) Oh, doctor, put your arms around me.
  COSTELLO:   Please, you're melting my pocket comb.
  ABBOTT:   Doctor! Stop fooling around with that nurse. What about the patient?
  COSTELLO:   Let him get his own girl.
  NURSE:   I love you, Sam! I love you, Sam! Now, you say it.
  COSTELLO:   I love you, Sam! This won't work! We're both in love with the same guy!

## Burns & Allen

(*George thinks they should go on television, but he's worried about working in the new medium. Gracie tries to console him.*)
- GRACIE:   Look at those puppets on TV. Even a dummy can work.
  GEORGE:   I'm not worried about you. It's me!
  GRACIE:   Don't worry, George. On television they say look at the character on that face.
  GEORGE:   What?
  GRACIE:   Or is it, look at the face on that character?

GEORGE:    Oh, stop kidding. I haven't any more sex appeal than … uh, Clark Gable. Once a girl heard me on the radio and fell in love with me on the radio.

GRACIE:    Wouldn't the couch be a better place?

- ANNOUNCER:    Women flock around me like moths.

  GRACIE:    Well, before I married George, women did the same with him and when we got married, he was plenty moth-eaten. Oh, George is handsome! And that's not just my opinion. It's his, too!

- GRACIE:    (*At the beach*) George, your green bathing suit looks like a watermelon.

  GEORGE:    That explains it. I was lying on my stomach and a lifeguard came along, tapped me on the shoulder and said, "You better get that out of the sun, or it'll be too ripe to eat."

  GRACIE:    All these women want to get you. When they pass by, they look at you and say, "Get him!"

  (*George is alone on the beach, when he is approached by a beautiful woman.*)

- WOMAN:    Hello, handsome.

  GEORGE:    Who? Me?

  WOMAN:    I want to sit with you.

  GEORGE:    Who? Me?

  WOMAN:    I'll be your slave. Anything you want. Here, I'll light a cigar.

  GEORGE:    Good. And light one for me, too. (Wow, these new swimming trunks are dynamite! I'd better cover myself with sand or I'll start a riot.)

## Al Jolson

- OSCAR:    You'd make a good painter. In fact, when people see you they say, "Here comes Jolson, let's give him the brush."

  HARRY:    (*Guest, Harry McNaughton from* It Pays to Be Ignorant) I went hunting. A bear saw me and chased me through the woods, into town, down three blocks, around a corner, where I finally ducked into a movie theater.

  AL:    Did the bear follow you into the movie theater?

  HARRY:    Oh no, he'd seen the picture!

# May 13, 1949

## Jimmy Durante

- DON:    (*Don Ameche*) Jimmy, that's a cow!

  DURANTE:    A cow? I thought it was a horse with vacuum cleaner attachments!

- DON:    I can swim like a fish, work like a beaver and run like a deer. Do I get the job?
  DURANTE:   No, but if I ever open a zoo, give me a call!

- DURANTE:   (*Western bit*) I was one of the James boys!
  DON:    Don't be silly. I've only heard about Frank and Jessie.
  DURANTE:   Well, I was the brother that stayed home.
  DON:    What was your name?
  DURANTE:   Home, James!
  DON:    What else have you done?
  DURANTE:   I shot Sitting Bull.
  DON:    Where?
  DURANTE:   Sitting Bull will sit no more!

## Eddie Cantor

(*Announcer, Harry Von Zell, has asked for a raise. Now trying to convince Eddie that he's flat broke.*)

- HARRY:   Here, Eddie. Have a cigarette butt.
  EDDIE:   A cigarette butt?
  HARRY:   Yes. Have a Pell.
  EDDIE:   Don't you mean Pell-Mell?
  HARRY:   No, someone smoked the "mell" out of it.

No luck getting the raise, Harry decides to become a prize fighter to make money.

EDDIE:   What makes you think you can become a prize fighter?
HARRY:   When I was in school, I could lick anybody in my class.
EDDIE:   What happened?
HARRY:   Then I was transferred to a boy's school.
EDDIE:   I can see you in the ring now. Your opponent hits you in the stomach. Again and again and again!
HARRY:   Doesn't he ever miss?
EDDIE:   With your stomach, he can't miss. He hits you again and you go down, down, down.
HARRY:   When we get to the main floor, I'm getting off!

## Red Skelton

(*Subject of the day: Dogs.*)

- RED:    I wanted to make friends with that dog, so I threw him a bone.
  ANNOUNCER:   That's using your head.
  RED:    But the dog bit me.
  ANNOUNCER:   Really? Where?
  RED:    Well, I can't say, but if I was a car I'd have a leaky gas tank.

- RED: That dog wouldn't hurt a flea. He's got millions of 'em and he never hurt one.

- RED: I saw a doggone dog walking down the doggone street, so I chased the doggone dog until along came a doggone cat, and the doggone dog chased the doggone cat up a doggone alley, and I got doggone tired and threw down the doggone net and guess what I said?
ANNOUNCER: What?
RED: I'll be doggoned!

- RED: Put that dog down so we can see which end is which. Oh, he's sitting down ... well, now we know! Anybody missed that joke, you can hear it next week on Berle's show.

- RED: I used to have one of them long dogs. He was about one dog high and three dogs long. I used to stand him in the living room and then run out into the kitchen and watch him wag his tail!

- ANNOUNCER: Oh, Red! Red! Oh, there you are. Say, you'd better get your hair cut. It's getting really long.
RED: That's the dog. I'm over here. The one without the tail.

# May 15, 1949

## Martin & Lewis

- DEAN: (*Finishes singing*) Jerry, how did you like my song?
JERRY: Well, Dean, a real friend would tell you how much he liked it and if he didn't like it, he'd change the subject.
DEAN: Well...?
JERRY: So, how's the family?

- JERRY: I went hiking and my feet got sore, so they told me to put my feet in hot water.
DEAN: Did that help?
JERRY: No, and it didn't do my shoes any good, either.

## Jack Benny

- ROCHESTER: Boss, what should I do with this leftover meat?
JACK: Save it, we'll make hash out of it.
ROCHESTER: What'll I do with these leftover potatoes?
JACK: Save them. We'll make hash out of it.
ROCHESTER: Well, what should I do with this thirty pounds of leftover hash?

- JACK: (*Going down into the depths to his vault*) (*SFX: Growl*) Gee, those sharks in the moat are so playful!

GUARD: Halt! Who goes there?
JACK: It's me. Jack Benny.
GUARD: What's the password?
JACK: You can take it with you.

- ROCHESTER: (*Driving Jack's old Maxwell car*) Boss, the wheels are out of line.
JACK: Are they much out of line?
ROCHESTER: I think so. One's in the garage and the other is on Wilshire Boulevard.
JACK: Oh, there's Phil Harris! Phil! Where are you going?
PHIL: I'm going to have my appendix out.
JACK: What?
PHIL: Yeah, it's in my insurance policy. I get a free operation.
JACK: Really?
PHIL: It was either that or have a baby.
PHIL: Where are you going with that violin?
JACK: I'm going to take my violin lesson.
PHIL: Don't kid me. You're gonna play on some street corner!

- JACK: (*At violin lesson*) I'd better tune up.
TEACHER: It doesn't make any difference!
(*Jack plays for a moment*)
TEACHER: Wait a minute! Wait a minute!
JACK: Why did you stop me from playing?
TEACHER: My baby's hair just turned grey!

## Fred Allen

- FRED: (*To Portland*) Get that frog out of your throat and the three of us will take a stroll down Allen's Alley.
(*SFX: Knocks. Door opens*) Well, if it isn't Titus Moody!
TITUS: Howdy, bub.
FRED: How do you like this weather we're having?
TITUS: Oh, I know all about weather. My brother is a weather man.
FRED: And he knows a lot about weather, eh?
TITUS: Yep. He keeps a small cloud in his closet.
FRED: He keeps a small cloud in his closet? Why?
TITUS: Every two or three days, he just steps inside and takes a shower.
FRED: Let's go next door. (*SFX: Knocks. Door opens*)
AJAX: Ohh, how do you do?
FRED: Ajax Cassidy! How are you feeling?
AJAX: A lot better. The doctor told me to take these pills with a little whiskey every day.
FRED: And how is the treatment coming?
AJAX: Well, I'm a little behind with the pills, but I'm six weeks ahead with the whiskey.

## Alan Young

- ALAN: I'm trying to find a girlfriend, so I put an ad in the newspaper. I finally got a reply, listen. It says, "I would like to meet you. Enclosed find a lock of my hair. I have answered two hundred letters like this. Signed, Baldy." I better talk to Hal March. He knows more about women than the window washer at the Y.W.C.A.

Jim Backus played Hubert Updike, III, a snob playboy on this show. Years later, Backus would bring that character to TV's *Gilligan's Island*. This time renamed as Thurston Howell, III.

- ALAN: Mr. Updike, where were you born?
  UPDIKE: I wasn't born.
  ALAN: Where did you come from?
  UPDIKE: I came from Sak's Fifth Avenue. Mother wouldn't accept anything unless it was gift wrapped.

# May 17, 1949

## Bob Hope

- BOB: Boy, those new cars are small. In fact, they're so small you don't get in them ... you put them on! If you get caught in a traffic jam, you can just gather it up in your arms and say, "Step aside, my baby's sick."
  COLONNA: I'll never do this again. Last night I kissed my girlfriend in the dark.
  BOB: Why not?
  COLONNA: I found out when she couldn't make it, she'd send her brother.

*(Lucille Ball was Bob's guest star. Scene: On a boat.)*

- COLONNA: Mr. Hope, where did you get that sailor suit?
  BOB: I got it from an old sea dog.
  COLONNA: Must've been a St. Bernard, there's a hole in the back.
  BOB: Yeah, he had a hole in the back so he could walk across the deck and swab it at the same time.
  COLONNA: There's a girl overboard! Girl overboard!
  BOB: (*To girl*) Hey, what are you doing in the water?
  LUCILLE: Well, the last thing I remember, the Captain yelled, "Throw all the old bait overboard!"

*(A court room scene.)*

- JUDGE: Have a cigar!
  BOB: Thanks.
  JUDGE: Match?

BOB:      Thanks.

JUDGE:    That'll be ten dollars more for smoking in the court room.

BOB:      There were so many drunks there, the mosquitoes would bite them, then come and bite me for a chaser.

(*SFX: Knock, knock*)

- VILLAIN:   (*Evil laugh*) Ha, ha, ha, hah!

BOB:      Who's there?

VILLAIN:   (*Evil laugh*) Ha, ha, ha, hah!

BOB:      Must be the Good Humor man.

LUCILLE:   I'll never give you the plans! I shan't! I shan't!

VILLAIN:   Oh … yes … you … shan!

BOB:      Leave her alone!

VILLAIN:   What are you going to do about it?

BOB:      I'll give you a tongue lashing.

VILLAIN:   (*Tough*) Oh … yeah?

BOB:      Stick out your tongue, I'll lash it!

# May 18, 1949

## Milton Berle

- BERLE:   My brother Frank is a man of the press. He prints five dollar bills. Somebody told him Grant's picture was on a five dollar bill. Anybody want two thousand five dollar bills with Cary Grant's picture on them?

(*The theme is boxing.*)

- BERLE:   I started out as a pugilist. Ended up as just plain, P.U.

GALLUP:   It's Battling Berle, the Boxer!

BERLE:    (*Entering the ring*) Who is that guy in my corner?

GALLUP:   That's the undertaker.

BERLE:    'Bye!

GALLUP:   Come on! Shake hands with your opponent. (*SFX: Crunch*)

BERLE:    Just give me back my ring and throw the rest away.

GALLUP:   (*During fight*) You bum! I told you … left cross, then right cross! What now?

BERLE:    Call the Red Cross.

GALLUP:   You were supposed to build up your muscles.

BERLE:    I did chin-ups twenty-five times every day.

GALLUP:   Any new muscles in your arms?

BERLE:    No, but you should see the muscles in my chin. Here's my arm. Feel that muscle.

GALLUP:   Where? Here? Or here?

BERLE:    No, farther down.

GALLUP:   Here? I don't feel a thing.
BERLE:    You went past it.
BERLE:    My wife was a middle weight. All her weight was in the middle.
She wrestled at Madison Square Garden. What a crowd! She wore trunks,
and what a crowd! I've never seen anything so tightly packed.
GALLUP:   The Garden?
BERLE:    No, her trunks.

- BERLE:  I love indoor sports. In fact, I'm about to engage in my favorite
indoor sport. Poker! (*After audience laughs*) Oh, losers, huh?
DAD:      Okay, son, we're playing poker and I want you to...
BERLE:    I know … to mark the cards.
DAD:      No, that would be stealing.
BERLE:    Is this my father talking?

## Abe Burrows

- SONG TITLES: *What Is the Doctor Doing When the Apple Keeps Him Away?* or
*Girls with Wooden Legs Should Stay Away from Old Flames.*

# May 22, 1949

## Martin & Lewis

- DEAN:   We need a bathroom door for our dressing room! That's what we
want. A bathroom door for our dressing room.
JERRY:    Yeah, we're gettin' tired of taking baths with our clothes on.
DEAN:     This lady you're going to meet is very wealthy and distinguished.
She and her husband are so ritzy, they have solid gold mice. Here she
comes now. Mrs. Buffington, this is Jerry Lewis.
LADY:     Oh, how cute! Is he pedigreed? Oh, I'm sorry. If you're Jerry Lewis
you have a right to look that way.
JERRY:    Listen here, Dean Martin! I'm not going to stand here and have you
endure me.

- DEAN:   Jerry wouldn't wear that suit to a pig's wedding.
JERRY:    Oh, yes, I wore it.
DEAN:     Where?
JERRY:    To a pig's wedding.

During this period it seems as though they were all doing jokes about the
new low-slung automobiles.

- JERRY:  Those new cars are so low you have to slide down a fireman's pole
to get in them.

(*Dean sings while Jerry does jokes.*)

- DEAN:   (*Sings one verse of* Cocktails for Two.)
  JERRY:   My girlfriend likes a variety of food. She eats different things.
  DEAN:   Nuts?
  JERRY:   Oh, Gad! Is she!

## Jack Benny

- DON:   This is National Pickle week.
  JACK:   Well, dilly, dilly!
  DON:   Jack, pickles aren't anything to laugh about.
  JACK:   I can tell that by our first joke.

- DENNIS:   Last week the doctor came to my house. He had really poor eyesight. He came in, hung his hat on my tongue, walked over to the coat
  hanger and said, "Don't just stand there with three coats on, if you're
  cold, go to bed!
  JACK:   That's terrible.
  DENNIS:   He also couldn't hear. I told him good-bye four days ago and he's
  still there.

(*A satire on boxing movies like* Champion.)

- JACK:   My name is Bruiser, the middleweight champion. They say I'm a heel.
  That I'd slug my own grandmother. But they're wrong. My grand-
  mother's a heavyweight! I was on my way to the fight in a new car. It
  was the latest model driven by a beautiful girl with a convertible top. I
  could tell by the part in her hair. What great hair! I promised myself
  when I got rich, I'd buy me some of it. I was introduced to my oppo-
  nent.
  TRAINER:   This is Slugger.
  SLUGGER:   Yeah!
  TRAINER:   He's fighting tonight.
  SLUGGER:   Yeah!
  JACK:   So you're Slugger?
  SLUGGER:   Yeah!
  JACK:   Thirty-six "yeahs" later, we arrived at the ring. I stripped and he
  said...
  SLUGGER:   That reminds me, we're having spare ribs tonight for supper.
  JACK:   He was tough, so when I got in the ring, I tried to avoid him. I got
  on my bicycle, but he caught me. My trunks got caught in the chain.
  (*Aside*) Gee, that new writer from Lux is terrific. I saw my girlfriend at
  ringside. She was wearing one of those new car dresses. The neckline
  was so low she had to step down to get into it. Do you want to know
  what happens next?

TRAINER:  Would I?

JACK:  Well, turn the page and find out. (*They turn the page*) He was right. That new writer from Lux had double-crossed me. I had to throw the fight.

TRAINER:  Take a dive in the third round!

JACK:  Why?

TRAINER:  My feet are killing me.

JACK:  You know, I spent twelve years in the ring.

TRAINER:  Twelve years?

JACK:  Yeah, then I came to and went home.

## Fred Allen

- COLONEL:  (*Colonel Stoopnagle*) I sang like a bird! When I was a baby, I'd sing in my cradle and before I knew it the cat would have me down on the floor.

  FRED:  Gad, so you've been singing all your life.

  COLONEL:  Yes, finally a teacher said they ought to send me away.

  FRED:  To study music?

  COLONEL:  He didn't say where.

- FRED:  I ate in a dark cafe last night. It was so dimly lit, I was feeling around for my spare-ribs and ate the meat off two of my fingers.

There was a trick ending on Fred Allen's show that night. Fred's show had a habit of running overtime, so tonight they had an actor, playing the part of an NBC executive, rush on stage and stop the program.

- MAN:  Stop the show! Stop the show! You're running overtime. I'm from NBC. If you don't stop, I'll ring my chimes!

  FRED:  Okay, okay! We'll finish our program on the Henry Morgan show.

And that's exactly what they did. Fred completed his program on the Henry Morgan show which followed his.

# May 26, 1949

## Abbott & Costello

- COSTELLO:  The cops chased me and I had the green light with me.

  ABBOTT:  That's no reason to chase you, if you had the green light.

  COSTELLO:  It was in the backseat of my car.

- MAN:  I'm a high-wire walker.

  COSTELLO:  Do you use a net?

  MAN:  No, my hair is just naturally curly.

- COSTELLO:   (*In doctor's office*) Doctor, I'd like to kiss your nurse.
  DOC:   What good would that do her?
  COSTELLO:   I don't know about her, but it would do wonders for me.

  (*SFX: Awk! Awk! Awk!*)
- ABBOTT:   What's that noise?
  COSTELLO:   I still have some Christmas seals left.

- MAN:   I'll kill him! I'll bash him! I'll break his neck!
  ABBOTT:   Who shall I say is calling?
  MAN:   A friend.

- COSTELLO:   This arm chair is no good. When I'm tired, it's not my arm I
  want to rest.

- ABBOTT:   So you say you can ride a horse?
  COSTELLO:   Are you kidding? I ride a horse like my pants were nailed to
  the saddle.
  ABBOTT:   How do you do that?
  COSTELLO:   I nail my pants to the saddle.

## Burns & Allen

- WOMAN:   My rich husband's ashes are in a vault.
  GRACIE:   How neat! George just throws his on the floor.
  WOMAN:   My new husband plays polo.
  GRACIE:   I hope he beats him.
  WOMAN:   Polo is a game you play with horses.
  GRACIE:   Well, he's bound to win. People are much smarter than horses.
  WOMAN:   Sometimes I have my doubts.

- GEORGE:   Hello, Gracie, how are you?
  GRACIE:   Let's go to Paris.
  GEORGE:   Gracie, you're not talking sense.
  GRACIE:   I can't stay here. My mind's in a vacuum.
  GEORGE:   Now, you're talking sense.
  GRACIE:   You'd like Paris. All that delicious French food.
  GEORGE:   I like hot-dogs, not pate de foie gras.
  GRACIE:   Well, if Patty's there, you be nice to her.
  GEORGE:   Pate de foie gras is a sausage.
  GRACIE:   I don't care how her figure looks, you be nice to her!
  GEORGE:   I will. I will. Let's start this again. Hello, Gracie, how are you?

- WOMAN:   Does your husband ride an Arabian steed?
  GRACIE:   No, he rides a horse.
  WOMAN:   What kind of horse?
  GRACIE:   One with four feet.

- GEORGE: I used to work with the Andrew Sisters.
  WOMAN: Women?
  GEORGE: Well, as far as I could tell.
  WOMAN: Aren't you a polo player?
  GEORGE: No, I'm not.
  WOMAN: What did you do with the Andrew Sisters?
  GEORGE: I played in vaudeville with them.
  WOMAN: Oh, so you're merely an actor.
  GRACIE: Well, I'm proud that George is nearly an actor.
  GEORGE: That's merely!
  WOMAN: I suppose you'd prefer him to have a title … like Count!
  GRACIE: No, I'm glad my husband is no 'count!

## Al Jolson

- GROUCHO: (*Guest*) Al, how would you like to be a traveling salesman?
  AL: Never. I want to stay home with my wife.
  GROUCHO: I have a better idea. You travel and I'll stay home with your wife. I even have a car I'll sell you. It's a steal at two hundred dollars. I ought to know, I stole it myself.
  AL: I don't think so.
  GROUCHO: It takes a size thirty-four pedestrian.
  AL: I don't need a new car.
  GROUCHO: I'm also in the ice business. Would you like four thousand pounds of ice?
  AL: What would I do with four thousand pounds of ice?
  GROUCHO: You could melt it. It'll make swell water.

- GROUCHO: I met my girl in the laundry. I knew it was wet wash at first sight. I offered her a pinch of my Lux. She didn't say anything, just went on, pausing only to damp dry my head.

# May 29, 1949

## Martin & Lewis

- JERRY: I offered my girl money, cars, boats, houses.
  DEAN: How could you do that?
  JERRY: I got a lucky box of Crackerjacks.
  DEAN: What's important is health. Remember … health is wealth!
  JERRY: What's that got to do with me?
  DEAN: You're bankrupt.
  JERRY: Hey, I may not be the smartest man in the world, but believe me, I'm plenty stupid.

DEAN:   I'm a lot stronger than you.

JERRY:   Prove it.

DEAN:   Okay, but I won't hit you hard. No harder than this…(*SFX: Sock! Thud!*)

JERRY:   (*Music to begin dream sequence*) I'm a boxer. They call me Killer Lewis. Hey, you! Take that! And that! And that!

TRAINER:   Your opponent isn't in the ring, yet.

JERRY:   Here's a left for you! (*SFX: Sock!*)

FIGHTER:   Well, here's a right for you! (*SFX: Sock!*)

JERRY:   Here's a left!

FIGHTER:   Here's your teeth.

JERRY:   I've got his strategy figured out.

TRAINER:   What is it?

JERRY:   He's trying to murder me!

## *Jack Benny*

- MARY:   Jack, did you hear? Phil Harris had an accident.

  JACK:   What happened?

  MARY:   He was carrying a bowl of goldfish when someone yelled, "Bottoms up!"

  JACK:   You mean…?

  MARY:   Fish, sand and all! He didn't mind the fish and sand so much, it was the water that got him.

  DENNIS:   To make Phil feel better, maybe I should write a song for him.

  JACK:   Dennis, what qualifies you to write a song for Phil Harris?

  DENNIS:   I used to work in a boiler factory.

  JACK:   You're wonderful, Dennis.

  DENNIS:   I can understand that, coming from you.

  JACK:   Why?

  DENNIS:   You're nuts about me.

- GIRL:   I'm hunting for men.

  JACK:   It's a shame nature gave you such bad ammunition

  SEXY GIRL:   Hello…

  JACK:   Now I know where all the ammunition went. Phil, what do you think of her?

  PHIL:   Praise the Lord and Pass the Ammunition! (*Popular song of the day*)

# June 1, 1949

## *Milton Berle*

- GALLUP:   Ladies and gentlemen…

BERLE: That's a clever remark. Mr. Gallup, for three years we've had this comedy show...

GALLUP: I've just heard.

BERLE: That it's been three years?

GALLUP: That it's a comedy show.

BERLE: And I want to thank you for not ruining my jokes.

GALLUP: You did it well enough by yourself.

- BERLE: I gave my girlfriend a big diamond star sapphire. I won't say it was big, but the star was Sidney Greenstreet.

GALLUP: You should get married. It's a great institution.

BERLE: Yeah, but who wants to live in an institution? Why don't you get married?

GALLUP: There are plenty of fish in the ocean.

BERLE: Yeah, I've seen the barracudas you go out with.

GALLUP: I like to keep my girl on a string.

BERLE: With a face like hers, she should be on a leash. But you're right about love. It's horrible! Look what happened to my mother and father.

GALLUP: What?

BERLE: Me! They entered the Sea of Matrimony and wound up ... up the creek! I met my girlfriend on a double-date. I thought it was a double-date, until I found out it was all her.

- BERLE: Ah, memories of my old girlfriend, Cynthia. Ah, Cynthia! Remember the night you smiled and showed me your teeth. And I smiled and gave them back to you. And you had such pretty hair. I told you to wear it. Remember when we were walking along the street. It was wonderful. Until a cop stopped me and asked if I had reported the accident. And remember, your Aunt Fanny who played with a band? She was billed as Aunt Fanny and Her Magic Tuba. Or was it Aunt Tuba and Her Magic...? Oh, forget it...

# June 5, 1949

## Ozzie & Harriet

(*Ozzie is in a department store buying a suit without any help from Harriet.*)

- OZZIE: (*Trying on suit*) Hmm, the pants are baggy. I like that. The coat makes me look too thin, but the baggy pants make me look fatter.

CLERK: I see. Well, actually, you'd look good in baggy clothes.

OZZIE: I am the baggy type, aren't I? I can see me now. I'll flop down the street in my baggy pants and baggy hat. I wonder where I can get a baggy pipe?

OZZIE: (*At home to show new suit to Harriet*) How do you like my new suit? Wait, I'll put on the light.

HARRIET:   Oh, does it have a light in it?
OZZIE:   There! The light's on.
HARRIET:   I think it'll look better without the light.

## Fred Allen

- FRED:   Mr. Moody, you look thin.
  TITUS:   I've been on a diet. I haven't eaten in so long, I've forgotten what my mouth is for. I thought it was a small pocket, so I've started carrying things in it … small change, a pocket knife.

## Henry Morgan

Morgan finally got a sponsor.

- HENRY:   We'll be back on Wednesday, July 6, sponsored by Bristol Meyers, makers of Ipana, Sal Hepatica and money.
  MAN:   My wife listens to your program off and on.
  HENRY:   How does she like it?
  MAN:   Off.
  HENRY:   Thank you. Now take off your propeller beanie and sit down. (As disk Jockey) I have a request for a song. She's Got Rings on Her Fingers, Under Her Eyes and in Her Nose. Also, here's a request from Sing-Sing. They want me to play that ever popular song, "A, you're in Alcatraz." I went to college and earned my LS. Later, I'm going back to get my MFT. (Ad slogan for Lucky Strike cigarettes: "LSMFT, Lucky Strike means fine tobacco.")

# June 8, 1949

## Milton Berle

- BERLE:   My brother, Frank, is a live-wire. I have to wire him money to keep him alive. There's one thing about him I like. One thing. But I keep forgetting what it is.
  GALLUP:   Mr. Berle!
  BERLE:   Mr. Gallup! You could at have at least had a smile on your face when you died. Which joke are you working on, anyway?

(Snowbound in a mountain resort.)

- GALLUP:   Brrr! It's cold here. Why don't you take off those blue pajamas?
  BERLE:   What blue pajamas? That's me!
  GALLUP:   I'm hungry.
  BERLE:   Me too. I could eat a horse.
  GALLUP:   Oh, you saw the menu.

BERLE:   Everybody's hungry. Look, they even ate the tablecloth. There's nothing left but the table with one leg chewed off.
GALLUP:   Here comes the waiter.
BERLE:   Good. Maybe he'll let me lick his apron.
GALLUP:   Here's the Forest Ranger to rescue us!
BERLE:   Forest Ranger, ever have any exciting experiences in the woods?
RANGER:   Please, we're on the air.
BERLE:   That's okay, nobody's listening. I've got to get out of here. I'm going out into the snow and there's only one thing that can stop me.
SEXY GIRL:   Hello ... big boy!
BERLE:   That's it.
SEXY GIRL:   I see you in my dreams and now, you're here, in person!
BERLE:   Yes....?
SEXY GIRL:   No resemblance.

## This Is Broadway

This was a summer replacement program featuring current stars on Broadway. The following is part of a monologue delivered by comic actor, Phil Leeds.

- LEEDS:   I had a rough childhood. My father used to say, "Leeds!" He never could remember my first name. So I ran away from home. He helped me pack. I got a job as a grease monkey. But it was no fun greasing monkeys. I worked and worked, until my boss told me I'd better slow down. We'd been closed for three months. I finally met a girl. She was sitting on the George Washington Bridge with her feet dangling in the water. She was a tall girl. She had everything a man would want ... muscles ... a mustache. She was Rita Hayworth and Betty Grable all rolled into one. Four hundred pounds of it. We got married and when I carried her over the threshold, I fell down. Oh, well, I'd always wanted a sunken living room. Soon there was the pitter patter of little feet around the house. My mother-in-law was a midget. Then one day I came home and found my wife in the arms of another. Then everything went black. He put his hat over the keyhole.

## June 10, 1949

## Eddie Cantor

- EDDIE:   My uncle was in vaudeville. In his act he wore eight costumes. He'd take off one costume and, voila! There was another costume underneath. Then he'd change again and again. Last week he got the biggest laugh of his career. He wore eight costumes and made nine changes.

# June 15, 1949

## Milton Berle

- GALLUP: In answer to thousands of requests this is Milton Berle's last program!
  BERLE: (*Singing*) "California, skies are blue … when I get there, Lassie's through."
  GALLUP: What is it, Berle?
  BERLE: You know, Frank, for thirty-nine weeks you've used the same line.
  GALLUP: I could stand here for thirty-nine years, look at you and still say, "What is it?"

- BERLE: (*To pretty girl*) Let me put my arms around your waist.
  GIRL: Okay, but be careful of my nylon stockings.
  BERLE: Around your waist?
  GIRL: They didn't have my size.

- BERLE: This audience is getting hostile. Look, there! Seated on the aisle. An angry woman clinching her teeth in her right hand.

# June 16, 1949

## Burns & Allen

(*A teenage girl is staying in their home for awhile.*)

- GIRL: I can't wait to get married. I can almost hear the roar of Niagara Falls.
  GRACIE: That's Mr. Burns, sleeping on his back again.

- GRACIE: George, I found her diary.
  GEORGE: You shouldn't read her diary. It isn't done.
  GRACIE: I know, but it's great as far as it goes.
  GEORGE: Gracie, it isn't nice.
  GRACIE: I'll say it isn't!
  GEORGE: Oh, brother. Anything interesting?
  GRACIE: She says she's going to marry a fellow named Rudy. Oh, no! She's going to marry Rudy Vallee!

(*Gracie goes to Rudy Vallee's house to try and convince him not to marry such a young girl. She knocks on the door and is greeted by the Chinese houseboy.*)

GRACIE: Are you Rudy Vallee?
BOY: No, I'm his Chinese boy.
GRACIE: Oh, well, I didn't know Mr. Vallee married a Chinese woman. Show me to your mother.

BOY:    Please, I just work for Mr. Vallee.

(*Gracie meets with Rudy Vallee and tries to convince him that the teenage girl is her daughter.*)

RUDY:    So, she's your daughter?
GRACIE:    Not only that, I'm her mother. I'm twenty years old and I've been married for fifteen years.
RUDY:    You were married at five?
GRACIE:    No, I think it was three-thirty.
RUDY:    Don't you have your figures mixed up?
GRACIE:    No, she has hers. I have mine.
RUDY:    Oh, be serious. You can play dumb, but...
GRACIE:    I'm not playing. You can't marry her. I know you look young. In fact, you looked younger when I first came in here.
RUDY:    I was younger. I've aged since you came in!

- GEORGE:    You know, I'm quite a singer. People want me to sing in night-clubs.
GRACIE:    Yes, they'll even buy one for you. Every time you sing, I hear somebody say, "Oh, if I only had a club!"
GEORGE:    I'll prove it. Just for that, I'm going to turn on all my personal magnetism and let it fly.
GRACIE:    Well, do it outside. I just swept the floor.

# June 19, 1949

## *Fred Allen*

- FRED:    The hotel is so close to the sea, your bed has oar-locks. The house detective is a crab and the cuckoo clock has a seagull in it. Boy, it's hot today. I feel like I'm sitting on a pressure cooker. I've been busier than a boy with his shirt-tail caught in an outboard motor. I don't have to do this for a living. I can always go back to my old job, demonstrating Mum. (*Deodorant*) You were a cute baby. You had a dimple you could hide a bowling ball in.

## *Jimmy Durante*

- ALAN:    Jimmy, how could you charge so much? You've got to live with your-self.
JIMMY:    With that kind of money, I could move to a different neighborhood!
ALAN:    Then, remember this. It's not the clothes, it's the man under them. Underneath this torn shirt...
JIMMY:    Yes?

ALAN:    Torn underwear.

JIMMY:    I can see you keep your money in a shoe. Washington is clutching a corn pad in his hand.

(*Doing a Western Private-eye sketch.*)

• JIMMY:    The bandit took a shot at me! I left the scene, crawled across the desert, swam a river, climbed up cliffs ... now, I'm dying!

ALAN:    He shot you, eh?

JIMMY:    No, he missed! It was the trip that killed me!

# June 26, 1949

## *Ozzie & Harriet*

• OZZIE:    Harriet, what are you doing in the kitchen?

HARRIET:    I'm cooking. We're having Beef Stroganoff.

OZZIE:    Is that a food, or have you invited a Russian wrestler for dinner tonight?

HARRIET:    What are you writing?

OZZIE:    I have to make a speech tonight at my club.

HARRIET:    How far have you gotten?

OZZIE:    Ladies and gentlemen.

HARRIET:    You'll need more than that.

OZZIE:    There's more. "Ladies and gentlemen, as I look down at your faces, I am reminded of a funny story.

HARRIET:    I don't think so.

• HARRIET:    Are you still trying to assemble that lawn furniture?

OZZIE:    Yes, and I don't want to call a carpenter.

HARRIET:    You can do it. Here, read the directions.

OZZIE:    (*Reads extremely complicated directions*) Where did you say that phone book was? (*SFX: Knock on door*) I'll get it. Probably another beggar at the door wanting a handout. (*SFX: Door opening*) Oh, it's you, Thorny. For a minute I thought you were a bum.

THORNY:    I've had the same idea about you for years.

## *Fred Allen*

(*Guest: Jack Benny.*)

• JACK:    Fred Allen is the only comedian who uses an air-wick for a straight man.

FRED:    When Jack's movies play in theaters, the streets are packed. I used to have a dog. A water spaniel. One summer it got so hot he percolated to death.

JACK:   Phil Harris drinks so much beer, when he perspires, his sweat has a a head on it.

# July 3, 1949

## Ozzie & Harriet

- ANNOUNCER:   Now it's time to visit the Nelsons. Ozzie is on his way to see his neighbor, Mr. Thornton. Here he comes walking across the lawn toward the hedge. Now, he jumps across the hedge. I said, now he jumps across the hedge. Ahem! Now he walks around the hedge and opens the gate.

OZZIE:   Hi, Thorny. I've got a great story to tell you.

THORNY:   No.

OZZIE:   Okay, have it your way. (*Pause*) It all started...

THORNY:   I'm not interested in what happened.

OZZIE:   You're not interested in what?

THORNY:   What happened.

OZZIE:   I'm glad you asked me that! It all started...

(*Ozzie goes on to tell story about the time he was a world champion diver. He brags so much, he has to prove it and winds up standing on a high diving board scared out of his wits, as he is introduced by the P.A. announcer.*)

- ANNOUNCER:   Now here's our champion diver, wearing a bathing suit with two stars on the back.

THORNY:   That must mean he's a rear-Admiral.

ANNOUNCER:   I know him! You know him! We all know him! Ooozie Nelson!

OZZIE:   That's Ozzie!

ANNOUNCER:   And now ... he dives! I said, Now he dives! Eh ... Mr. Nelson, are you ready?

OZZIE:   Well, not exactly, you see ... I ... er ... uh ... Oops! (*SFX: Slide whistle and Splash*)

THORNY:   Gee, I never knew I could aim so well with a Roman candle.

# July 4, 1949

## Joan Davis

A great visual comedienne, Joan Davis was on the air as a summer replacement for the first thirty minutes of *The Lux Radio Theater*.

- JOAN:   (*Reading paper*) Here's an ad: Man with mallet would like to meet woman with bow-legs. Object ... croquet. Hmm, here's another. Ladies pants, half off. Well, that ought to attract a lot of women. Come to think of it, that ought to attract a lot of men, too.

(*Joan goes shopping in department store and is mistaken for a shoplifter.*)

- MANAGER: You thief! You stole that alligator bag.
  JOAN: I did not.
  MANAGER: Then how come that alligator bag is right next to you?
  JOAN: I don't know. Maybe he followed me into the store.
  COP: These are handcuffs. Put out your right hand.
  JOAN: Why? Are we going to make a right turn?
  MANAGER: Now, let me get this straight. You are Miss Davis?
  JOAN: I am, Mr. Jones. I am, Mr. Jones? Wait a minute. You're Mr. Jones!
  MANAGER: I am, Miss Davis.
  JOAN: You're Miss Davis? I thought I was Miss Davis.
  MANAGER: You're going to jail and I don't want to hear one peep out of you.
  JOAN: (*Quietly*) Peep!
  MANAGER: You're like all crooks ... yellow! A coward.
  JOAN: Oh yeah? Well, while your back was turned I peeped four times.

- JOAN: Lana Turner, hah! What have I got that she ain't got?
  HANS: No, no. It's what has she got that you ain't got. You've got it back-wards.
  JOAN: That's right. I've got it backwards.

# July 6, 1949

## Henry Morgan

- HENRY: (*Talking to his new sponsor*) I want to thank you for my contract.
  SPONSOR: Oh, it was nothing.
  HENRY: I know.
  SPONSOR: That's funny. You're just saying that.
  HENRY: Ha. Is that so? My announcer is Ben Grauer. Ben you're going to be my straight man and it's very easy. I start a joke and all you have to say is, "Really? Is she? Or is he? Or, Is that so?" Okay? I'll start a joke. Ben, my aunt is eighty-six and...
  BEN: Really? Is that so?
  HENRY: No, no. Wait, I haven't finished. My aunt is eighty-six and she's still growing.
  BEN: Really?
  HENRY: She's growing flowers.

BEN:   Is she? Really? Is that so? No kidding? Really? Is he? Is that so?
HENRY:   Never mind. Never mind.

# July 10, 1949

## Ozzie & Harriet

*(Ozzie is bringing a huge trunk into the house.)*

- OZZIE:   Gad, it's heavy.
  HARRIET:   What is that?
  OZZIE:   I got it at the high school rummage sale.
  HARRIET:   What is it, the auditorium?
  OZZIE:   I can't get it open.
  HARRIET:   Here's a knife.
  OZZIE:   Am I supposed to open it, or kill it? (*SFX: Trunk creaking open*) There! It's open.
  HARRIET:   What's in there?
  OZZIE:   A box of cans without labels.
  HARRIET:   This one has a label. It's spaghetti sauce.
  OZZIE:   What are we going to do with a trunk full of spaghetti sauce?
  HARRIET:   Put an ad in the paper: Man with spaghetti sauce would like to meet woman with lots of pasta.

- HARRIET:   A letter came in the mail for you. It was just a bill.
  OZZIE:   You opened my mail? Now, really, do I ever pry into your mail?
  HARRIET:   Yes.
  OZZIE:   Then you know how annoying it is.

# July 13, 1949

## Henry Morgan

- HENRY:   I went to a movie. The sign outside said, "Comfortably cool." So I bought a ticket, went inside and it was as hot as blazes. Turns out, the name of the movie was, *Comfortably Cool.*

- HENRY:   (*To pretty girl*) You look lovely tonight. Your skin is so smooth.
  GIRL:   It's that new pancake makeup I'm wearing.
  HENRY:   What kind is it?
  GIRL:   Aunt Jemima.
  HENRY:   Aunt Jemima?
  GIRL:   Yeah, I'm well-stacked.

• BUM: Hey, buddy, can you spare some change?
HENRY: Here's a quarter.
BUM: A whole quarter! Wow! Now I can buy a meal fit for a prince. Here, Prince! Here, Prince!

# August 26, 1949

## Joan Davis

• JOAN: There's a new vitamin out now. They don't know what it's good for. It's to give to people who don't know what's wrong with them. Hmm, they're auditioning people for that new movie they're filming here. I better go try out. Hmm, I wonder if I'll get a good part? I wonder if I'll look good? I wonder how I trapped myself into asking that question?

*(Joan arrives at movie set to audition. Meets the director.)*

• DIRECTOR: I haven't time to bandy words with you.
JOAN: Bandy words? Is that anything like bandy-legs?
DIRECTOR: I don't get it.
JOAN: Don't worry, you've got 'em. Ha, ha, ha, ha! There's nothing like a good joke to start off the day.
DIRECTOR: Yes, and that was nothing like a good joke.

*(Joan gets a part in the movie. She plays an elevator operator.)*

JOAN: I only have one line? All I have to say is, "Second floor! Second floor!" How do I say that line?
DIRECTOR: Oh, you're an idiot!
JOAN: I see. So I'd say it like this: Duuhhh! Second floor!
DIRECTOR: Just say the line. I'm the director. Just keep your nose out of it.
JOAN: Sure, you can smell it up all by yourself.

*(The scene begins. Joan is the elevator operator. Her passengers on the elevator are a man and a woman who are getting romantically involved.)*

WOMAN: Oh, darling, put your arms around my...
JOAN: Second floor!
MAN: My sweet! How I love to look into your...
JOAN: Ladies shoes!
MAN: There's something about you. I don't know what it is. It's your...
JOAN: Ladies girdles!

*(Now, only a bit player, Joan falls asleep and dreams she's a big movie star.)*

DIRECTOR: Remember, the less you wear, the bigger the star you are.
JOAN: No wonder Lassie is such a big hit.

DIRECTOR:    For the premiere, we'll have a parade.

JOAN:    I was in a parade once. Walked right behind a horse named Trigger. Oh, well, in this business those are the things you have to face.

# September 11, 1949

## Our Miss Brooks

(*SFX: Doorbell rings*)

- CONKLIN:    That's the door, isn't it?
  BROOKS:    No, that's the bell. The door makes more of a creaking sound.

- BOYNTON:    He isn't fond of Mr. Conklin, is he?
  BROOKS:    Oh, it isn't that he isn't fond of him. He hates him.

- DENTON:    How will I find the principal's office?
  BROOKS:    You can't miss the office. You'll see a grey-haired teacher standing beside the door. Just push me aside and go in.

# November 11, 1949

## Jack Benny

Jack did a ground breaking show with this one. He was on a sightseeing bus and didn't appear on the program until the last two minutes when the bus driver announced that they were at CBS. Then, Jack said, "This is where I get off." He gets off and then finds that he'd left the script for tonight's show on the bus. Here are some gags from the show performed by other people as the bus goes from house to house in Beverly Hills.

- DRIVER:    (*On sightseeing bus*) There's Lassie!
  WOMAN:    That's my kid. He needs a haircut.

- MAMA:    Dennis, I thought you took a shower last night.
  DENNIS:    This is the same one. I can't figure out how to turn it off.

- MAMA:    How can you be so stupid?
  DENNIS:    I'm not stupid. I'm smart. (*SFX: Crash*)
  MAMA:    What happened?
  DENNIS:    I tied my shoelaces together.

# September 14, 1949

## Henry Morgan

Morgan was famous for kidding sponsors. Here are some takeoffs on commercials.

- HENRY: Our soap is so mild, you can use it to wash other soaps. When it sees tough dirt, our soap runs away. If it gets in your eyes, it cries!
- HENRY: Try our new breakfast cereal "Hooky." The only breakfast cereal that tastes like a hot-dog. It makes you sick, so you can stay home from school. Remember, our product is untouched by human hands. Now, I ask you. What's wrong with human hands?

# September 18, 1949

## Our Miss Brooks

- BOYNTON: The students are crazy about Miss Brooks.
  CONKLIN: Yes, they are crazy.
  (*Miss Brooks enters*)
  CONKLIN: Miss Brooks, that sweater you're wearing looks like a hot water bottle with sleeves.
  BROOKS: You know, Mr. Conklin, sometimes I think you're out of this world, but I know that's just wishful thinking.
- BOYNTON: (*As they plan a dirty trick*) Have we overlooked anything?
  BROOKS: Just the car out front with the motor running.

## Jack Benny

- JACK: Dennis, why are you so crazy?
  DENNIS: My mother dropped me on my head when she burped me.
  JACK: When you were a baby?
  DENNIS: No, last night.
  JACK: When Dennis was a kid, he took his pet frog to school with him. He didn't pass, but the frog did.
- JACK: Phil, you say your car broke down and you and your girlfriend were trapped in your car for six hours?
  PHIL: (*Lustily*) Yehhhhhhhh!
- MARY: (*Looking at baby*) Gee, he's only a year old and he's got a full set of teeth.
  JACK: So that's where they are! I've been looking all over for them.

# September 21, 1949

## Henry Morgan

- VOICE: Oo-ee-ee-oo-ah-oo-ee-oo-ah-ooblee — dahhhh!
  ANNOUNCER: What's that? Be-bop?
  HENRY: No, that's a man lowering himself into a hot bath.
- SINGER: (*To tune of* Stout-Hearted Men) Give me a man who's a real man's man and I will show you a man!
  HENRY: And goodnight, music lovers, everywhere.

- ANNOUNCER:   So how did your uncle make all his money?
  HENRY:   Greasing channel swimmers. He's the World's Richest People Greaser.

## Burns & Allen

- GRACIE:   We went to a wax dummy museum, and I couldn't get George out of the place.
  BEA:   Why not?
  GRACIE:   The owner kept grabbing him and standing him in the corner.
  BEA:   George is a wonderful man, Gracie. They don't make men like that anymore.
  GRACIE:   Yes, that model's been obsolete for years.

- GEORGE:   (*As he and Gracie get out of a taxi*) How much do I owe you?
  TAXI DRIVER:   Nothing. It's on me. I'm selling this experience to Reader's Digest.

- GEORGE:   Gracie when we got back from our trip I found thirty bottles of milk on our doorstep. Why didn't you stop the milk?
  GRACIE:   For three months? How long do you think a poor cow could hold back?

- SPONSOR:   Well, well, well! You must be Gracie.
  GRACIE:   Yes, George is taller and wears his hair wavy.
  SPONSOR:   And what did you see while in England?
  GRACIE:   We saw Westminster Abby, Stratford-on-the-Avon…
  SPONSOR:   Shakespeare's home?
  GRACIE:   Well, I don't know. We didn't knock.
  SPONSOR:   (*To his lawyer*) Are you sure these people are sane?
  GRACIE:   Here, sign our contract.
  SPONSOR:   Well, all right. Could I have a glass of water?
  GRACIE:   Oh, no. Sign it in ink!

# September 25, 1949

## Our Miss Brooks

- MRS. DAVIS:   (*The landlady*) Miss Brooks, Miss Brooks! You told me to wake you at six-thirty.
  BROOKS:   I was lying.
  DAVIS:   Did you have an exciting date last night?
  BROOKS:   (*Sarcastic*) It was a rip-snorter.
  DAVIS:   Tell me all about it. I'm dripping with emotion.
  BROOKS:   There's a blotter in the hall closet.

DAVIS:     I remember dating my late husband. I faced his face, face to face.
BROOKS:     From the picture *Let's Face It,* no doubt. You've been reading too
much Ogden Nash.

- WALTER:     (*Student*) Miss Brooks, I couldn't help overhearing your conver-
sation.
BROOKS:     You couldn't?
WALTER:     No, I had my ear to the keyhole.

- BROOKS:     Ah, Mr. Conklin. Is this your feeding time? ... eh ... lunch time?
CONKLIN:     Look at this desk. I find a little nick here, a little nick there...
BROOKS:     (*Sings*) Here a nick, there a nick, everywhere a nick-nick!
CONKLIN:     Are you making fun of me?
BROOKS:     Why, Mr. Conklin, how dare you accuse me of doing what I just
did.

(*Miss Brooks is making a play for the bashful biology teacher, Mr. Boynton.*)

- BOYNTON:     Miss Brooks, I hope you know what you're doing.
BROOKS:     I hope you get your hope!
CONKLIN:     My lunch! Look at this chicken. It's just skin and bones.
BROOKS:     Well, he's been working hard, lately.

## Jack Benny

- JACK:     (*Riding in the Maxwell*) That's nice, Rochester. How did you know
I wanted the top down?
ROCHESTER:     Who knew? We just went under a low tree.
JACK:     What?
ROCHESTER:     With no brakes, who needs push buttons?
MARY:     You have no brakes? What do you do when you come to a railroad
crossing?
ROCHESTER:     We jump out and pick up coal. Those diesels are ruining us!

- JACK:     That Phil Harris! I'd tear up his contract if he didn't have it tattooed
on his back.

- JACK:     I've never danced so much in all my life.
RED:     (*Red Skelton, guest*) Yeah! Imagine those girls trying to cut in on us.

## Phil Harris

Thanks to his popularity on the Jack Benny program, Phil Harris got his
own show. He co-starred with his wife, the movie star, Alice Faye. He continued playing the role of the hard-drinking, carousing bandleader.

- PHIL:     Hey, I keep regular hours! I go to bed at four in the morning and
get up promptly at three in the afternoon.
JACK:     What do the boys do until three o'clock in the morning?

PHIL:    (*Sarcastic*) We're making a patchwork quilt!
JACK:    What's Frank Remley doing?
PHIL:    He's teaching the band the Alphabet song as soon as he learns it.
JACK:    You mean he doesn't know a simple tune like that?
PHIL:    It's not the tune that bothers him, it's the alphabet!
JACK:    What do you have there?
PHIL:    A great new thermos bottle. Holds a fifth of milk.
MAN:     Hello?

(*Miscue. Actor has entered before the SFX: Door opens.*)

PHIL:    (*Ad-lib*) Here's a guy that talks before they get the door open! Little quick this afternoon? Been on another malted milk bender or something?
JACK:    Let's back up. Why did you call it a fifth of milk?
PHIL:    It comes from cows with hangovers. Can you imagine cows with bags under their … eyes?

## Henry Morgan

- HENRY:    (*Satire on Hollywood gossip columnists*) Here's the news from Hollywoooooooooduhhh! Clark Gable, Spencer Tracy, Alan Ladd, Cary Grant, James Cagney and Gary Cooper are six different people. Remember, you heard it here first. Attention! Lana Turner … hello there! This just in! Margaret O'Brien has been seen with Mighty Joe Young. Her mother doesn't approve. Neither does his! Neither does mine. Attention, Lana Turner … hello there! Zsa-Zsa, Magda and Eva Gabor are sisters. Groucho, Chico and Harpo are not sisters. You heard it here first!

## Burns & Allen

- GRACIE:    (*Talking to her neighbor*) I wish George was more romantic.
  BEA:    I know. It's amazing how men wind up.
  GRACIE:    I can't even wind George up!
  BEA:    To put the spark back in marriage some girls wear low-cut dresses. Try that on George.
  GRACIE:    What? With his figure?
  BEA:    Somehow you've got to get George hot. Try building a fire under him.
  GRACIE:    What a strange place for a man to get cold.

  (*They go on a date and plan to act like a couple of teenagers.*)

  GEORGE:    Gracie, I'd be too embarrassed to go in and order a vanilla soda with two straws.
  GRACIE:    Aw, go ahead, George. Let's go in the drug store. You can do it.
  CLERK:    (*Laughing*) Ha, ha, ha! Hello, folks! You know a funny thing just happened. A couple came in and ordered a soda with two straws! Ha,

ha, ha, ha! Isn't that the silliest thing! A soda with two straws! Ha, ha, ha! Well, what'll you have? (*Long pause*) I said, what'll you have?
GEORGE:   Who? Us?

(*They spot a young couple talking romantically.*)

GRACIE:   George, go over and hide behind that couple and listen to him and his girl. You might learn something.
GEORGE:   Who me? That's not nice. He might say something I shouldn't hear. He might even … uh, wait here!

(*George goes over to eavesdrop on the couple.*)

GIRL:   What's that noise?
MAN:   Just a gopher.
GIRL:   Go look and see.
MAN:   Okay. (*Pause*) Say, do gophers smoke cigars?
GIRL:   Let me look. (*Pause*) By golly, they do!

• GRACIE:   (*Man holds a gun on George*) Don't hold that gun at George's head! It's liable to go off and wake the whole neighborhood.

(*Gracie holds up a new French gown to entice George.*)

• GEORGE:   Gracie, I dare you to try that French gown on me.
GRACIE:   Okay, but I still think it'd look better on me!

# October 2, 1949

## *Our Miss Brooks*

• BROOKS:   That football player is a three-letter man. After the ABC's he's a goner!
BOYNTON:   Miss Brooks, Mr. Conklin has a juicy idea and I've got a juicy idea. Do you know what it is?
BROOKS:   You're opening a juicy orange juice stand?
CONKLIN:   I've got a juicy bit of news. How are you, Miss Brooks?
BROOKS:   Just juicy!
BOYNTON:   Don't you want to hear our ideas?
BROOKS:   No, if you'll excuse me, I think I'll go lie down under a street car.
BOYNTON:   Before we go ahead with our plan, we need your sanction. Your okay.
BROOKS:   What?
BOYTON:   Your okay.
BROOKS:   You're okay, too, but what do you want?

## Jack Benny

- JACK:   Phil, when we went to that show, why did your girlfriend get up and parade up and down the aisle?
  PHIL:   The band shouldn't have played, *A Pretty Girl Is Like a Melody*.
  JACK:   And where did she get those balloons?
  PHIL:   Where did you get the pin?

- DENNIS:   I gotta go home, now. We're putting a moose head in the shower.
  JACK:   A moose head in the shower? Why?
  DENNIS:   The other end would look silly.

  (*Phil bumps his head.*)

- JACK:   Hey, he's out cold! Dennis, go get a glass of water.
  DENNIS:   I'd rather have a Coke.
  JACK:   It's not for you!
  DENNIS:   Here's the water.
  JACK:   Well, throw it! (*SFX: Splash!*) Not at me! Him!

  (*Show ends with Jack getting hit on the head and suddenly becoming generous.*)

## Amos 'n' Andy

- ANNOUNCER:   As we look in on them today, Andy is driving Kingfish downtown.
  KINGFISH:   I come and pick up a check every week. Now where is that unemployment office? Oh, there it is. Park here.
  (*SFX: Crash!*)
  ANDY:   Is that all right?
  KINGFISH:   Fine, but I think we ought to observe the common courtesies of the road. Pick up the man's fender and put it in the backseat of his car.

  (*Kingfish poses as an old man in an effort to collect social security.*)

- AGENT:   You don't look old.
  KINGFISH:   That's because I come from a family of long livers.
  ANDY:   That's right. One of his Uncle's livers is four feet long!

  (*Down at the Lodge House, a recruiter from a school comes to call. He's looking for people to enroll in the Farnsworth Business Institute. He introduces himself as follows.*)

  MAN:   I'm from the FBI.
  KINGFISH:   Oh, no! The FBI!
  ANDY:   I told you not to try and collect social security.
  MAN:   Shall I put you down for eighteen months, or the full four year term?
  KINGFISH:   I didn't know I had a choice.

MAN:   I'm happy to find that you qualify. We'll put you in the Co-ed building.

KINGFISH:   This might not be so bad after all.

MAN:   Yes, we find people learn a lot more that way.

KINGFISH:   I can understand that.

## Bergen & McCarthy

- CHARLIE:   (*As Hollywood gossip reporter*) Splash! I mean … Flash! This is your Hollywood reporter Hedda McCarthy. I have a nose for news and tonight, I have a snootful!

  BERGEN:   Charlie, Charlie, you know this is just gossip. There isn't a word of truth in it. Remember those three little monkeys.

  CHARLIE:   Your ancestors?

  BERGEN:   Those three little monkeys. See no evil, speak no evil and hear no evil. Look at the first little monkey. What do you see?

  CHARLIE:   He has his hands over his eyes.

  BERGEN:   That means he can't see anything bad. And the second monkey?

  CHARLIE:   He has his hands over his mouth.

  BERGEN:   So he can't say anything bad. And the third little monkey?

  CHARLIE:   He has his hands over his ears.

  BERGEN:   And what does that mean?

  CHARLIE:   Go ahead. Surprise me.

  BERGEN:   Ah, where was I?

  CHARLIE:   Standing right here. Laying an egg.

- BERGEN:   Ah, Mortimer Snerd. You're mighty tardy.

  MORTIMER:   Nope, I'm Morty Snerdy.

  BERGEN:   Where were you yesterday?

  MORTIMER:   I went to movies without a ticket.

  BERGEN:   I suppose they threw you out on your ear?

  MORTIMER:   Well, not exactly out on my ear. I hear much higher up than that. At least, I think.

  BERGEN:   Mortimer, you're easily confused.

  MORTIMER:   It's a good thing, too. If it was hard, I'd never make it.

  BERGEN:   Remember one thing, Mortimer. The early bird gets the worm.

  MORTIMER:   I'll bet the worm don't know it, or else he'd stay in bed.

- WOMAN:   (*To Charlie*) My husband's a woodcarver. He might saw you up and make bookends out of you.

  CHARLIE:   What a nasty way to meet my end!

## Red Skelton

- RED:   I've been so nervous lately. Last night, I put my pants to bed and I hung over the chair all night. (*Ad-lib*) Boy, I tell you, that eight year old writer has got to go! I had a great idea, though. I wanted to get rid of mice so I put some limburger cheese in the trap. Guess what? I caught a mouse backing into it.

RED:   (*As Clem Kadiddlehopper*) I been dating a beautiful girl with hair all the way down her back. None on her head, but plenty on her back! I tell you, at the Boston Tea Party, she was one of the bags they threw overboard.

MAN:   Excuse me, sir. What are you doing in that bucket of sand? That's for cigarette butts.

RED:   Well, I'm not digging for gold, you know!

*(As Junior, the mean widdle kid. He is crying.)*

- MAMA:   Junior! I wouldn't cry like that.
  JUNIOR:   Well, everyone has their own technique. You hit me! You hit me and I can't talk! I can't talk!
  MAMA:   You're talking, you're talking!
  JUNIOR:   I thought I heard voices.
  RED:   That eight year old writer has got to go!

Be sure and see Bob Hope and Lucille Ball in *Fancy Pants* and selected shorts!

## You Bet Your Life

*(Groucho is interviewing a man from the Department of Motor Vehicles.)*

- MAN:   For example, Groucho, how long should you put your arm out before making a left turn?
  GROUCHO:   Depends on how long your arm is. Now, young lady, it says here that you're a softball player.
  GIRL:   What?
  GROUCHO:   What position do you play?
  GIRL:   What position do I play?
  GROUCHO:   We're beginning to sound like Abbott and Costello. Pull yourself together while I talk to this masseur here. Tell me, minute-rub, do you massage just anybody?
  MAN:   Sure. I massage fat people.
  GROUCHO:   Sort of a pot holder, eh?
  MAN:   Yes, I massage all sorts ... fat, slim, short, tall...
  GROUCHO:   Sort of a melting pot, then? Let's go back to the girl. Tell me, while pitching softball, have you ever been chased to the showers?
  GIRL:   Yes, a couple of times.
  GROUCHO:   They ever catch you?

# October 12, 1949

## *Burns & Allen*

(*Gracie wants her Uncle John to stay in their house. Now, she's trying to keep George happy, so he'll let him stay. It's morning and George is still in bed.*)

- GRACIE: George, would you like breakfast in bed? I'll cook anything.
  GEORGE: Okay, and how about the morning paper?
  GRACIE: Fine, and how will I cook it?
  GEORGE: Never mind. I'll eat it raw.
  GRACIE: (*Watching George eat*) Gad, you're strong! Look at the way you bend that bacon.
  GEORGE: Yeah, I'm a tiger.
  GEORGE: Gracie, you're waiting on me hand and foot.
  GRACIE: Yes, now what will your foot like?

(*George's birthday. Gracie goes to a bakery to buy a birthday cake.*)

- GRACIE: I baked a birthday cake for my husband, but when I put it in the oven, the candles melted all over it.
  CLERK: A cake for your husband? Egg layer?
  GRACIE: Well, he laid a few in vaudeville.
  CLERK: I was referring to the cake. How about a sponge?
  GRACIE: No, I want a cake.

(*Gracie finds some old love letters that George sent her years ago. She shows them to her neighbor.*)

- GRACIE: Look at all these love letters.
  BEA: Are they written in George's hand?
  GRACIE: No, on paper. What are these little x's?
  BEA: Those are kisses.
  GRACIE: Gee, I wonder how George got his lips into that shape? Listen to this one. "I love you lots, I love you plenty. Darling, I'm broke. Send me twenty."

(*Gracie goes to sporting goods store to buy George a gift.*)

- CLERK: We have the largest supply of goods in sports next to Abercrombie and Fitch in New York.
  GRACIE: Well, I wish you had it here.
  CLERK: We have it all here. How about a bowling ball?
  GRACIE: Bowling? Oh, no.
  CLERK: What's wrong with bowling?
  GRACIE: Well, it can't be nice if you do it in an alley. What's this? Fifteen dollars for snowshoes?

CLERK:   Madam, that's a racket.
GRACIE:   It certainly is!
CLERK:   We also have hunting rifles.
GRACIE:   My husband doesn't own a gun.
CLERK:   Lucky for you.

# November 13, 1949

## *Red Skelton*

- ANNOUNCER:   Here we are in New York and you're nervous.
  RED:   I am not.
  ANNOUNCER:   You are, too. Look, you've put your shorts on over your pants!
  RED:   Okay, so I dress casually.
  ANNOUNCER:   You folks in the first three rows, move back. If his teeth fall out, they'll chop your heads off.

# November 18, 1949

## *Joan Davis*

- JOAN:   (*Posing as a French masseuse*) I'm Yvette.
  MAN:   Oh. Bonjour, Yvette.
  JOAN:   No, just Yvette. Bonjour is my sister.
  MAN:   Bonjour means good-bye.
  JOAN:   Oh, I'm sorry. I haven't been in America long.
  MAN:   Oui!
  JOAN:   Not we! Just me.
  MAN:   I need a massage in the worst way.
  JOAN:   Well, that's the way you're going to get it.
  MAN:   You make a good living as a masseuse?
  JOAN:   Yes, I live off the fat of the land.

## *Jimmy Durante*

- DURANTE:   I called my girl. She said to come on over. I hung up, rushed over and she looked at my nose and said, "You sure must've hurried, you forgot to hang up the phone!

  (*Durante is packing his suitcase in preparation for a train trip to New York.*)

- DURANTE:   Let's see ... black and yellow checked pants, green coat with a belt in the back. That takes care of my business clothes. Now for my sports outfit. Hm, and I'll need some reading material. (*SFX: Rip, rip*)

That ought to do it. Two pages! This suitcase is really full. Can't close it. I'll have to sit on it. (*SFX: Click! Closing suitcase*) There! See what you can do when you put your mind to it.

While boarding the train, Durante gets on the cattle car by mistake.

- DURANTE:   Look at this. A gangplank! What class! Although I think some-one is tampering with the air conditioning. Golly, it's dark in here. I just felt my cowhide bag and one of the gloves is sticking out.

# November 20, 1949

## Jack Benny

(*Once again, Jack and Rochester are driving to the studio in his old Maxwell car.*)

- JACK:   Gee, it's a beautiful day. Rochester, put the top down.
  ROCHESTER:   Do I have to? It's a lot of trouble pulling down the tent and pulling up those stakes.

## Bergen & McCarthy

- BERGEN:   We're having quite a Thanksgiving dinner. We have smoked ham.
  CHARLIE:   Where did you get it, at a fire sale?
  BERGEN:   And turkey. This turkey really tickles the palate.
  CHARLIE:   What did you do? Leave the feathers on?

## Lux Radio Theater

*Sorrowful Jones* starring Bob Hope and Lucille Ball. Remake of Damon Run-yon story *Little Miss Marker*. Bob plays bookie who has to take care of little girl who was left as an IOU for a gambling debt. Lucille Ball played his girlfriend. Lots of gambling and racetrack horse jokes, etc.

- BOB:   (*About horse*) He's so old they have to mix his oats with adrenaline. His jockey is Grandma Moses.
  LUCILLE:   I guess you lost your shirt.
  BOB:   Yeah, look at me. I have to starch my underwear and tie the hair on my chest into a Windsor knot.
  LUCILLE:   What are you giving that horse?
  BOB:   It's a four-way cold tablet. He won't know which way to run. (*After winning*) Look at all this money! I may have to open a branch mattress. (*Audience is not laughing, so Hope ad-libs*) I wonder if it's too late to get into television?

  (*Bob takes the little girl to a nightclub.*)

LUCILLE:   What are you doing in a nightclub with this little girl?

BOB:   Her scout troop's holding a meeting here. The Vic Damone Beaver patrol.

LITTLE GIRL:   I'm hungry. I wanna eat.

BOB:   Eat? Hey, do you want to look like a four year old Kate Smith? Well, okay. Waiter, bring this little lady the works. A bowl of cornflakes. And two spoons.

WAITER:   (*Snide*) Two spoons?

BOB:   Look, after the tip you get your family will be back on cornflakes, too.

(*The little girl has to stay with Bob in his hotel room.*)

BOB:   This is a small room. I have to sleep with one leg out in the hall. (*Girl giggles*) Honey, you mustn't laugh on this show. You might start a trend. Here, take this pillow. The one stuffed with Lux wrappers. Can I get you anything? A slug of Pablum?

LITTLE GIRL:   I'm lonesome. Sing me a song.

BOB:   If I start singing with this audience in here, we'll both be lonesome. Okay, I'll sing a song and put you to sleep. (*Sings:* Muletrain) Oh, sorry. That only puts mules to sleep.

LUCILLE:   (*Enters the room*) What a lousy room! What time do the bats fly out?

BOB:   I don't keep track of 'em as long as they pay their rent.

LUCILLE:   You must think you're some kind of lover.

BOB:   Are you kidding? Cary Grant is so jealous of me he's having another hole drilled in his chin.

(*The little girl is in the hospital. If they bring the horse to her it might help.*)

LUCILLE:   You'll just have to steal the horse.

BOB:   Yeah, I'm sure no one will notice the lump under my coat. If they catch me, they'll have to roll me into the hospital on four different tables.

(*As Bob is stealing the horse.*)

HORSE:   (*SFX: Horse whinny*)

BOB:   Why didn't you think of that before we left the stable? I don't know how to mount you. Tell you what. I'll spread my legs and you crawl under me.

(*In a fist fight with crooks.*)

BOB:   Wait! I'll give him my rabbit punch! (*SFX: Punch*) Didn't work. That's funny, it always worked on rabbits.

## November 23, 1949

### *You Bet Your Life*

- GROUCHO: (*Interviewing contestant*) How did you meet your wife?
  MAN:   I was drinking coffee when I met her.
  GROUCHO:   And that was grounds for marriage?
  MAN:   We went for a drive and my battery went out.
  GROUCHO:   And who did it go out with?
  MAN:   So I bought her a ring.
  GROUCHO:   Expensive?
  MAN:   I'd say roughly in the neighborhood of two thousand dollars.
  GROUCHO:   That's a pretty rough neighborhood.
  WOMAN:   I went to a party and it looked like rain.
  GROUCHO:   What did? The party?
  WOMAN:   No, I was wearing a long, full dress.
  GROUCHO:   And you looked long and full?
  WOMAN:   It began to rain and you know how dresses get when they get wet.
  GROUCHO:   Yes, I have trouble with them all the time.
  WOMAN:   It drew up. Shrunk real small while I was waiting for the bus.
  GROUCHO:   So your dress was almost gone? Where was the bus driver all this time? Well, tell me. Do you have any visible means of support?
  WOMAN:   A girdle, but I hope it isn't visible.

### *Burns & Allen*

- GEORGE:   After Gracie stuffed the turkey, she tried to sew it up, but it kept slipping off the sewing machine.

  (*Gracie is talking to her neighbor.*)

- BEA:   I just got through listening to Bing Crosby.
  GRACIE:   Bing is nice, but George is a better singer.
  BEA:   Everything Bing sings is immortal.
  GRACIE:   Well, George's songs are clean!
  BEA:   Look, this recipe calls for coconut milk.
  GRACIE:   Coconut milk? My you must have to sit on a mighty low stool to milk that.

  (*Gracie goes to store to buy a turkey for Thanksgiving.*)

- CLERK:   You're too late. I haven't got a single turkey left.
  GRACIE:   Well, then I'll take a married one.
  HARRY:   The turkey was alive! She didn't cook it!
  GEORGE:   You're kidding. A live turkey on a dinner table?
  HARRY:   Kidding, eh? Well, how come when I reached for a drumstick, it shook hands with me!

- GRACIE:   George the electric garbage disposal doesn't work. I can't get the garbage can in it.
- GUEST:   My plane arrived ahead of schedule. We had a tailwind.
  GRACIE:   Oh, you must be chilly. Stand with your back to the fireplace.

## Milton Berle
- BERLE:   It's the first Thanksgiving. I'm a pilgrim. I'm in love with Priscilla. Yes, I'm a pilgrim, but I'm not making any progress.
  MAN:   What are you doing in jail?
  BERLE:   Nothing right now, but tomorrow I'm trying out for the ball team.

# November 27, 1949

## Jack Benny
On this show, they did a takeoff on the movie, *The Farmer's Daughter.*
- DON:   Now, we present, *The Farmer's Son!*
  JACK:   Now, there's a switch! I'm the farmer. I have a pig. (*SFX: Pig squeal*) I have a cow. (*SFX: Cow moos*) I have a dog. (*SFX: Dog bark*) I have a horse. (*SFX: Horse whinny*). And I have a jackass.
  DENNIS:   How do you do!
  MARY:   Paw, where's Lem. Is he with Clem?
  JACK:   I don't know. I ain't seen Clem since eight PM! (*SFX: Drums beat to tune of* Shave and Haircut, Two Bits) Now cut that out!

## Red Skelton
- RED:   What a week! With these slippery sidewalks and horseback riding, boy, have I got a tail of woe.
  WOMAN:   I'm a newspaper woman.
  CLEM:   (*As Clem Kadiddlehopper*) Newspaper, eh? I never met one of those before. I thought that was skin.
  WOMAN:   Tell me, did you study singing? Where did you study? Did you study abroad?
  CLEM:   Yeah, in Italy. She was selling Hershey bars.

- ANNOUNCER:   He's on the roof!
  CLEM:   Roof?
  ANNOUNCER:   Roof! Roof!
  CLEM:   Somebody throw him a bone.

## Bob Hope
JACK BENNY:   (*Guest*) One more remark like that and I'll plug your hearing aid into a long playing record of Mel Torme.

**– 1 9 4 9 –**

BOB:   (*As a doctor*) I'm the doctor. I didn't want to be a doctor at first. I wanted to be a nurse. But, I gave it up. Too much trouble.

JACK:   Doctor, I found your watch in my stomach. Butterfingers!

BOB:   I hate to tell him, but my portable radio is missing, too.

JACK:   Doctor, you've taken out my kidney, my appendix, my spleen and I'm still not well.

BOB:   Yes, but you should see my scrapbook. All my life I've wanted to work on something big, but Kate Smith already has a doctor. Once as an experiment, I stayed locked in a room with four thousand rabbits for six months. I'll never forget one day while I was sitting on my haunches, wiggling my nose and munching a carrot…

# December 2, 1949

## *Joan Davis*

- SHIRLEY:   Joan, cheer up. You look sad. Look at yourself.
  JOAN:   That ain't gonna make me any happier.
  SHIRLEY:   Well, pour some coffee, and prepare yourself for a shock.
  JOAN:   Why?
  SHIRLEY:   The percolator has a short circuit.
  JOAN:   And who is this little girl?
  SHIRLEY:   She's my sister, silly.
  JOAN:   How are you, silly? Funny name for a kid.
  SHIRLEY:   My sister is Millie!
  JOAN:   Millie? Well, that's silly.
  MILLIE:   And you are Joan?
  JOAN:   It's me. Or is it … it is I? Me sounds better. It is me!
  SHIRLEY:   Miss Davis, I is correct.
  JOAN:   You is correct? You ain't even in this, honey-chile. This is just between us two me's.

## *Martin & Lewis*

- JERRY:   I got a date with a gal and I'm not so sure I want to keep it.
  DEAN:   Why not?
  JERRY:   Her name is Doris Karloff.

- GIRL:   I love Rod. He loves me madly, insanely, passionately! He is what I call a hot Rod!
  JERRY:   Monday, Dear Diary: Today I weigh only ninety pounds. The doctor says I need more iron. More iron. Tuesday, Dear Diary: Ate my erector set today.

# December 6, 1949

## *Bob Hope*

- BOB: (*At the bank*) I want to talk to the President and nobody else.
  PRESIDENT: I am the President. I've just canceled all my appointments with Harry Truman about the billion dollar loan just to see you. Now what do you want?
  BOB: Well, your calendar came and I don't like it.

- BOB: (*To Jack Benny, guest*) Jack, Where did you get that Santa Claus suit?
  JACK: You'd be surprised what you can do with a bottle of catsup and some long underwear.
  BOB: Jack, can you really play the violin?
  JACK: Can I play the violin? Are you kidding? I've got so much talent, it scares me.
  BOB: Scares me, too.
  JACK: (*Plays a few notes*) There. How did that sound?
  BOB: Sounds like something the muletrain left behind!
  (*Note:* Muletrain *was a hit song recorded by Frankie Laine.*)

# — 1 9 5 0 —

## January 8, 1950

### *Jack Benny*

- JACK:   Okay, I'll show you what a great lover I am. Come here, babe! Put your arms around me. Tighter, tighter. Now, I'll put my arms around you. Tighter, and closer and ... what do I do now?

- DENNIS:   My dog is smart. He can add.
  JACK:   Okay, dog. What's two plus two?
  DOG:   *(Barks four times)*
  JACK:   Amazing. Now, what's the square root of 3,507? *(Long pause)* Put down that pencil and paper and figure it out in your head. Stupid dog!

On this show the Sportsmen Quartet made a blooper while singing and it all fell apart.

- JACK:   That was the lousiest thing I've ever heard! One rehearsal. That's all!

*(Later, riding with Dennis and the dog.)*

- JACK:   Turn left. *(Pause)* I said, turn left!
  DOG:   Bow-wow!
  JACK:   You were supposed to turn left, you stupid dog! How he got his driver's license I'll never know!

# Bergen & McCarthy

- BERGEN:   When would you like me to sing?
  CHARLIE:   You sing? When that day comes, a man with horns and a tail will knock on your door and say, "It's frozen over, Bergen!"

- BERGEN:   Mortimer, how old are you?
  MORTIMER:   Oh, I'm a boy about my age.
  BERGEN:   You know, Mortimer, when I'm with you I could die laughing.
  MORTIMER:   Well, that's the least you could do.
  BERGEN:   I know when I'm not wanted. I guess I'll go find someone who appreciates me.
  MORTIMER:   Well, that should take you quite some time.

# Henry Morgan

- ANNOUNCER:   Time now for Mr. Question Man. Here's a question sent in by a listener. "Why is it called a honeymoon?"
  HENRY:   (*As Mr. Question Man*) Why is what called a Honeymoon?
  ANNOUNCER:   Mr. Question Man … would you say men or women are more nervous?
  HENRY:   Certainly. Men or women are more nervous.

# Jack Benny

- ROCHESTER:   Here's your teeth, boss. Now smile at me!
  JACK:   (*In cheap hotel*) It's great being in New York. I could have sworn it was snowing.
  ROCHESTER:   That was the plaster falling off the ceiling.

  (*Later, Jack imitates Fred Allen doing Allen's Alley.*)

- JACK:   (*Nasal voice*) Well, Portland it's time to take a stroll down Allen's Alley.
  (*SFX: Knock on door*)
  TITUS:   (*Played by Dennis Day*) Howdy, bub.
  JACK:   Ah, Titus Moody! And what's new with you today?
  TITUS:   Having problems with my chickens.
  JACK:   Problems with your chickens, eh?
  TITUS:   Yep. My hens lay eggs every time they hear gunshots on television.
  JACK:   Your hens lay eggs when they hear gunshots on television? What's wrong with that?
  TITUS:   It was okay, but when they pulled out a machine gun, my hens dropped dead trying.

# February 12, 1950

## Amos 'n' Andy

- ANDY: What a gal. Wasn't she the one who wore hip boots to the Senior Prom?
  KINGfiSH: Age didn't bother my grandfather. He chased girls until he was real old. In fact, the only way I could stop him was to take the tires off his wheelchair.

## Bob Hope

- BOB: I'm Bob Hope.
  COLONNA: Bring the garbage around to the rear, please.
  BOB: Colonna, what are you up to?
  COLONNA: I've invented a mouse trap that only catches boy mice.
  BOB: What do you use for bait?
  COLONNA: Girl mice.

## Milton Berle

- BERLE: Young man, what is your name?
  MAN: (*Weak, timid voice*) My name is Humphrey Bogart. But I'm not the real Humphrey Bogart. I'm not! I'm not! I'm not!
  BERLE: Okay, I know you're not the real Bogart.
  MAN: Really? Who told you?

- BERLE: I'm tired, but every night when I come home there's a tub waiting for me.
  FRANK: A hot bath?
  BERLE: No, my wife.

  (*Comedy sketch about the Air Force. "Smilin' Jack Berle."*)

- FRANK: Smilin' Jack Berle was the pilot. Suddenly, he barked out an order! (*SFX: Dog bark*) Yes, Berle?
  BERLE: That's an order!
  FRANK: Yes!
  BERLE: On rye bread.
  FRANK: Captain, we've contacted another plane. Listen!
  RADIO: I'm lost! Lost! I'm at longitude 48 and latitude 56! Altitude three feet and the fog is closing in. Where am I?
  BERLE: Be quiet. You're in the steam room of the YWCA.
  FRANK: Captain, I see you're wearing both eagles on the same shoulder.
  BERLE: Mating season.
  FRANK: How long have you been flying?
  BERLE: I began flying the mail. I was the first to send mail by tying it to Walter Pidgeon's leg.

- BERLE:   Men, this is the zero hour. And you know what that means.
  FRANK:   What?
  BERLE:   Nothing!
  FRANK:   Roger.
  BERLE:   You've known me for twenty years and there's something I should tell you … I'm yellow!
  FRANK:   We're falling! We're falling!
  BERLE:   Who's flying the plane?
  FRANK:   You are.
  BERLE:   I am?

## You Bet Your Life

- GROUCHO:   (*Interviewing contestant*) What's your name?
  MAN:   My name is Jesse James.
  GROUCHO:   Oh? Where's your horse? Is it parked outside? Is the motor running?
  MAN:   I'm from Texas!
  GROUCHO:   Which part?
  MAN:   All of me.
  GROUCHO:   So why did you fall in love with him?
  WOMAN:   He was very quiet and comfortable.
  GROUCHO:   You could have gotten that with a feather mattress. (*To the man*) So you run a dance hall. How many girl dancers are there?
  MAN:   One hundred.
  GROUCHO:   One hundred girls? That's in round figures I suppose.
  MAN:   We have one hundred girls who dance.
  GROUCHO:   Imagine, dancing with one hundred girls. Old octopus Marx they call me. As a matter of fact, one girl did call me that. Where is this dance hall?
  MAN:   In Alaska.
  GROUCHO:   I entertained in Alaska. They had a cold wave up there. She wouldn't go out with anyone.

## Red Skelton

- CLEM:   I owe so much money, when I light a candle, the guy from the electric company comes over and blows it out.

- CLEM:   I once worked in an ice cream factory. I worked in the Tutti-Frutti department. I separated the Tutti from the Frutti. Sometimes you can get too much Tutti in the Frutti there and you have to get it out. One day a little Tutti got through and got into the Frutti and the boss wanted to start trouble, so I says, what difference does it make if I have more Tutti in the Frutti than Frutti in the Tutti?
  ANNOUNCER:   What did he say?

CLEM:    You're fired.

• RED:    Ever see these sexy books they publish nowadays? The covers are better than the whole book. I saw one the other day, it was called, "She!" And on the cover was a picture of a beautiful girl and she's wearing a low-cut dress. A real low-cut dress. I mean really low-cut … it was cut all the way down to … well, all the way down to … the bottom of the page.

# Notes and Comments

## Abbott & Costello

Bud Abbott and Lou Costello began as a team in burlesque. The routines they brought with them to radio were honed to perfection after years on the boards in those bawdy theaters. Bud Abbott was the definitive burlesque straight man, the "take charge" type who bossed Lou around and ultimately got them both into one scrape after another. Lou was the hapless, child-man, bumbling his way though life, confusing words and taking everything Abbott said literally. The results were a stream of misunderstood words and puns that was the root of their humor. Their "Who's On First?" routine holds up even today as a classic example.

Abbott and Costello were enormously successful in a string of hit movies including: *Buck Privates*, *In the Navy*, *The Naughty Nineties*, *It Ain't Hay* and *Pardon My Sarong*. Later, they brought it all to television, and today those shows are collector's items for anyone interested in studying classic burlesque routines.

Despite the fact that their jokes were familiar, their skillful performances made the material seem new again. Abbott and Costello were comic artists in the truest sense of the word.

## Fred Allen

Fred Allen was the most cerebral of all the great radio comedians. As a writer, he was often regarded as a satiric humorist on the same level with Mark Twain. As a performer, his dry, nasal voice made him a natural for radio and served to emphasize his acerbic wit.

Allen's career in radio was long and varied, spanning some 17 years from 1932 until 1949. His most successful radio shows happened in the mid-nineteen forties with the introduction of a feature called *Allen's Alley*. During this, he and his wife, Portland Hoffa, would take a stroll down the imaginary Alley, knocking on doors which would be opened by a range of wonderful ethnic characters representing a broad range of Americana. There was Miss Nussbaum, who spoke of her schnook husband, Pierre. Then came Ajax Cassidy, an Irish blowhard, followed by Titus Moody, a dry Vermont farmer and finally, to cap it all off, the quintessential southern politician, Senator Claghorn, so southern he only drank out of Dixie cups. It was this feature that listeners looked forward to each Sunday night.

Fred's humor was topical and satiric. He did parodies on cultural subjects like Gilbert and Sullivan operettas, and spoofs of current Broadway shows. Even though his humor was sophisticated, Fred's popularity was widespread. His mock feud with Jack Benny became legendary and helped secure him a top spot in the ratings.

While Fred's show was funny at the time, little of it holds up today. The humor was topical and hearing it now, the bite is lost. While other radio shows of that period dealt with day-to-day human verities, Fred's shows do not retain the strength they once had. Nevertheless, they were brilliant for their time, and Fred Allen remains as one of America's greatest humorists.

## Amos 'n' Andy

*Amos 'n' Andy* has been called America's first great radio show. It was so popular in the early days that movie theaters would interrupt the movie and play the show over the speaker system so fans wouldn't miss it. It would appear that everything stopped when Amos and Andy came on the air.

It began as Sam and Henry in 1926. Later, with a title change to Amos and Andy, it continued in popularity until 1949 before turning to television in 1951. Freeman Gosden and Charles Correll, both white, played the African/American characters Amos and Andy throughout its radio career. At the time their show was enjoyed by blacks and whites alike. As with Red Skelton, the characters were lovable, and the humor was meant as harmless fun. During the early days, Gosden and Correll portrayed all the characters, male and female, with their natural talents for voice changes. When the show went to a half-hour, other actors were hired to play the female parts and supporting characters. As the show progressed, the character of Amos was moved into the background when the more dominant, Kingfish, literally took over the show and became its pivotal character.

The plots generally ran along a familiar theme with Kingfish trying to con Andy out of something or into something that invariably turned out to be a mess of trouble. Puns, mispronunciations, along with catch-phrases and quick one-liners became the main source of humor that connected the simple plot lines.

Although controversy eventually plagued the show, especially on television, it remained popular for thirty-four years, which made it the longest running program in the history of radio.

## Jack Benny

One of the greatest comedy performers of all time, Jack Benny and his gang created a formula that has proven successful for a host of other comedians from radio right on up to this day in television. Comedians like Bob Newhart and Jerry Seinfeld have used Benny's formula, whether knowingly or unknowingly, with astounding results. That formula is this: The main character (Benny, Newhart, Seinfeld) is mostly a straight-man surrounded by a cast of kooky characters.

To many people, Jack Benny was the greatest straight-man who ever lived. He very generously gave the punchlines to his cast, and let himself become the butt of the jokes. Jack was the core, the center around which the chaos revolved. It was how he reacted to what was going on that made him funny. What pulled it all together was the character that Benny developed over the years — that of a vain, boastful, inept man who surpassed even Scrooge in his stinginess. The character Benny played was so cheap he'd steal paper napkins from restaurants to use in his home. He would put an old tube of toothpaste on the railroad tracks and let a train run over it to get just one more squeeze out of it. That's how cheap Jack Benny was pictured to be. Offstage, of course, Jack was one of the kindest, most generous and loved men in show business.

All of this gave his supporting cast a lot of ammunition to feed off, hurling a barrage of insults and one-liners his way, which would bring on the famous Benny reaction, sometimes a long stare or simply a "Hmm." Or when he had heard enough, a loud, "Now cut that out!"

The Jack Benny show was a perfect ensemble piece relying completely on characterization from everyone involved. From wise-cracking Mary Livingstone (his wife in real life), to his heavyweight announcer, Don Wilson, brash Phil Harris, back-talking Rochester, idiot singer Dennis Day, racetrack tout Sheldon Leonard, Artie Auerback as Mr. Kitzel, Frank Nelson, the abrasive man who was put on earth to annoy Jack, and Mel Blanc, who played a host of characters from Benny's violin teacher, to a parrot, a train announcer, and Jack's automobile, the Maxwell. Even the Sportsman Quartet was played for comedy integrating commercials into the songs they sang.

All of this blossomed from some of the finest comedy writers the entertainment industry has ever known — Milt Josefsberg, George Balzer, John

Tackaberry and Sam Perrin to name a few. Every line was approved and edited by Jack himself whose innate comic sense guided the show every step of the way and helped develop it into a national icon.

With the passing years, a lot of radio comedy might seem old hat, out of date and just plain corny, but the radio shows of Jack Benny remain just as funny now as they were when they were first broadcast over fifty years ago.

## Bergen & McCarthy

At first the idea of a ventriloquist on radio seemed absurd. After all, listeners would be unable to see Edgar Bergen's uncanny talent, that ability to throw his voice into a dummy sitting on a stand beside him. However, the naysayers were proven wrong, because radio was a medium that was made to order for people who did voices and vocal characterizations. So fully developed was the character of Charlie McCarthy, that people began to think of him as a real boy. The same thing happened with all of Bergen's characters, from Mortimer Snerd, a slow talking, incredibly stupid rustic, to Effie Klinker, the gossipy old maid: both were completely believable. And the reason for all this was simple — to Edgar Bergen they were real. It has been noted that at the Bergen residence in Hollywood, Charlie McCarthy had his own room with a complete wardrobe in his closet. This makes sense when you realize that actors have to believe their characters are real while performing in order to make them convincing.

The program was basically a variety show with guest stars, musical numbers and comedy sketches. Don Ameche and Francis Langford began their famous Bickersons skits with *Bergen & McCarthy*. A famous feud developed between comedian W. C. Fields and Charlie. It became as famous as the so-called feud between Jack Benny and Fred Allen. Bergen appeared as the very conservative father figure, while Charlie was the mischievous wise-cracking boy who would throw one zinger after another at guest stars and flirt with any female guest who showed up on the program. Mortimer Snerd was a sweet, dopey country bumpkin who took everything literally and could be stumped by the question, "How do you do?"

The fact that Bergen was a ventriloquist became irrelevant. As the show moved along in years, so did Bergen's lips, but by then, nobody cared. All that mattered were the wonderful, warm characters he brought into our homes each Sunday night.

## Milton Berle

Primarily a visual comic, Milton Berle did not fare too well on radio. However, between 1947 and 1949, it was his radio show that paved the way for his astounding success on television. For years, Berle had tried various formats in radio, none of which seemed to fit his unique talents. Finally, in 1948, he began his association with Texaco on the radio with the Texaco Star Theater. This was basically a variety show with Berle doing an opening monologue, and then some play-by-play with announcer Frank Gallup, before going into an outlandish comedy sketch with Arnold Stang, Pert Kelton and various guest stars.

Why Berle's show wasn't more popular remains a mystery. The gags were funny, his trading of insults with announcer Frank Gallup worked beautifully, and the sketches were far-out and amusing. Whatever the reason, perhaps because he was such a visual type, the show did not do well in the ratings. It did, however, form the nucleus for his television show that was soon to follow and earn Milton Berle the title of "Mr. Television" back in the early fifties. While Berle may have been called "The Thief of Badgags," one can only agree with his philosophy that jokes are public property, because the same formulaic jokes we heard on radio over fifty years ago still show up on television today.

## The Bickersons

The Bickersons gained their first real popularity on the *Bergen & McCarthy* show. However, it actually began on Drene Time, a shampoo sponsored variety program. Don Ameche was perfectly cast as John Bickerson with Francis Langford as his long-suffering wife, Blanche. Most of the scenes took place in bed and should have been shocking in its time, but weren't because of the incessant nagging bestowed upon John by his wife.

Their skits always began the same way with John's snores keeping Blanche awake, causing her to wake him up and start in with myriad of complaints. Their bickering (hence the name) was sharp and cutting with John muttering outrageous insults at her under his breath. This kind of husbandly back-talk was unheard of on radio at the time, and listeners found it hilarious. Ameche and Langford were perfect foils for each other and gained a cult following that is still around to this day on recordings.

## Blondie

The transition of the popular comic strip Blondie from newspaper to radio was highly successful. Arthur Lake, who played Dagwood actually was a Dagwood type character himself. Nowhere in the history of show business has typecasting been so on the mark. Penny Singleton, as Blondie, was perfect, also. They were soon both teamed in a series of movies that grew out of the radio program. Blondie was among the first "family" situation comedies and was immediately popular.

Dagwood, the bumbling Bumstead, forever in trouble with his boss, Mr.

Dithers, invariably sought and received help from his not-so-dumb blond wife. The radio program had a built-in audience from Chic Young's established comic strip, and it became one of those not to be missed shows on radio during its time. All of the comic strip characters were included — Blondie, Dagwood, and their son, Alexander, who began life as Baby Dumpling, and their dog, Daisy. Later, a sister named Cookie was added. All of this was supposed to represent a typical middle-class family, although it was far from that.

Dagwood's boss, Mr. Dithers was played by Hanley Stafford, and Frank Nelson, from the Jack Benny program, took the part of Mr. Woodley, the Bumstead's next door neighbor. Arthur Lake remained in the role of Dagwood throughout the series, while various actresses took the part of Blondie. However, because of the movie versions, Penny Singleton remains fixed as the definitive Blondie. The show ran from 1944 until 1950 when television began to take its toll on the radio audience.

## Burns & Allen

The formula dates back to early vaudeville and burlesque. It's a surefire routine, the straight man and the dizzy female. For years comedy teams used this approach, but not one ever came close to matching the success with it as did George Burns and Gracie Allen. When they brought their act to radio, they were instantly popular, and continued on into television.

Truth was, Gracie was far from dumb. She simply took whatever anyone said literally, so that when analyzed there was a kind of crazy logic in her every response. What she said actually made sense in her context. The fact that it did not fit what was actually going on made no difference to her. That was the source of their humor.

George Burns was by far one of the smoothest straight men ever to grace a stage. He used to say that he had a great job, the easiest in show business. All he had to do was walk on-stage with Gracie and say, "How's your brother?" Then stand back and let her talk. He would puff on his cigar and occasionally feed her another straight line like, "And then what happened?" and off she'd go again, while George stood there calmly smoking his cigar.

Of course, there was a lot more to it than that. George was the genius behind it all, carefully crafting their comedy with the writers on scripts based on mistaken identity and misunderstandings brought on by Gracie. The result? Millions of listeners tuned in each week for years to see what fix Gracie would get them into next.

Far from being just a straight man, George fine tuned every line spoken by Gracie and the entire cast. Needless to say, they continued on radio and survived the transition to television easily, where they remained high in the ratings until Gracie retired in 1958.

## Abe Burrows

As one of the top writers in the entertainment business, Abe Burrows had a brief career as a radio performer. His 15 minute show was highly sophisticated and featured Burrows at the piano playing and singing his own song parodies, peppered with satirical wit and occasional guests.

Burrows was best known on Broadway as a play doctor, which is simply a writer who is brought in to work on ailing Broadway shows. He co-authored the show *How to Succeed in Business Without Really Trying*, and wrote the libretto for *Guys and Dolls*.

## Eddie Cantor

Like Al Jolson and most of the stars from the golden age of radio, Eddie Cantor came to radio from vaudeville and Broadway. Cantor was an all-around performer — singer, dancer and comedian whose strong point was a frantic energy compounded with an "in your face" attitude toward authority. His skits were peppered with quick insult one-liners and off the wall humor supplied by Bert Gordon as the Mad Russian, and a wild man named Parkyakarkus, played by Harry Einstein. Einstein must've had quite a sense of humor. He named his son Albert, who later changed his name and is now known to all of us as comic actor Albert Brooks. Brilliant, original humor seems to run in that family.

This cast, coupled with Hollywood stars as guests, helped Eddie Cantor create a solid comedy-variety radio program that ran from the nineteen thirties right on up until 1949. Cantor loved to take credit for discovering new talent and showcasing them on his show. Dinah Shore, Deanna Durbin, Bert Parks and Bobby Breen were just a few of his "discoveries."

Eddie's ego matched Jolson's (no mean feat in itself) and he seldom missed a chance to toot his own horn. None of this, however, dimmed his audience appeal and his show ran at the top of the ratings for many years before competition from other big stars forced his show down a peg or two to a lower, but respectable spot on the charts.

Cantor and his wife, Ida, had five daughters, and that fact became fuel for running gags throughout the rest of his career. Television beckoned in 1950 and he went on to carry his brand of entertainment to the Colgate Comedy Hour.

## Jack Carson

Another vaudeville performer who made his way into radio was Jack Carson. Along with his partner, Dave Willock, who played his smarter nephew, Tugwell, the Jack Carson show featured an impressive cast which included Arthur Treacher, Mel Blanc, Irene Ryan (later to become Granny on TV's *Beverly Hillbillies*) and even the distinguished actress Agnes Moorehead, who eventually wound up on television's *Bewitched*.

Jack Carson's character was simply that of a big, dumb guy. It was a role that he was to use throughout his radio, television and movie career. Eventually, Jack was teamed with singer Dennis Morgan in an obvious attempt to compete with Hope and Crosby, in a series of "Two Guys from..." movies, as in *Two Guys from Milwaukee*.

Jack's radio show ran in various formats from 1943 until 1955. However, his biggest success came from an astounding number of classic movies such as *Mildred Pierce* and *Cat on a Hot Tin Roof*.

## Bing Crosby

While Bing Crosby was primarily known as one of the greatest pop singers of his day, he also had a flair for casual comedy that held him in good stead. His style was, like his singing, mellow, and his laid-back delivery allowed him the opportunity to say his lines in a throwaway style that caught people off guard and made them laugh. Laughter often comes from the unexpected, and that worked well for Bing on radio and with Bob Hope in movies.

He actually began early on radio in 1930, but it was the Kraft Music Hall that brought him the most success. It was a variety program with Bing engaging in low-key comic dialogue with guest stars along with songs and duets. The stars who appeared as guests on the show would make up a veritable "Who's Who" in show business. The feeling generated to listeners was that of an easy-going variety show with light-hearted, conversational style jokes, a format that Bing Crosby maintained throughout his career.

Crosby's movies with Bob Hope remain classic "buddy" type films and were helped in popularity by Hope's occasional appearances on Bing's radio program. They continued this team spirit right on into television, with each guesting on the other's show from time to time.

More than anything else, Bing Crosby was a great pop singer. The term "crooner" describes Bing perfectly, and many who followed were influenced by him. Dean Martin and Perry Como are prime examples. Bing's recording of "White Christmas" remains a standard, and to this day people know that Christmas is near when they hear the sound of Crosby crooning Irving Berlin's classic on the radio, in stores and malls across the nation.

## Joan Davis

*Leave It to Joan* was an outgrowth of her earlier show, *Joanie's Tea Room*. Her character was that of a nutzy female always on the lookout for a man. Her distinctive voice and delivery added greatly to the characterization. This, coupled with good writing led the show quickly into the top ten ratings.

Most of the comedy came from misunderstandings, misinterpretation and outrageous puns with Joan playing dumb most of the time. Not dumb like Gracie Allen, who had her own logic behind her, but dumber than dumb would best describe Joan.

The show was set first in a small store, which later became a tea room, in a small town. Joan Davis was a natural comedienne. Visually funny, she could mug with the best of them, but her unusual voice made her perfectly suited for radio. The show ran high in the ratings until 1950. In 1952 it was transferred to television as *I Married Joan* were it ran until 1955.

## Durante & Moore Show

Jimmy Durante came to radio from saloons, Broadway and grade B movies. His first radio attempts met with little success until he was teamed with a young, brash radio performer named Garry Moore. The contrast between the old pro and the newcomer was an instant hit, and they stayed together from 1943 until 1947 when Moore left and was replaced by comedian Alan Young.

Durante was so famous for his large nose, that he became known as "Schnozzola." It was said that he actually had his nose insured with Lloyds of London for a million dollars. Jimmy was by nature a warm, sweet lovable man. It was impossible to dislike him and no one has ever uttered an unkind word about him. He played a great ragtime piano, wrote crazy novelty songs epitomized by his theme, "Inka Dinka Doo." He pounded away on the piano, interspersed his songs with long yarns about a fictional character named Umbriago, and then railed out in mock rage at the orchestra when he felt it had gotten too loud, and to anyone who interrupted him. "Stop the music! Stop the music!" he shout. "Everybody wants to get in the act!"

Garry Moore, a sophisticated comedian with an intellect for the absolutely silly, was a sharp contrast to Durante's mangling of the English language. Moore was the mock highbrow, Durante, the lowbrow, a great combination that endeared them to all who tuned in. The show usually began with a Moore monologue, then an exchange with Durante and one of his songs. This would be followed by the comedy sketch with a guest star. The scripts were corny and brilliant, all at the same time, but it was the chemistry and love that these men shared for each other that came across the airwaves to listeners across the nation.

## Fibber McGee & Molly

After a long career playing small-time vaudeville and several years on various radio programs, Jim and Marian Jordan finally made the bigtime when they debuted *Fibber McGee & Molly* in 1935. This was a show that personified small town America with a cast of typical mid-American characters whom listeners could easily identify. Fibber, named that because of his non-stoppable urge to expand the truth, was a lovable blowhard whose ineptness was kept in check by his long-suffering wife, Molly. The formula was simple: The McGees were usually at home while various characters came knocking at their door in what amounted to two or three minute vaudeville routines. Those characters became famous on their own and included the great Gildersleeve, who was the first supporting player in broadcasting to spin-off into his own show. Then there was the Old Timer, who told outlandish stories and challenged McGee's fabrications with "That ain't the way I heered it, Sonny!" And Mr. Wimple, who spoke of his "bird book and his big old wife." Mayor LaTrivia, Doc Gamble and Beulah, their cook, who also spun off into her own show, were others in the cast. Marion (Molly) also doubled as the little girl from next door.

Of course, the highlight of the show each week was Fibber's closet which, when opened, sent what seemed like hundreds of piles of junk crashing out onto the floor. Listeners waited in anticipation for someone to inadvertently open that closet door. It was the one sound effect on radio that became immortal, perhaps rivaled only by Inner Sanctum's squeaking door.

The dialogue, written by the incredibly talented Don Quinn, remains a hallmark in radio comedy. Characterization and situation were the keys and catch-phrases from the show swept the nation. "T'aint funny, McGee," was quoted throughout the land years after the show went off the air. It was a warm, wonderful, funny show that epitomizes the Golden Age of Radio.

### Phil Harris and Alice Faye

The *Phil Harris and Alice Faye* program evolved right out of the Jack Benny Show with Phil retaining his loud-mouth, hard-drinking, egotistical bandleader role. A lot of the supporting players from the Benny show also appeared with Phil. The major difference was Alice Faye, Phil's wife in real life. Alice Faye was already a major movie star in her own right, and as a singer and actress, she was the center that grounded all the zany goings on around her. It gave the carousing Harris a home life with a wife and two daughters.

The plots mostly revolved around Phil and his guitar-playing drinking buddy, Frank Remley, portrayed by the great radio actor, Elliot Lewis. Together they were constantly getting into trouble with hilarious results. The show was one of the funniest ever on radio and remained popular from 1946 until 1951. Phil Harris was, as he used to say, "Solid, Jackson! Solid!"

### Bob Hope

Like most of the top comedians of that era, Bob Hope came to radio by way of vaudeville and the Broadway stage. Bob began his career initially as a song and dance man, but when asked to fill in for a master of ceremonies during a vaudeville show, he discovered a natural flair for standup comedy. His rapid-fire, rhythmic delivery soon established him as the finest monologist of his time. However, Hope turned out to be much more than just a standup comic. He became a gifted actor, singer and dancer, which earned him the title of "best all-round comedian." From comedy skits to duets with Bing Crosby, Hope could do it all. He even danced with James Cagney, who also began his career as a dancer in *The Seven Little Foys*, a marvelous sequence which is the highlight of the entire movie. His "Road" pictures with Bing Crosby established them both firmly as super-stars in the 1940s.

Radio was the root source for all of this, and there Hope followed the tried and true formula of surrounding himself with comic stooges. His most famous sidekick was Jerry Colonna, who could say the wildest lines and make them work. Then there was Vera Vague, a man-hungry female always on the prowl for a man, any man.

During World War II, Bob Hope discovered the GI audience, which was starved for entertainment. When he found they would laugh easily at just about anything he said, GI's became his core audience. From them on Hope's broadcasts emanated from military bases across the nation and eventually around the world. It became his mission, and for this he was awarded medals, plaques and enough honors to fill rooms. He became personal friends with each President who occupied the White House, regardless of political party, and is revered and respected by all to this day.

Hope's radio show followed a strict formula. First the opening monologue, followed by an exchange with one of this stooges, usually Colonna, then a comic sketch with his guest star, and a final word (sometimes serious) to close out the show. The radio show lasted until the early 1950s when Hope went on to a fabulously successful career on television.

### It Pays to Be Ignorant

Easily the corniest show ever to appear on radio, *It Pays to Be Ignorant* fooled the critics and ran for over nine years. It was a very funny spoof of quiz programs with Tom Howard acting as quizmaster, while his panel of "experts," Harry McNaughton, George Shelton and Lulu McConnell held forth on everything except the correct answer. Chaos reigned throughout as the panelists pretended not to hear the question, understand it or even care about it and proceeded to digress into a series of outrageous puns, insults and even poems. The program was so packed with vaudeville type jokes that laughter came from the sheer volume of it all. As a listener, one fact became evident — if you stayed with it, you were bound to laugh.

Quiz programs, those homages to greed, are certainly ripe for satire, and *It Pays to Be Ignorant* served that purpose admirably by skewering them all.

## Al Jolson

When Bing Crosby left the Kraft Music Hall in a format dispute, singer Al Jolson took over the spot. Jolson was already a legendary stage and screen performer having had a successful career on Broadway and in the movies. He appeared in the first talking movie, *The Jazz Singer*, and had been in and out of radio from the very beginning of the medium, in 1929, in various variety show formats.

Primarily a singer who often appeared in blackface, Jolson was from the old school of stage belters who never needed a microphone to get their songs across. His ego matched his talent (some say it surpassed it) but his love of performing endeared him to audiences everywhere. On Broadway he even had a runway built that ran out from the stage into the audience, so he could get closer to them while he sang.

His most successful venture into radio was on the Kraft Music Hall from 1947 until 1949. There he was teamed with the sharp wit and superb pianist, Oscar Levant. Ken Carpenter remained as the Music Hall's announcer and often served as comedy foil for the two stars.

Two movies — *The Jolson Story* and *Jolson Sings Again* — starring Larry Parks (with Jolson's voice singing the soundtrack) brought his life to the screen and his popularity continued until he passed away in 1950. He used to tell his audiences, "You ain't heard nothing, yet!" And he was right about that.

## Lux Presents Hollywood

The program opened cold with an announcer saying these words, "Lux presents…Hollywood!" A drumroll and then the theme and the Lux Radio Theater was on the air, the most prestigious dramatic show in radio. The format was simple, broadcasting radio adaptations of current popular movies. Its purpose was two-fold. It brought the movies into your living room and it brought people out to see movies.

Originally, its host was none other than one of the most important movie directors in Hollywood at the time, Cecil B. DeMille, who held that position until 1945. Various hosts followed and continued the dramatizations until 1954. It was a class act all the way and with production values of the highest standards. Practically every major movie star in Hollywood appeared on the show at one time or another. One of those "not to be missed" programs from the Golden Age of Radio.

## Ted Mack's Original Amateur Hour

Actually, the original amateur hour was created in 1934 by Major Edward Bowes. He served as host to thousands of amateur talents of all descriptions.

Major Bowes became a very rich man exploiting these show business hope-fuls who most of the time went no further than an appearance on his pro-gram. The more talented of the group were hired and went on road show tours which served to further the popularity of the radio show. For many of them it was exciting fun and their first and only experience with the realities of show business.

When Major Bowes died in 1946, the program took a two year hiatus, and returned to the air with a new host, Ted Mack. Mack had been a mas-ter of ceremonies for one of the road shows and seemed the best choice to take over the Major Bowes role.

It was a standard amateur show which included a spinning "wheel of for-tune" and a gong which sounded if the amateur performer didn't measure up. This was radio's version of the old "hook" that used to remove vaudeville per-formers from the stage if their act was a flop.

A few performers who appeared on the Amateur Hour went on to great success. Frank Sinatra and Beverly Sills were two who appeared very early in their careers and later rose to incredible stardom. Ted Mack's version even-tually made its way to television where it met with moderate success.

### Martin & Lewis

Dean Martin and Jerry Lewis were a very popular comedy team appear-ing in nightclubs when they were snapped up by NBC and given their own radio show. While mildly amusing on radio, their comedy was primarily visual and audiences at home found themselves wondering what the studio audience was laughing about. Jerry Lewis could get laughs just by walking on stage. Dean Martin, who patterned himself after Bing Crosby's relaxed, casual style, acted as Jerry's straight man. The combination was hilarious. The only problem was you had to see them to really appreciate their humor. Radio just wasn't their medium, even though each show contained some good jokes and sketches.

The team went on to a very successful movie and television career until they went their separate ways. Unlike most comedy teams who break up, both Dean Martin and Jerry Lewis continued to enjoy great careers individually and became legends in the entertainment industry.

### Henry Morgan

Henry Morgan was a product of radio right from the beginning. Unlike most comedians who got their training in vaudeville, Morgan began his career as an announcer on a local station in New York City. He made a name for himself by kidding his sponsors. He was unmerciful and relentless, ad-lib-bing his way around the written copy, inserting very funny, but sometimes cutting remarks about the products.

This brought him a lot of attention and soon he was given his own fifteen minute radio show where he was granted free rein. Of course, sponsors came and went, but Morgan remained and developed a local following. Fred Allen was one of his regular listeners who admired his work, and suggested Morgan as a summer replacement for his show.

Now on network radio, Morgan continued his acerbic comedy. His sidekick and stooge was comic actor, Arnold Stang, whose nasal voice and nerdy character made him a highlight on the show. Another actor who appeared with Morgan was Art Carney, who later gained fame as Norton on Jackie Gleason's *The Honeymooners* on television.

Morgan was fluent in many dialects — German, French, Russian and British. His humor was intellectual silliness, and sharp cutting wit. His parodies were esoteric, the humor elitist which eventually missed the mark in middle America. Low ratings and sponsor dissatisfaction brought an early end to his short network radio career. However, Henry Morgan was a very funny man and soon found his niche on television as a panelist on Garry Moore's *I've Got a Secret*. There the audience could see his whimsical, warm face and appreciate his clever jibes.

## Our Miss Brooks

Revered by everyone (especially teachers) *Our Miss Brooks* broke the stereotype of old maid teachers with a sharp tongue equaled only by Groucho Marx. Eve Arden was so right for the role that she remained with it for the rest of her life. Sarcasm was built into her voice so strongly, that she could say "hello," and make it sound like an insult. Zingers and sharp retorts fell from her lips with ease.

Miss Brooks was no dummy, either. Quite the opposite, she exuded wit, combined with intelligence, as she endured the pompous windbag of a principal, Osgood Conklin, played by Gale Gordon. Her pursued, but never obtained, love interest was Mr. Boynton, a biology teacher, who seemed incredibly unaware of her advances at all times. The actor Jeff Chandler took that role, while Richard Crenna was teenager Walter Denton, who continually got Miss Brooks involved in all manner of plots and situations.

In keeping with her low salary, Miss Brooks lived in a boarding house owned by a screwball landlady named Miss Davis, played by Jane Morgan. The trials and tribulations of a teacher's life were great fuel for humor and Eve Arden was so believable in the role that she was offered many teaching jobs in schools across the nation.

The show was a hit from the moment it hit the airwaves and remained so right on into television where it ran from 1952 until 1956.

## Ozzie & Harriet

The full title was *The Adventures of Ozzie and Harriet* with the adventures being implemented by Ozzie, who each week would get his mind fixed on something and not let up until certain disaster loomed upon the family. Supposedly, they were a typical middle-class family, and like *Blondie*, were anything but that. They had two sons, David and Ricky, who eventually played themselves in 1949 beginning when they were age 4 and 8.

The Nelsons were a clean-cut family. Almost too clean-cut from today's perspective, but it was a staunch, reliable family show, a hit across the nation because it represented the kind of family that a lot of people aspired to. In spite of their misadventures, they seemed to be the ideal family, even though that ideal was far removed from real life.

The joke among listeners was that Ozzie didn't seem to have a job. He was always home, hanging around the house, getting obsessed with his latest tangent. Actually, Ozzie Nelson had been a successful band leader long before his radio sitcom came to radio. He must have assumed that listeners knew his background. Ozzie was a band leader who was home a lot. Simple. He knew that, even if the rest of America wondered what his character did for a living.

The show moved easily into television and ranked among the top shows until 1966. Son, Rick, went on to become a famous rock star until his untimely death in a plane crash in 1985. Their legacy as a warm, funny family show remains strong in the hearts of all who were privileged to have followed them on radio and television.

## Red Skelton

Red Skelton was America's greatest clown. Primarily a visual performer, it was a miracle that he succeeded on radio at all. But, succeed he did, remaining a ratings giant through the 1940s until finding even greater success in the cool light of that new medium called television. However, it was radio that did the trick for Skelton and first brought him national attention, fame, and stardom. From that came some twenty-five movies which further insured his stamp on the American consciousness.

How could a visual performer, adept at mugging and a genius at pantomime become a radio star? The answers were the characters he brought with him from vaudeville, burlesque, the circus and even medicine shows. Red had plenty of them — Clem Kadiddlehopper, Willie Lump-lump, Dead-eye, Cauliflower McPugg, Bolivar Shagnasty and his "mean widdle kid," Junior, whose expression "I dood it!" became a national catch-phrase. These were strong, solid characters each of whom endeared themselves to the radio audience.

Perhaps, the standout ingredient that made Red Skelton a star could be summed up in the word "lovable." Red came across to the listeners as a warm, sweet guy and so did his characters. No matter how corny the jokes were or how predictable, it didn't matter. Red's fans laughed, because they loved him. He was our friend and each week we welcomed him into our homes.

## Sweeney & March

Bob Sweeney and Hal March teamed together in a comedy variety show that ran for a couple of years on CBS radio. They performed comedy sketches interspersed with songs by a young singer named Doris Day, who went on to become a major motion picture star. Bob Sweeney played the meek, milksop type fellow, while Hal March was the straight man. While the show was funny, the jokes were corny and they never developed a cast of regular players to keep listeners coming back for more. They achieved a moderate success, then Hal March went on to become the quiz master of the first of the big money game shows, *The $64,000 Question*. Later, this show ended in a huge scandal. Hal March died prematurely at age 49. Bob Sweeney continued his career as a character actor in movies and on television.

## This Is Broadway

*This is Broadway* was a talent show that differed from *Ted Mack's Original Amateur Hour* in that it dealt strictly with professional performers. It consisted of a panel of experts who watched performers take their turn in the spotlight, and then gave advice about what path they should take next with their careers. Panel members included, Abe Burrows, Clifton Fadman (of *Information, Please*) and playwright George S. Kaufman. The show had a very brief run in 1949 and died, some say, of natural causes.

## You Bet Your Life

As the literate, outrageous, wise-cracking member of the Marx Brothers team, Groucho was already an international star when he came to radio. He and his brothers had failed several times in earlier attempts, and it was not until *You Bet Your Life* came along that Groucho finally hit his stride on radio.

*You Bet Your Life* was a game show in which the money was not important. Billed as a comedy-quiz program, it was the by-play between Groucho and his contestants that made the show an instant hit. Three couples were contestants during the half-hour program. They were carefully pre-screened to allow Groucho ample opportunity to ad-lib a barrage of one-liners and insults their way. The show was supposedly spontaneous, relying on Groucho's quick wit and freewheeling style. Even though some of the "ad-libs" were worked out ahead of time, no one knew what Groucho might come up with, so the program was taped for a hour and then trimmed down to a nice tight thirty minutes.

Each week hundreds of people vied to get on the program just so they could be insulted or ridiculed by Groucho. Out of those, only six would get on the air. So outrageous was Groucho that whatever he said became accepted on or off the air. In his well-defined character, Groucho could get away with just about anything, so no matter where he went in public, people expected Groucho to be himself. And he gave it to them in spades throughout his life.

*You Bet Your Life* revitalized Groucho and allowed him to continue a successful career long after the Marx Brothers were dissolved as a team. He became, and remains to this day, an icon in American comedy.

## Alan Young

Meek, timid, shy, naive, inept, bashful, innocent — all these words describe the character of Alan Young on radio. As luck would have it, that was exactly the way he was in real life. Alan Young simply played himself with great success.

Called in to replace Garry Moore on the popular *Durante & Moore* show, Alan so impressed sponsors that he gained his own program while still working as a comedy foil for Jimmy Durante.

Alan found himself surrounded by a wonderful cast including Jim Backus, who played the incredibly wealthy snob, Hubert Updike, III. Backus would later bring that same character to television's *Gilligan's Island* as billionaire Thurston Howell, III. Hal March also appeared in straight parts and would later go on to host the famous quiz program, *The $64,000 Question*. Don Wilson, moonlighting from the Jack Benny program, supplied the announcing duties.

It was a funny show that should have been more popular than it was. In 1950, Alan moved onto television with a comedy variety show and eventually won his greatest fame as co-star to Mr. Ed, the Talking Horse. However, radio was where Alan perfected the bashful, innocent character he would portray with great success for the rest of his career.

# Index

*Abbott & Costello* 43, 47, 52, 55, 57, 61, 130, 137, 143, 147, 157, 193
Adams, Franklin P. 32
Allen, Fred 7, 9, 15, 18, 22, 25, 27, 29, 30, 32, 34, 38, 42, 44, 45, 48, 51, 53, 56, 59, 60, 63, 66, 67, 69, 70, 75, 77, 78, 82, 83, 85, 87, 90, 98, 100, 102, 105, 108, 109, 114, 117, 121, 123, 127, 133, 135, 141, 146, 152, 157, 162, 165, 166, 193
Ameche, Don *see The Bickersons*
*Amos 'n' Andy* 5, 11, 13, 16, 19, 30, 33, 38, 44, 54, 56, 68, 73, 76, 135, 177, 190, 194
Arden, Eve *see Our Miss Brooks*

Backus, Jim 153
Ball, Lucille 44, 153, 182
Benny, Jack 5, 9, 21, 24, 27, 29, 31, 36, 38, 42, 53, 55, 58, 60, 73, 74, 77, 81, 82, 83, 88, 90, 93, 96, 97, 99, 102, 104, 106, 107, 109, 112, 113, 116, 119, 122, 125, 127, 140, 146, 151, 156, 160, 166, 171, 172, 174, 177, 182, 185, 188, 189, 195
*Bergen & McCarthy* 6, 9, 18, 21, 24, 27, 29, 32, 34, 36, 44, 45, 48, 51, 53, 56, 59, 62, 67, 70, 75, 76, 78, 82, 83, 85, 89, 93, 98, 178, 182, 196
Berle, Milton 6, 11, 13, 16, 19, 23, 26, 30, 33, 42, 44, 46, 49, 54, 56, 60, 62,

63, 64, 67, 84, 86, 88, 95, 98, 100, 102, 105, 107, 112, 114, 118, 121, 123, 126, 133, 136, 142, 146, 154, 160, 162, 164, 185, 190, 196
*The Bickersons* 14, 17, 20, 35, 63, 82, 83, 89, 91, 97, 197
Blanc, Mel *see* Benny (occasional)
*Blondie* 29, 197
Booth, Shirley 10
Boyd, William 144
*Burns & Allen* 86, 94, 100, 101, 103, 108, 110, 114, 124, 131, 138, 144, 148, 158, 164, 173, 175, 180, 184, 198
Burrows, Abe 70, 155, 199

Cantor, Eddie 150, 163, 199
Carson, Jack 92, 115, 199
Chandler, Jeff *see Our Miss Brooks*
Colman, Ronald (and often Benita) 83, 104, 117
Colonna, Jerry *see* Hope
Crabbe, Buster 38
Crosby, Bing 61, 200

Davis, Joan 167, 170, 181, 186, 200
Day, Dennis 145; *see also* Benny
Durante, Jimmy (and *Durante & Moore*) 7, 13, 14, 18, 21, 24, 26, 28, 36, 43, 50, 52, 58, 60, 62, 63, 66, 67, 70, 71, 72, 79, 80, 87, 111, 149, 165, 181, 201

*Edgar Bergen & Charlie McCarthy* see Bergen

Faye, Alice *see* Harris
*Fibber McGee & Molly* 6, 16, 19, 39, 64
Fontaine, Frank 136

Gallup, Frank 33, 46, 84, 105, 106, 114, 121, 123, 126, 133, 136, 142, 146, 154, 160, 162, 164
Gordan, Gale *see Our Miss Brooks*

*Hallmark Players* 90
Harris, Phil 36, 177; and Alice Faye 174, 202
*Here's Morgan* see Morgan
Hope, Bob 6, 8, 11, 13, 17, 20, 23, 27, 30, 33, 35, 39, 43, 45, 46, 49, 51, 54, 57, 60, 64, 65, 68, 69, 71, 73, 75, 77, 79, 81, 84, 88, 91, 94, 97, 108, 117, 127, 128, 130, 153, 182, 185, 187, 190
Horton, Edward Everett 29
Howard, Tom *see It Pays to Be Ignorant*

*It Pays to Be Ignorant* 41, 50, 203

Johnson, Van 122
Jolson, Al 125, 131, 145, 149, 159, 204

Langford, Francis *see The Bickersons*
Leahy, Frank 33
Leeds, Phil 163
Leonard, Sheldon 116
Levant, Oscar 131, 139
Livingston, Mary *see* Benny
*Lux Presents Hollywood* 204

Mack, Ted: *Original Amateur Hour* 136, 204
March, Hal *see Sweeney & March*
*Martin* [Dean] *& Lewis* 84, 91, 126, 127, 132, 134, 139, 145, 151, 155, 159, 186, 205
Martin, Tony 46
Marx, Groucho 47, 49, 52, 55, 58, 78, 85, 88, 106, 113, 119, 131, 134, 143, 159, 179, 184, 191, 208

McConnell, Lulu 21; *see also It Pays to Be Ignorant*
McNaughton, Harry 149; *see also It Pays to Be Ignorant*
Moore, Garry *see* Durante
Moore, Victor 50, 123
Morgan, Henry 68, 114, 121, 127, 133, 141, 162, 168, 169, 171, 172, 175, 189, 205

Nelson *see Ozzie & Harriet*

*Our Miss Brooks* 171, 172, 173, 176, 206
*Ozzie & Harriet* 92, 93, 96, 104, 107, 112, 119, 121, 125, 161, 166, 167, 169, 207

Peck, Gregory 97, 101

Rains, Claude 114
Rockwell, Doc 127

Screen Guild Players 11
Shelton, George *see It Pays to Be Ignorant*
Skelton, Red 5, 7, 8, 12, 14, 17, 20, 23, 26, 31, 34, 37, 39, 43, 45, 46, 49, 55, 57, 61, 62, 64, 65, 66, 68, 69, 72, 74, 77, 79, 80, 87, 92, 111, 150, 174, 178, 181, 185, 191, 207
Smith, H. Allen 32
Stewart, Jimmy 102
Sweeney, Bob *see It Pays to Be Ignorant*
*Sweeney & March* 13, 21, 28, 208

*This Is Broadway* 163, 208
Treacher, Arthur 10, 52, 100, 133

Vallee, Rudy 107, 165
Von Zell, Harry 150

Willock, Dave *see* Carson
Winchell, Walter 54
Wyman, Jane 124

*You Bet Your Life* see Marx, Groucho
Young, Alan 7, 10, 15, 18, 22, 25, 30, 32, 35, 37, 38, 117, 129, 153, 209